PN
1997.2
.P3
M33
2004

Mel Gibson's
Passion and
philosophy

JUN 1 5 2005

D0020726

Popular Culture and Philosophy™
Series Editor: William Irwin

VOLUME 1
Seinfeld and Philosophy: A Book about Everything and Nothing (2000)
Edited by William Irwin

VOLUME 2
The Simpsons and Philosophy: The D'oh! of Homer (2001)
Edited by William Irwin, Mark T. Conard, and Aeon J. Skoble

VOLUME 3
The Matrix and Philosophy: Welcome to the Desert of the Real (2002)
Edited by William Irwin

VOLUME 4
Buffy the Vampire Slayer and Philosophy: Fear and Trembling in Sunnydale (2003)
Edited by James South

VOLUME 5
The Lord of the Rings and Philosophy: One Book to Rule Them All (2003)
Edited by Gregory Bassham and Eric Bronson

VOLUME 6
Baseball and Philosophy: Thinking Outside the Batter's Box (2004)
Edited by Eric Bronson

VOLUME 7
The Sopranos and Philosophy: I Kill Therefore I Am (2004)
Edited by Richard Greene and Peter Vernezze

VOLUME 8
Woody Allen and Philosophy: You Mean My Whole Fallacy Is Wrong? (2004) Edited by Mark T. Conard and Aeon J. Skoble

VOLUME 9
Harry Potter and Philosophy: If Aristotle Ran Hogwarts (2004) Edited by David Baggett and Shawn E. Klein

VOLUME 10
Mel Gibson's Passion and Philosophy: The Cross, the Questions, the Controversy (2004)
Edited by Jorge J.E. Gracia

IN PREPARATION:

More Matrix and Philosophy (2005)
Edited by William Irwin

Superheroes and Philosophy (2005)
Edited by Tom Morris and Matt Morris

Mel Gibson's *Passion* and Philosophy

The Cross, the Questions, the Controversy

Edited by
JORGE J.E. GRACIA

OPEN COURT
Chicago and La Salle, Illinois

Volume 10 in the series, Popular Culture and Philosophy™

To order books from Open Court, call toll-free 1-800-815-2280, or visit our website at www.opencourtbooks.com.

Open Court Publishing Company is a division of Carus Publishing Company.

Copyright ©2004 by Carus Publishing Company

First printing 2004

All rights reserved. No part of this publication may be reproduced, stored in a retrieval system, or transmitted, in any form or by any means, electronic, mechanical, photocopying, recording, or otherwise, without the prior written permission of the publisher, Open Court Publishing Company, a division of Carus Publishing Company, 315 Fifth Street, P.O. Box 300, Peru, Illinois, 61354-0300.

Printed and bound in the United States of America

Library of Congress Cataloging-in-Publication Data

Mel Gibson's Passion and philosophy : the cross, the questions, the controversy / edited by Jorge J.E. Gracia.
   p. cm. — (Popular culture and philosophy ; v. 10)
    Includes bibliographical references and index.
    ISBN 0-8126-9571-2 (trade pbk. : alk. paper)
    1. Passion of the Christ (Motion picture) 2. Jesus Christ—
Passion.   I. Gracia, Jorge J. E. II. Series.
    PN1997.2.P39M35 2004
    791.43'72—dc22
                       2004019747

Contents

Preface: Philosophy Confronts *The Passion*   ix

Acknowledgments   xiii

1.   Who Do You Say That I Am? Mel Gibson's Christ
   RALPH McINERNY   1

I   Did Christ Have to Suffer Violently?   7

2.   Seeing the World Made New: Depictions of the Passion and Christian Life
   MARK A. WRATHALL   9

3.   Christ's Atonement: Washing Away Human Sin
   JERRY L. WALLS   25

4.   The Focus of *The Passion* Puts the Person of Jesus Out of Focus
   CHARLES TALIAFERRO   40

5.   Gibson's Sublime *Passion:* In Defense of the Violence
   WILLIAM IRWIN   51

6.   God and Man Separated No More: Hegel Overcomes the Unhappy Consciousness of Gibson's Christianity
   JAMES LAWLER   62

II   Is *The Passion* Anti-Semitic?   77

7.   *Passions of the Christ:* Do Jews and Christians See the Same Film?
   THOMAS E. WARTENBERG   79

8.   *The Passion* as a Political Weapon: Anti-Semitism and Gibson's Use of the Gospels
   PAUL KURTZ   90

9.   Is *The Passion of the Christ* Racist? Due Process,
     Responsibility, and Punishment
     J. ANGELO CORLETT   101

10. The Passion of the Jew: Jesus in the Jewish
     Mystical Tradition
     ERIC BRONSON   111

III What Is the Truth?   125

11. Pilate's Question: What Is Truth?
     WILLIAM IRWIN   127

12. How Can We Know What God Truly Means? Gibson's
     Take on Scripture
     JORGE J.E. GRACIA   137

13. The Women Who Loved Jesus: Suffering and the
     Traditional Feminine Role
     CYNTHIA FREELAND   151

IV   Why Was Christ Killed?   165

14. The Craftiness of Christ: Wisdom of the Hidden God
     DALLAS WILLARD   167

15. The Death of Socrates and the Death of Christ
     GARETH B. MATTHEWS   179

16. Dances of Death: Self-Sacrifice and Atonement
     BRUCE R. REICHENBACH   190

17. The Crisis of the Cross: God as Scandalous
     PAUL K. MOSER   204

V   Who Is Morally Responsible?   219

18. Christ's Choice: Could It Have Been Different?
     JONATHAN J. SANFORD   221

19. Forgiving Judas: Extenuating Circumstances in the
     Ultimate Betrayal
     ANNA LÄNNSTRÖM   234

20. Resist Not Evil! Jesus and Nonviolence
     GREGORY BASSHAM and DAVID BAGGETT   246

About the Authors   261
Index   265

Philosophy Confronts
The Passion

Mel Gibson's *The Passion of the Christ* has become one of the most controversial films ever made, and it is already a blockbuster of cinematography. Its defenders passionately regard it as one of the most moving and influential pieces of religious art ever created. But its detractors argue with comparable vehemence that the violence and gore it contains, its alleged anti-Semitism, a particular take on the Christian message, and a lack of historical and biblical accuracy, make it nothing more than a kind of political propaganda. Father Thomas Rosica praised it as one of the great masterpieces of religious art, but the secular humanist Paul Kurtz thinks of it as a political weapon in the hands of the religious right. Film critics are divided in their judgment, giving the film anywhere from no stars to five stars. Regardless of what one thinks of the film, however, its impact both personal and social is beyond question. Discussions about it are frequently heard everywhere, and not too long ago the news reported that a Christian minister had died of a heart attack while seeing the film in Brazil, so moved was he. *The Passion* deeply stirs people.

Who is right and who is wrong? Good question. But perhaps more important than the question are the reasons behind it. Many other works of popular culture raise important issues and produce controversy. Movies like *The Matrix* or *The Lord of the Rings* pose interesting quandaries about good and evil, the nature of reality, the ultimate end of humanity, time and morality, happiness, and free will and determinism, for example. Unlike many of these works, however, *The Passion* goes beyond a theoretical interest and well into the heart of many people's deeply treasured beliefs and values. Although other films may raise similar issues to those posed by this movie, Gibson's work puts them in a religious and social context that gives them particular significance. Audiences who see the movie cannot help but be disturbed and challenged by a message that concerns the very roots of their faith and the understanding of the world around them. The significance of Jesus himself, the tragic story of his life, and the subsequent history of Christianity touch deeper cords than a science-fiction story like *The Matrix* or a fantasy like *The Lord of the Rings*. After all, there has not been any other person with greater impact than Jesus in the history of the world. People have died for the Christian message and people have died because they have rejected it, so we are not talking here about a light matter. *The Passion* challenges both Christians and non-Christians to look again at the story of Christ's trial, conviction, and crucifixion, as seen from the perspective presented in the movie.

A work as powerful as this film provides an unusual opportunity to raise and address some of the most fundamental philosophical questions concerning the human predicament in a context in which the general public can relate to them. Philosophy began on controversy and thrives on controversy, so it was to be expected that it would take up some of the challenges posed by *The Passion of the Christ*. This collection of essays addresses some of these. It begins with a chapter that raises the fundamental question: Who is Christ? We are asked to think about how Gibson's depiction of Christ's passion and the excruciating suffering he endured contribute to the understanding of Christ's identity.

This brings us to one of the two most debated questions concerning *The Passion*, which is also the title of the first part of the book: "Did Christ Have to Suffer Violently?" Obviously Gibson not only thought so, but believed it was necessary to portray the violence in the film, which brings us to the issue of how comprehensible such violence is to us and in terms of what concepts it can become intelligible. This leads to the notion of atonement. Does the depth of human sin require the kind of suffering that Jesus is portrayed as having endured in *The Passion*? If so, what does this tell us about humanity, sin, and Christianity? Does such suffering make sense, both as atonement and cinematically? Does *The Passion* distort the whole person of Christ by concentrating on the gore and violence? And does this emphasis contribute to the value of the film as a work of art?

The second most debated question about *The Passion* has to do with its purported anti-Semitism and the role that Jews played in Christ's death. So the next section of the book is entitled, "Is *The Passion* anti-Semitic?" Does the film blame all Jews for the death of Jesus? Is the film racist? And does the movie take into account that Jesus was a Jew well entrenched in a Jewish mystical tradition? What explains the different reactions that people have to the film, particularly in the context of anti-Semitism?

At the center of the film, and related to the questions raised so far, is the understanding of God's message and the relation between faith and truth. Foremost for philosophers is the question of what truth itself is, and how it is related to faith. In general, how can one know the truth, and in particular how can one know that what is believed through faith is true? Even more pointed still, if the Gospels are taken as the word of God, we need to ask about the best way to approach them, and how effectively Gibson meets this challenge in the movie. How does the transfer from word to film affect the message of the words? And finally, what do we make of the women who loved Jesus? What is their true role in the story of the passion? These issues are explored in a part entitled "What Is the Truth?"

This is followed by a part entitled, "Why Was Christ Killed?," pointing both to the reasons for and the significance of Christ's death. It begins by exploring what is characteristic of the death of Christ, which involves redemption and its meaning. What is crafty and wise about Christ's choice to redeem humanity? What is the significance of his self-sacrifice? What does the cross entail for philosophers in particular and the world at large, and does it answer some of the questions philosophers have not been able to answer? Indeed, how does Christ's death compare with that of another martyr, Socrates, who is considered the philosopher *par excellence*?

Christ's choice to die for humanity naturally leads to questions of freedom, divine foreknowledge, and moral responsibility which are at the center of both the Christian faith and *The Passion*. Was Christ free to choose death when, as God, He knew from all eternity that He would do so? The question of freedom does not only apply to Christ as God. Humans also face a problem, which can be put in the context of Judas's predicament: How can Judas be considered morally responsible for his betrayal of Jesus when God knew that he would do so and his action was necessary for the accomplishment of human redemption? This logically leads to questions about how much humans are capable of resisting evil and the best way to do it. And this brings us back to Christ's nonviolent behavior and his teaching on nonviolence. These matters are explored in a section headed by the query: Who is morally responsible?

These topics are explored by twenty well-known philosophers and scholars in short, direct, and provocative essays in this volume. Their background helps to make the treatment of the issues they raise lively and challenging, while keeping a sense of their serious nature. All of them feel strongly, perhaps passionately, about the issues they discuss, but they take different perspectives arising from deeply held convictions. Some of the authors are Evangelical Christians, some Roman Catholics, some Jews, at least one is a Mormon, some have no religious faith, and some are militantly anti-religious. Different genders and ethnic backgrounds are also represented, all of which provides a good sample of the diverse viewpoints people take both toward the film and the philosophical issues it raises. The pieces are aimed at both depth and accessibility, and should generate discussion and reflection.

The book as a whole takes no sides in the controversies surrounding *The Passion*. It is intended as a work of philosophy, even if much of its content is rooted in, and deals with, religion; and the task of philosophy is to deepen and broaden our understanding of topics that are often dealt with superficially and summarily. It is neither an apology nor an attack on any particular point of view, although it poses problems and issues that go well beyond the boundaries of an academic exercise, prompting the authors to take sides. It is up to those who read these essays to make up their minds about them; we are merely providing a point of departure.

Acknowledgments

Full credit for this collection goes to the authors. Apart from their willingness to participate in the project and the hard work of preparing essays under extremely tight time constraints, their patience and good nature were exemplary. They put up with many inconveniences, and were willing to consider many suggestions for revision. Dealing with them has been a true pleasure and I only hope that I did not tire them out with my repeated pestering.

I am particularly grateful to William Irwin, who edits the Open Court Series on Philosophy and Popular Culture. Without his interest in the project, his constant support and expert advice, and his willingness to work with me throughout the editing process, the collection would never have seen the light of day. He has effectively functioned as an overseer and I have learned much in the process. In addition, I am indebted to Gregory Bassham, who like Irwin, read all the essays and offered many suggestions for enhancing their value. His help has been indispensable. Abigail Myers and Mitu Pandya read many of the essays in draft form and offered keen insights to improve them. Finally, I should express appreciation to Sandro D'Onofrio, who compiled the index, to *Free Inquiry* for permission to reprint Paul Kurtz's essay with a few modifications, and to David Ramsay Steele of Open Court for his support and help.

1

Who Do You Say that I Am? Mel Gibson's Christ

RALPH McINERNY

When Dorothy Sayers wrote a radio play about Christ many believers professed to be shocked that a human actor should play the role of Jesus. Perhaps this said more about the secularization of the stage than anything else. In the history of drama that Graham Greene wrote on a slow boat to Africa during World War II, he of course located the origins of European drama in the medieval mystery plays, in which the great events of the faith were portrayed as a kind of complement to the liturgy. It is a long way from *Quem Quaeritis* to Oscar Wilde and Noel Coward, no doubt, but I suppose that Greek drama would be more suggestive of the former than the latter.

When the Word becomes flesh in Jesus, the great mystery is that a particular man in a given time should by his actions reveal the divine. Or perhaps conceal the divine, as the great Protestant philosopher and theologian Søren Kierkegaard (1813–1855) suggests through Johannes Climacus. How could the historical and contingent express the eternal? That great mystery can be domesticated for the believer, even its culmination in the passion of Christ. In Catholic churches the walls are lined with depictions of the stations or stages of Christ's passion, often quite stylized, just as many crucifixes give us a dying Christ whose suffering is tamed. To this *The Passion of the Christ* is an almost shocking antidote. Surely the cruelty of the *via crucis*, or way of the cross, and the crucifixion have never before been so graphically put before the eyes.

The reaction of some Jews to the movie must puzzle the Christian. Surely it cannot be the portrayal of the priests and Sanhedrin that provoked, as if a little editing could take the sting out of the fact that the Jewish people were divided by the events shown in the film. The first Christians were of course Jews and those Jews who refused Christ could be taken to define themselves thereby. The reaction is not confined to them however. After all, Friedrich Nietzsche (1844–1900) announced himself as the Antichrist. If there is any either/or in human history it is defined by one's acceptance or rejection of Jesus's claim to be the Messiah. For the believer, the charge of anti-Semitism must seem a distraction. Like Uncle Sam in the recruiting poster, Jesus looks into the eye of every viewer as if to say, "I want you." In a long life I have never heard the passion story invoked as a means of criticizing Jews. The message taught was that this is being done for me, I am somehow responsible for this, but by his stripes I will be healed.

In the Ignatian method of meditation, the first stage is to imagine as graphically as one can some scene in the life of Christ whose meaning for oneself one will seek to discern. Of course it would be bizarre to think of a Jesuit devoting half an hour of his morning reminding himself how awful the Jews who condemned Christ were.

The Mass is being said somewhere in the world right now. It always is. This continuous memorial of Christ's passion is the heart of the Catholic liturgy. The institution of the Eucharist the night before Christ died established the connection between the bread and wine and his body and blood. "Do this in memory of me." As Thomas Aquinas (1224/5–1274) put it in a hymn, Christ's divinity was cloaked by his humanity but in the Eucharist he is as it were twice hidden, there under the appearance of bread and wine.

One reads that a great number of Catholics, perhaps most, no longer know what the real presence means. To be then told that they do not know if they accept it goes without saying. Kierkegaard in the nineteenth century saw his task as the introduction of Christianity into Christendom. He saw all around him a domesticated Christianity that seemed light years distant from the Gospels. How to get a nominal Christian to realize that his life was being lived in non-Christian categories, as Kiekregaard would put it? What was needed was a form of indirect communication, a rhetoric that would in many ways mimic the Socratic method to bring the reader to the point where he put the question to himself, in the privacy of his own soul. In the *Philosophical Fragments,* Kierkegaard provides the means for his reader to remember that the Incarnation is not something that can be assimilated into our ordinary modes of thinking. Rather, it goes against them, contradicts them. All efforts to keep religion within the bounds of reason alone are bound to be a distortion of Christianity.

It would doubtless be fanciful to think of Mel Gibson as a latter day Kierkegaard, but not perhaps fantastic. There is no way the passion story can be divorced from its meaning. Hollywood biblical epics of the past prettied up the scene and did not quite suggest that the persecutions of Diocletian were occasions for pagan boys and Christian girls hooking up in the Coliseum. (As a boy, I read *Quo Vadis?*, envying the pagans who disported themselves as I thought with moral impunity.) What surprises in Gibson's film is the involvement it suggests, not simply of actors in their roles, but of the whole film in the significance of these events of so long ago. Of late, there have been films that have depicted Christ in a way that seemed meant to infuriate believers. For all that, the reactions were fairly tame. Demythologizing may work for jaded theologians, but it is absurd to portray Jesus as hankering for Mary Magdalene. Nonetheless, such leveling efforts seem more in tune with our post-Christian time. Any residual faith that engenders a shocked reaction is all too easily assuaged. By contrast, Gibson's film has all the directness of St. Francis de Sales. It is a cinematic way of inviting the viewer to the Amen Corner. No wonder it got the reactions it did.

Anne Catherine Emmerich (1774–1824) was a German nun displaced from her convent by the political events of the day. She was a visionary for whom the events of the Gospels were forever being shown on the private screen of her imagination, the familiar scenes made more concrete by a flood of details. Clemens Brentano was so enthralled by her accounts of what she saw that he devoted himself to being her amanuensis, writing it all down as she talked. The written version is a subject of controversy. How much of it is due to the literary gifts of Brentano, how much of it is Anne Catherine Emmerich? An insoluble problem, of course, and one of little interest to the reader of the volumes that emerged from Brentano's dedication to his task. These visions have no interest apart from the Gospels they embroider with details. Much the same must be said of Gibson's film.

Were one to appraise the film in purely aesthetic terms, if its story were to be examined as self-standing, it would I think disappoint. It would be like, I beg your pardon, the movie *A Bridge Too Far*, the story of a failed military operation where the failure never achieves any significance above its individual details. The last days of Christ are gruesome events whose meaning arises from a recognition of their transcendence. They involve a transvaluation of values, standing human, and aesthetic, expectations on their head. One responds by rejecting or accepting that transcendent meaning.

It is the nominal Christian, *l'homme moyen sensuel*, who is the chief addressee of the film. Like Kierkegaard's reader, the viewer of this film is meant to be disturbed, to be made uneasy, to realize how distant he is from his alleged beliefs. Kierkegaard did not claim to be an official spokesman for Christianity, quite the opposite, and Gibson too has produced a film that overwhelms the heart. To embrace it too immediately, in the Kierkegaardian sense, would be not wholly unlike the impassioned rejection of it. Like its protagonist, it is a sign of contradiction. That the movie screen should provide the means of this contemporary thumb in the eye of our complacency is only as it should be. How many trivial images have flickered forth to our imaginations, titillating, diverting, sometimes more. Gibson's film is one of a kind. To thank him for it must seem inappropriate. He provided the medium, but the message is the old one we are forever forgetting.

SOURCES

Anne Catherine Emmerich. 2003. *The Dolorous Passion of Our Lord Jesus Christ*. Translated by Klemens Maria Brentano. El Sobrante: North Bay Books.
Soren Kierkegaard. 1985. *Philosophical Fragments*. Princeton: Princeton University Press.

QUESTIONS FOR DISCUSSION

1. What is unique about Christ?

2. How does Gibson's portrayal of Christ differ from yours?

3. Do the conceptions of Christ's identity of Catholics and Protestants differ? Why?

4. How does dwelling on Christ's suffering in the passion affect our view of him?

5. What is the place of mystical visions in understanding Christ?

I

Did Christ Have to Suffer Violently?

2
Seeing the World Made New: Depictions of the Passion and Christian Life

MARK A. WRATHALL

Fra Angelico's *Santa Trinita Altarpiece* depicts the scene as Christ's body is removed from the cross. On Christ's right hand side, a group of women mourn while Mary kneels and kisses his feet. To his left hand side, a column of men stands apart. Unlike the women, these standing men, with one notable exception, seem outwardly serene. In the front of the column, one man, in the dress of a scholar, holds the implements of Christ's torture–the crown of thorns, and three spikes used to nail him to the cross. His face is turned away from Christ and the scene unfolding behind him as he converses with the man to his left. One man alone among this group betrays any signs of sorrow. Largely hidden by those in front of him, he turns his face away and covers his hands, evidently trying to disguise his weeping.

In its graphic intensity, Gibson's depiction of Christ's suffering in *The Passion of the Christ* has more in common with Lovis Corinth's *Red Christ* than the serenity and beauty of a Fra Angelico. This is one of the strengths of his movie. Unlike Gibson and Corinth, Angelico depicts a remarkably dispassionate passion. One sees few visible signs of the trauma that a tortured and crucified man's body would in fact manifest. In works like *The Mocking of Christ*, Angelico's Christ endures suffering with the equanimity of a Socrates drinking the hemlock, precisely as one might expect of one who knows both the worthlessness of this transient world and the good to be won by enduring his momentary suffering. Angelico shows us outwardly on Christ's body the tranquil state of mind of an all-knowing God.

Yet, even if God himself can be unmoved by Christ's suffering, and even if he can comprehend it, it doesn't follow that *we* can or should be unmoved by it–a point Gibson's movie makes in the opening scenes in the Garden of Gethsemane. Finding his Apostles asleep, Christ notes disapprovingly: "You could not watch even one hour with me." Gibson intends the same rebuke, I take it, for those members of the Christian public at large who might also be tempted to turn away in order to avoid confronting the intensity of Jesus's suffering.

One of the central lessons of the *Santa Trinita Altarpiece* is likewise that the true followers of Christ must remain true to his suffering by refusing to turn away from it or reason it away. The figures on Christ's left-hand side are worthy of criticism for being too dispassionate, too scholarly and rational in their response, as the inscription under their feet indicates ("Behold how the just man dies, and no one takes it to heart"). Too reflective a response prevents some from being moved by or "taking to heart" the event. Thus, the small space between Christ's body and the scholar on Fra Angelico's canvas shows us the infinite space between theology and faith. Angelico, too, sees the passion as something that ought to move us, to produce in us a certain response to the world.

But the way Angelico conceives of the ideal emotional response is quite different from Gibson's way. For Angelico, the passionate response to Christ's suffering is restrained, and not permitted to destroy our attachment to the world. The wounds his Christ bears elicit our pity, but don't confront us with horror. And the world surrounding his Christ is a bright, luminous, spring day, that reminds us of the rebirth of creation itself. Gibson, by contrast, situates his depiction in a dark, gloomy, nearly barren world, and has presented us with a vision that doesn't allow us to avoid the horror and irrationality of Christ's torment. As Gibson noted in an interview:

> I think we have gotten too used to seeing pretty crosses on the wall, and we forget what really happened. . . . But when you finally see it and understand what he went through, it makes you feel not only compassion, but also a debt. You want to repay him for the enormity of his sacrifice. You want to love him in return. (Lazzeri 2004)

Fra Angelico's dispassionate passion. Angelico shows us outwardly on Christ's body the tranquil state of mind of an all-knowing God. It arouses pity, not horror. We see a world made new. Fra Angelico, Descent from the Cross, Santa Trinita Altarpiece *(ca. 1430), illustration used by permission of Alinari/Art Resource, New York.*

Like all good depictions of Christ's suffering, the intended result of Gibson's film is, then, to produce a passionate response in us, the viewers. But we need to be mindful of the kind of response it provokes.

On Christ's Suffering

A commonly voiced objection to Gibson's film has focused on the level and graphic intensity of the violence and suffering it depicts. The often unstated assumption behind the objection is that such a depiction at best does nothing to advance the Christian message, and at worst actually obscures or distorts it. A.O. Scott's review of the film is a clear example. "*The Passion of the Christ*," he writes, "is so relentlessly focused on the savagery of Jesus's final hours that it seems to arise less from love than from wrath, and to succeed more in assaulting the spirit than in uplifting it. . . . It is disheartening to see a film made with evident and abundant religious conviction that is at the same time so utterly lacking in grace." Scott infers from the violence of the film that it must be intended "to terrify or inflame" the audience: "The desired response of the audience to this spectacle is, of course, not revulsion but something like . . . cowering, quivering awe." He concludes that a Christian viewer is forced into a "sadomasochistic paradox" in which her faith in the necessity of Christ's sacrifice compels her to squelch "the ordinary human response"—namely, "wish[ing] for the carnage to stop" (Scott 2004). Others assume that the violence of the depiction is attributable to Gibson mindlessly plugged Jesus into formulaic action or horror genres.

A more charitable response would be to ask: what purpose might be served by such a vivid and disturbing depiction? This question can't be answered without an inquiry into the nature of Christian faith, something that, perhaps understandably, most critics neglect. One simply cannot assess whether the graphic depiction of Jesus's suffering will obscure the message of his death without some sense for the role played by his suffering and death in the life of the believer.

Before analyzing Gibson's film in these terms, it's useful to contrast his depiction with two other visual depictions–the two we've already mentioned. The body of Fra Angelico's Christ is largely unmarked by the suffering he has endured. His face, in

Lovis Corinth focuses on the horror and absurdity of Christ's suffering. We see the world as brightly lit, yet bewildering and meaningless. Lovis Corinth, The Red Christ *(1922), illustration used by permission of Bridgeman-Giraudon/Art Resource, New York.*

death, looks peaceful. Rather than a barren and stony Golgotha, Angelico's crucifixion occurs in a flowery garden on a bright spring day. The viewer of this scene can discern neither horror nor violence in Christ's death. Instead, the viewer is shown how to look beyond the pain of this world, and see the world as an admittedly imperfect realization of God's ideal of it. While Angelico's depiction takes a number of liberties with the literal facts of the crucifixion—another criticism, incidentally, that is often leveled at Gibson's film—it does so to better focus our attention on what it takes to be the true significance of the event. It thus goes out of its way to minimize the horror which, after all, rarely produces a rational and measured response, and is almost certain to obscure our ability to see the world as instantiating God's idea of things.

Corinth, too, takes liberties with the facts. In his *Red Christ*, a soldier on Christ's left hand side offers him a sponge full of vinegar to quench his thirst (Matthew 27:48), while a soldier on his right hand side thrusts a spear into his side (John 19:35)—an event that was supposed to occur after Christ had died. But Christ in Corinth's painting is still very much alive, and he looks out at the viewer apparently confused and bewildered at the violence he is suffering. Unlike Angelico's Christ (but very much like Gibson's) Jesus's body is battered and bloody. His skin has obviously been flayed, and his flesh is discolored by the trauma it has suffered; blood explodes from the wound as the spear is thrust into his side, and streams of blood run down from the wounds in his hands. Unlike Gibson's world, the world of Corinth's crucifixion is brightly lit by the sun. But Corinth's sun doesn't bathe the world in the bright, cheerful colors of Angelico's crucifixion; instead, its bright blood-tinged rays color the whole world in shades of red and pink. The overall effect is therefore unlike either the lustrous, springtime depiction of Angelico's or Gibson's dark and brooding film. But before explaining how this contrast ought to be understood, let's return to the question with which we began, namely, What purpose is served by the graphic depiction of Christ's suffering?

We have to assume that for Gibson, as for Corinth, the absurdity and horror of Christ's suffering is itself an important feature to which the believer is supposed to respond. One might argue that if we make sense of it, if we rationalize it, we at the same time undermine our ability to experience it as an evil. At the same time, and for exactly the same reason, we will be tempted to dismiss the suffering of others. The problem is this: we think that if suffering is the price of sin, and if Christ has suffered for the repentant, then the human suffering we witness is either deserved (the result of unrepented sin), or will be compensated for through the atonement and the reward that Christ purchased for all those who believe in him. Either way, there is no need for the faithful to worry over the suffering of others. It is only the unfaithful who would feel any need to try to alleviate suffering, for in so doing they are presuming to act to correct what God himself has already taken care of.

The existentialist philosopher-novelist Albert Camus (1913–1960), himself an atheist, explored these arguments brilliantly through the character of Father Paneloux in his novel *The Plague*. Camus puts into Paneloux's mind the following thoughts: "For who would dare to assert that eternal happiness can compensate for a single moment's human suffering? He who asserted that would not be a true Christian, a follower of the Master who knew all the pangs of suffering in his body and soul" (Camus 1991, p. 224). Obviously, Father Paneloux realized that being faithful to Christ requires that one "keep faith with that great symbol of all suffering, the tortured body on the Cross" (ibid.), and acknowledge the absolute injustice and incompensable nature of Christ's suffering. This acknowledgment, in turn, would force the follower of Christ to face up to all the other suffering she encounters in the world, to allow herself to be moved by it, and to devote her life to alleviating it.

If this is true, then it would be a strength of any depiction of Christ's crucifixion that it resist placing his suffering into a rational economy of exchange, that is, as a payment for the debt incurred by our sins. On this view, the intensity of Gibson's depiction of Christ's torment is a virtue. At some point, every rational viewer must be shocked by it, and should be willing to concede that it is excessive, unnecessary, and that it doesn't make any sense. Monica Bellucci, who plays the role of Mary Magdalene in the film, put the point most concisely: *The Passion of the Christ*, she noted, is "a reflection on the horror and absurdity of violence" (Donn 2004, p. 29). In recognizing this horror and absurdity, one is ready to be moved by Christ's suffering and, consequently, the suffering of all men.

But Gibson's absurd world is unlike the existentialist's absurd world in one very important respect–a respect illustrated by the difference between Gibson's and Corinth's depiction. Remember that in Angelico's world, Christ's suffering shows us the presence of God in the world. In Corinth's painting, divinity is neither instantiated in, nor withdrawn from, the world. Corinth shows us, instead, a world wholly unmarked by divinity—it does not even appear as the place from which God has withdrawn. The sun shines brightly in Corinth's depiction, but it doesn't infuse the world with meaning. This world is the only world, and it is a bewildering and absurd one. In Gibson's world, by contrast, Christ's suffering ultimately shows us how God's presence is withdrawn from the world. The absurdity of this world ought, for Gibson, to lead us to look beyond it toward another world. But in this way the absurd is incorporated into a more profound meaning, and the point of Christ's suffering is to make us despair of this earthly existence so we can set our hearts on the transcendent world.

Christ's Passion as World Disclosure

Gibson's depiction makes perfect sense if the point is precisely to show that Christ's suffering is not rationalizable, and that one's response to the absurdity of his suffering must be put at the center of one's faith. Indeed, if philosophers like Camus are right, then there could be a very powerful ethical impact of such a depiction. But the contrast with Corinth should help us to reject the idea that all depictions are equally acceptable as long as they force us to face the horror and absurdity of Christ's suffering. There can be important differences in what we learn from the absurdity.

But now we have a new paradox: what standards can we use to critique these different depictions if we give up the idea that Christ's Passion is ultimately rationalizable? We need to be able to critique something rationally without rationalizing it. Is this possible? Philosophers in the tradition of Blaise Pascal (1623–1662), Martin Heidegger (1889–1976), and Maurice Merleau-Ponty (1908–1961), at any rate, have thought that we can. Pascal argued that, in matters of faith, the purpose of reason is a merely instrumental one—it can clear away obstacles to belief (Wrathall 2005). Heidegger and Merleau-Ponty both philosophized descriptively. The point was to describe the world in such a way that we can see more clearly the phenomena without pretending to have either a logical account or a scientific reduction of the phenomena to causal structures. Such descriptions have critical "bite," because they show us what is wrong with rationalist or cognitivist accounts of the phenomena. But, for such thinkers, the point of a philosophical account or explanation is not to produce a new theory, but rather to lead one to a direct apprehension of the phenomena in question. Having achieved such an apprehension, the philosophical account is given no further weight, for it is the apprehension which produces understanding.

If we are going to philosophize about religion, or any other field where the goal is not to learn to *think* properly, but rather to be *moved* in the right way, some such approach must be the correct one. Religious theories, by the same token, ought to avoid philosophical disputes about matters that lie beyond our experience. Christianity does, of course, make claims that can't be verified by worldly means. Accepting such claims as true is a necessary condition for our being Christians, and thus there is what one might call a cognitive dimension to Christianity. But such cognitive states are not sufficient for Christianity because belief doesn't automatically effect a change in the way one experiences and acts in the world (recall in the film how Peter's mere belief that he would never betray the Christ was worthless without the action to back it up). In general, Christianity values the cognitive state of belief, not as an end in itself, but as a means for producing a Christian life. And a Christian life, on the view I'm suggesting, aims at disclosing the world in a new way.

The Passion recognizes the disclosive dimension of religious faith through a pervasive emphasis on perception. In what is, to me, the pivotal scene of the whole movie, Christ looks up to Mary and says: "See, mother, I make all things new," which is a line drawn, not from the Gospels, but from the Book of Revelation (Revelation 21: 5-6). The challenge for the Christian is precisely to learn to see all things new, to see how Christ's suffering must change our experience of the world. Christian "knowledge" consists in this changed experience, it is a knowing how to see the world, and to respond to people and events in the world, in the light of God.

Gibson's film thus shares with philosophers like Pascal a sense that the function of Christian faith is not exhausted in adopting a certain mental attitude toward an unseen reality, but rather in attuning us to the world we see in such a way that we can see it for what it is. Jesus' passion produces this attunement when we learn of it, are moved by it, and respond to it passionately. I call this approach to faith the *world-disclosive* approach.

It is on the basis of the world-disclosive view that we can address the paradox discussed above. We can think through and assess different depictions of Christ's suffering, not in terms of whether they adequately rationalize his suffering, but rather in terms of how they show us the world. If the world-disclosive approach to religious faith is right, then an introduction into the faith consists in an introduction to the practices that will let us see the world in the right way, for it is our practices that train our passions and thus allow us to see the world in the way that we do (Pascal 1995, pp. 156–57).

Our ability to see the world as meaningfully structured—and this means, our ability to see the world at all—depends on our having the skills to respond to the meaning in the world. Gibson depicts this idea nicely in the scene where the young Jesus and Mary playfully discuss a tall, modern-style table that he has been crafting for a rich client. "Does he like to eat standing up?," she asks. "No," Jesus responds as he takes up the bodily stance of one sitting at a table, "he prefers to eat so. Tall table, tall chairs." Mary tries to adopt a sitting posture at the table for a moment, and then concludes "This will never catch on." Mary, lacking the practices and bodily skills involved in sitting on chairs at a table, is unable to even imagine how the table could work until Jesus pretends to sit at it. Just as Jesus needs to show her the practices for chair sitting to enable her to see the table in a new light, so he needs to show us new practices of submission and love to let us see the world in a new way. The new revelation of the world will only really take hold, however, when we master the skills and practices that let us see the world.

This same thought is the key to understanding the relative advantages and disadvantages of a visual depiction. A written description cannot directly show us how to act or how something feels. It can at best refer to bodily actions and experiences with which we might already be independently familiar.

Linguistic representation is, compared to a visual depiction, remarkably pallid and weak when it comes to capturing passionate bodily experiences, because when we experience something or do something, our experience or action is primarily a bodily rather than a mental experience or action. If we don't already have the skills or experiences to draw on, the written description can't tell us much. A picture, by contrast, can let us directly experience how something feels, how something looks, how something is to be done. It can also show us the bodily attitudes which constitute the feeling and the appropriate bodily stance to adopt for a practice. A film, in addition, can show us the actual bodily movements. It can thus move us directly to grasp the scene, free of the mediation of language.

The difference is, to put it simply, the difference between, for example, reading in John 19:1 that "Pilate therefore took Jesus, and scourged him," on the one hand, and seeing a man scourged on the other. A description of a scourging, no matter how detailed and precise, can't communicate the quivering that our muscles feel, the tension that builds in our limbs, and the beating of our hearts, as the pain another's body feels speaks directly to our bodies. When we see another person in pain or in the throes of any emotion, we see it through our own bodily experience, not through mentally projecting ourselves into the other's state of mind. This gives a pictorial depiction an advantage over written description. The written description could try to go inside the mind, to describe the "inner" content, of another's experience (something, interestingly enough, that the Scriptural accounts of Christ's suffering never do). But this cannot live up to the power of a visual depiction which can, itself, speak to our bodily sense for the world. As Merleau-Ponty put it:

> A movie is not thought; it is perceived. This is why the movies can be so gripping in their presentation of man: they do not give us his *thoughts*, as novels have done for so long, but his conduct or behavior. They directly present to us that special way of being in the world, of dealing with things and other people, which we can see in the sign language of gesture and gaze and which clearly defines each person we know. (1964, p. 58)

This is not to say that we are not moved by a written depiction. The written account of Christ's suffering and death have long been experienced themselves in a passionate, bodily way. But in order to produce such an effect, the words need to be translated into a bodily experience, whereas a visual depiction shows us the experience itself. No matter what and how much one says, there is something that the description can't capture—namely, what the thing looks like, and how it feels to perceive it. And the linguistic description can only represent the look and the feel of a thing provided that we already have an experiential sense for it.

Another way to recognize the important difference between linguistic and pictorial depictions is to reflect on the incommensurability between the linguistic order and the pictorial order. This incommensurability is manifest in that linguistic description is always compatible with an indefinite number of different, mutually incompatible pictorial depictions, a fact we've already illustrated with the different depictions of the crucifixion. And this point, in turn, puts us on the track of the danger of a visual depiction. The strength is that it communicates immediately to our bodies and can show us directly how to experience the world. The danger is that, being moved by a depiction, we will uncritically accept it as true.

Movies assume a passive audience, and encourage us to lazily accept an interpretation of the world as it is fed to us. Indeed, one might prefer books to films precisely because they demand more of their audiences. But we should always be alert to the fact that a film is artificially constructed, and if it comes closer to replicating the direct experience of the world than language, it also falls short in important ways. For example, the world offers direct feedback as we respond to what we see; a film cannot. In real life, we can explore on our own the scene as it is unfolding, and we reap the rewards of acting correctly, as well as the consequences of acting incorrectly. The picture doesn't allow us to explore the scene, but shows us only what it wants us to see. In addition, a film can manipulate appearances and the interactions between things in a way not possible in the real world. For all these reasons, if one had to choose between a true written account of an event and a illusory pictorial depiction of the same event, it is obvious what one should choose—at least if the goal is to achieve a correct orientation to the world.

We should always be ready to ask of a depiction: Is it a true depiction, one that makes us feel as we ought to feel and respond as we ought to respond to the world around us? Being true to the written account isn't enough, because there are an indefinite number of different ways to be true to the written account. One way is to orient us to the world, to disclose the world to us in the way that the written account strives to do. So, what of Gibson's Christ? How does he show us the world anew?

Gibson's Version of the Passion

So far, I've argued for the importance on the Christian account of being moved by Christ's suffering, and I've suggested that to be so moved, we need to be confronted by the horror of that suffering. But the particular way that the suffering is portrayed, the way that it shows us the world, will disclose the world differently for us, and move us to respond in quite particular ways. I want briefly now to describe how Gibson's movie does this.

One who is moved by the absurdity of Christ's torment cannot appeal to an intellectual belief in the ultimate rationality of the world as an excuse for tolerating the existence of human suffering. In addition to believing that Christ is innocent and completely undeserving of any suffering, Christians also believe that we are all responsible for the fact that he does suffer. Gibson's film forces us to confront the fact that the world contains undeserved and unjustifiable suffering for which we are responsible. In this sense, the movie is inaccessible to non-Christians, who will have no reason to accept that Christ's suffering is connected in any way to us. But Christians, once we are brought to recognize our responsibility for undeserved suffering in the world, should, first of all, feel compelled to try as much as possible to avoid being the cause of any more undeserved suffering. We do this by freeing ourselves of the desires that produce suffering.

Gibson tries hard to show us how pride, and the lust for power or wealth, produce suffering. "My kingdom," Christ explains to Pilate, "is not of this world." In the following scene, we discover that Pilate, by contrast, will subject Christ to torment and ultimately death because of his efforts to hold onto power and satisfy Caesar. The film illustrates the same point in a number of ways—one visually quite compelling instance shows how Christ, during a debate between Pilate and the High Priest, adopts an attitude of complete indifference to the competing parties, and looks instead at the dove, the symbol of the Holy Spirit, flying above the courtyard.

Through the use of such motifs, Gibson points to a central focus of the Christian experience of Christ's suffering: If we are moved by it, then we learn to see certain desires as producing misery and unhappiness for others. Beyond this passive response of trying not to cause more suffering, Christians hold faith with Christ by actively trying to alleviate the suffering that we encounter. The recognition that suffering can be unjustified and unrecompensable, together with a realization that we are implicated in producing suffering in unintended ways, ought to call us to actively seek to help others, which is a central message of Christ's sermons.

I find Gibson's film quite compelling insofar as it shows us how to see the world in a new way. But this is not the same as seeing the world made new. Indeed, the world as the suffering Christ sees it is remarkably like the world as the suffering Judas sees it. For Judas, his sin has made the world appear as a demonic and miserable place. The film depicts this admirably, not by showing him as bearing inner torments, but by showing how the world itself actually looks dark, miserable, unbearable. The thick night mists are full of demonic sounds and occasional apparitions. Children are transformed into tormenting fiends, and he is ultimately driven by the appearance of death and decay all around him to take his own life and depart the world.

Unfortunately, when Gibson shows us a Christ's-eye perspective of the world, things don't look significantly different. Indeed, the world seems to be just as God-forsaken for Christ as it is for Judas. While appealing to God the Father in the Garden, Jesus prays, "Shelter me, O Lord. I trust you. In you I take refuge," and looks toward the light of the moon. But the moon clouds over, darkness spreads, and Christ sinks to the ground forsaken. If even Christ himself sees the world as God-forsaken, one wonders what hope there is for the rest of us. Christ, like Judas, sees the people surrounding him as demons—a fact Gibson brings home to us by frequently placing Satan himself in the midst of the jeering, tormenting crowds. The most disturbing such scene shows Satan gliding through the crowds that are witnessing his scourging, clutching a deformed child in his arms. The child's smile is juxtaposed with the leering soldiers, communicating the not so subtle message that most of mankind have allowed themselves to become children of Satan rather than their Father in Heaven.

Given the way the world looks even to Christ himself, it is no surprise that he "embraces his cross, " as one of the thieves crucified with him observes. Gibson's Christ is ultimately a pessimist, and the world he shows us is, sadly, not a world made new, but a world to be abandoned as soon as possible. Even Mary comes to wish for both his, and her own, departure from the world. "My son," she asks during his scourging, "when, where, how will you choose to be delivered of this?" And, standing before him on the cross, she pleads: "My son, let me die with you." The viewer is left, then, with a despair at a world that seems more corrupt than ever.

A useful corrective to Gibson's version of Christianity would be Dostoevsky's. In *The Brothers Karamazov*, Dostoevsky even has a character, Father Ferapont, who represents Gibson's pessimistic version of Christian world disclosure. Ferapont, like Gibson's Christ, sees devils among the people around him, and this vision leads him to withdraw ascetically from the world. For Dostoevsky, pessimistic Christianity misses the true import of Christ's life, which shows us the "beauty and glory" of a world made new through Christ's love, and impels us to connect in love to others. Dostoevsky's Christianity is summed up by the dying Christ-like character, Markel who reprimands his mother for focusing on his suffering: "Don't cry, mother, life is paradise, and we are all in paradise, but we won't see it; if we would, we should have heaven on earth the next day."*

SOURCES

Albert Camus. 1991. *The Plague* Translated by Stuart Gilbert. New York: Vintage.
Allegra Donn. 2004. *The Passion* Shows Us All How Violent We Really Are. Interview with Monica Bellucci. *Evening Standard*, London (25th March).

* I am indebted to James Faulconer, Randy Paul, Hubert Dreyfus, Benjamin Huff, and Kenneth West for their helpful and thought-provoking comments on earlier drafts of this paper.

Fyodor Dostoevsky. 1990. *The Brothers Karamazov*. Translated by
    Richard Pevear and Larissa Volkhonsky. New York: Vintage.
Martin Heidegger. 1998. Phenomenology and Theology. In William
    McNeill, ed., *Pathmarks* (Cambridge: Cambridge University Press),
    pp. 39–62.
Antonella Lazzeri. 2004. Making This Film Was Difficult: Watching It Is
    Even Harder. *The Sun*, London (22nd March), p. 26.
Maurice Merleau-Ponty. 1964. The Film and the New Psychology. In
    Merleau-Ponty, *Sense and Non-Sense,* translated by Hubert L.
    Dreyfus and Patricia A. Dreyfus (Evanston: Northwestern University
    Press).
Blaise Pascal. 1995. *Pensées*. Translated by Honor Levi. Oxford: Oxford
    University Press.
A.O. Scott. 2004. Christ's Passion, Told Without Grace. *International
    Herald Tribune,* Paris (26th February).
Mark Wrathall. Forthcoming. Revealed Word and World Disclosure.
    Journal of the British Society for Phenomenology 36, 2.

QUESTIONS FOR DISCUSSION

1. Pessimism is the view that nothing in this world has genuine
   worth or eternal significance. In what ways is Gibson's film
   a pessimistic movie?

2. Is Christianity an inherently pessimistic religion? How would
   you justify your answer?

3. Despair is the condition of needing, but being unable, to find
   satisfaction for our profoundest longings in this world. Does
   Gibson's Christ offer a solution to the problem of despair?

4. Can a visual depiction of a Scriptural story really contribute
   anything to our understanding of that story? Are there some
   things that can only be taught through a visual depiction?

5. What is the proper relationship between philosophical and
   artistic efforts to understand a phenomenon?

3

Christ's Atonement: Washing Away Human Sin

JERRY L. WALLS

There is something more than a little ironic in the fact that a movie about a Bible story, a story that is told every week to Sunday School children, could cause such an uproar in our society. Movies with far more graphic violence, movies with explicit and often tasteless sexual content, movies with controversial political messages, are released on a regular basis and hardly cause a ripple. Why all the passion about *The Passion*?

The answer to this question comes into focus very early in the movie when Christ is praying in the garden and Satan comes to test his resolve. Satan asks him whether he really believes one man can bear the full burden of sin, and goes on to suggest that no man can carry such a burden, and that the price of saving souls is too costly. As Jesus wrestles with these questions, he prays to his Father for strength and help. Satan then presses a further question, "Who is your Father?" and then follows this up by asking, "Who are you?"

In this brief but intense encounter, we are given in capsule form the explanation for why *The Passion of the Christ* could hardly avoid being controversial. While several factors are no doubt involved, the most profound reasons for the controversy go far beyond the graphic violence of the film, as well as the fact that many of the Jews portrayed in the film are shown in a negative way that makes them appear responsible for the death of Christ. The Romans are depicted even more unfavorably, with some of them cast as bloodthirsty thugs who relish the torment they exact from Christ.

To be sure, *The Passion* is a brutal affront to polite sensibili-
ties and gentle manners. The cruel fashion in which Christ died,
the agony of crucifixion, has perhaps never been portrayed for
us in a more jarring fashion. To cite just one example, after
Christ has been nailed to the cross, the soldiers callously turn it
over and let it fall on top of him while they secure the nails from
the back. Then they turn it over and roughly drop it again. *How*
Christ died is the most obvious focus of the film, and that is
what has understandably impressed most viewers. But the
deeper root of the controversy is what the film claims about *who*
it was that died on the cross and *why* he died.

One of the key scenes pertaining to these questions includes
the flashbacks while Christ is on the cross. As he is dying, the
film cuts back several times to "the Last Supper," that meal
Christ had with his disciples shortly before he died. In this
meal, Christ identifies the bread as his body, broken for his disciples, and the wine as his blood shed for the forgiveness of
sins. Moreover, he claims that he is the way, the truth and the
life, and goes on to say that no one can come to the Father
except through him.

Implicit here are the most basic doctrines of Christian theology, particularly the doctrine that God is a Trinity, a being who
exists in three persons, the Father, the Son, and the Holy Spirit.
Here lies the Christian answer to Satan's questions, "Who is your
Father?" and "Who are you?" His Father is God the Father, the
First Person of the Trinity. Jesus's claim that no one can come to
the Father except through him points up his own identity,
namely, that he is the second person of the Trinity, the Son who
was begotten of the Father from eternity. It also underscores the
Christian account of why the eternal Son of God took on human
nature and was born as Jesus of Nazareth, namely, to provide
salvation for the whole human race. In doing so, he provided
the only way to a right relationship with God.

These claims are the deepest roots of the controversy
sparked by Gibson's film. It is the belief that Jesus was the Son
of God incarnate that makes it such a scandal that he was
unjustly put to death. It is bad enough to kill any innocent person, especially in a degrading and cruel fashion, but if that person is God, the offense takes on much larger and more serious
proportions. Moreover, if the Christian claims are true, they are
matters of extreme importance. What is at stake is nothing less

than the truth about God and how to be rightly related to him. Given the importance of these claims, no one can rationally be indifferent about them. The passionate reactions of those who have supported the film, as well as those who have opposed it, are altogether understandable in this light.

In this chapter, I want to focus on one of these controversial claims, namely, that the death of Christ provided atonement for the sins of the whole world. But as my comments have already made clear, the concept of atonement cannot be considered in isolation from other basic Christian doctrines like the Trinity and the Incarnation. These doctrines are interwoven with each other, and one cannot grasp any one of them without at least some understanding of the others as well.

Why Do We Need Atonement?

While our specific concern here is the Christian understanding of atonement, it is worth noting that the idea of atonement and its related notion of sacrifice are not exclusive to Judeo-Christian theology. Indeed, Colin Gunton has argued that the notion of sacrifice "derives from something deep in human nature, of such a kind that it appears to be rooted in a universal or near universal feature of our life on earth" (Gunton 1992, pp. 210–11). The doctrine of atonement, then, resonates with a universal sense that we are not right with ultimate reality, and some sort of sacrifice is needed to make us right.

This is suggested by the basic meaning of the English word 'atonement,' which can be seen by dividing it up as at-one-ment. At its most basic level, atonement has to do with reconciliation and unity. That is, it has to do with uniting, or making "one" persons who were previously separated or estranged. In Christian theology, the estranged persons involved are God and humanity, so atonement is about uniting and reconciling human beings with God. When Jesus says he is the way to the Father, and that no one can come to the Father except through him, he is saying that he is the only way for humans to be "at one" with God. He is the only way "at-one-ment" with God can be achieved.

But all of this raises a prior question. Why are we separated from God and why do we need help from Jesus or anyone else to be "at one" with him? The Christian answer is because of sin. Now 'sin' is a word that has lost much of its currency in contemporary culture. Indeed, the word is often used in a joking manner when people want to make light of the idea that one of their actions might be perceived as naughty, or perhaps even rude or somewhat offensive to someone. But in its original context, the idea is no joking matter, and without that context the idea of sin cannot help but seem like a quaint notion best suited for an easy laugh on Saturday Night Live.

In short, the essential context necessary for making sense of sin is the conviction that the ultimate reality that we must come to terms with is a holy God, a God of supreme power who is perfectly righteous and just. Without this conviction, the idea of sin is a trivial notion. It is like a word from a foreign language and culture for which we have only vague associations, and those associations seem mildly amusing to us. Part of what Gibson's film has done for us is to help us recover the notion of sin as a concept with serious content. The very fact that the terrible ordeal Christ suffers is presented as the consequence of his choosing to bear our sins makes it ever more clear as the story unfolds that sin is not merely a matter of harmless pranks or charming mischief. As he absorbs our sin and evil, sin is shown in its true colors. His broken and bleeding body is a vivid image of what sin looks like when it has its way.

But still, the question persists, what is it that makes sin so terrible? Well, the basic idea is that sin is an offense against a holy God. To sin is to fail to acknowledge God, to act against him and his will. The Genesis story of the fall brings this into focus. Some theologians take this story quite literally, while others take it metaphorically. But what is more generally agreed is that the story conveys for us the nature and dynamics of sin. The heart of the story is that Adam and Eve were forbidden by God, on pain of death, to eat from the tree of the knowledge of good and evil. The story implies that their needs could be fully met in eating from the other trees, this tree alone was forbidden to them.

Their famous disobedience came at the inducement of the serpent, who suggested to them that God's motives for not allowing them to eat from the one forbidden tree were less than honorable.

> "You will not surely die," the serpent said to the woman. "For God knows that when you eat of it your eyes will be opened, and you will be like God, knowing good and evil." (Genesis 3:4–5)

In other words, the serpent suggests that God is holding out on Adam and Eve, that what he forbids is really good for them, and that their true happiness and well being is to be found in disobedience to God. In short, God is not really good and cannot really be trusted to promote their true happiness and flourishing.

This means that the heart of sin is a wrong attitude toward God, an attitude of suspicion and mistrust. The failure to obey God is not simply a matter of breaking an impersonal law or code of behavior. It is more a matter of failing to trust and return the love of a God who not only knows what is best for us, but also passionately desires it. Sin is most crucially a breach in a relationship.

But perhaps most interesting for our purposes in the Genesis story is that God was not content to leave this breach in his relationship with his creatures. Before this episode in the story ends, we see the first clue that God will find a way to cross the breach and restore us to himself. Although Adam and Eve are expelled from the garden, and must now face the world without the close relationship with God they previously enjoyed, there is a ray of hope in the somewhat enigmatic words God spoke to the serpent: "And I will put enmity between you and the woman, and between your offspring and hers; he will crush your head and you will strike his heel" (Genesis 3:15). Many Biblical scholars see in this text the first promise of atonement, a promise that would find its fulfillment in the life, death, and resurrection of Jesus.

Giving the Devil His Due?

If our problem is that we have caused a breach in our relationship with God, how is it that the death of Christ on the cross can save us from our sins and reunite us with God? That Christ died for our sins and that his death and resurrection provide our salvation is a matter of broad consensus among Christians. But just *how* his death saves us has been a matter of considerable disagreement among theologians. It is also a point of general agreement that we are saved through faith, that we must believe in Christ and accept his gift of atonement. But this only raises further questions. How can faith or belief save us if our problem is a problem of moral and relational failure?

It seems obvious to some people that it cannot, and that the whole idea of atonement is therefore absurd. Indeed, some see the idea that Christ's death on a cross could save us as barbaric or superstitious. For those inclined to this notion, Gibson's film, with its gory depiction of Christ's death, may be cited as one more piece of evidence that such criticisms are deserved.

One prominent philosopher who was critical of traditional Christian views of atonement was Immanuel Kant (1724–1804). He saw the God of traditional belief as a God who was easy to please, a God who would accept various religious observances and professions of faith as a substitute for genuine moral transformation. As Kant saw it, traditional religious faith is deeply misguided: "It is a superstitious illusion to wish to become well-pleasing to God through actions which anyone can perform without even needing to be a good man (for example, through profession of statutory articles of faith, through conformity to churchly observance and discipline, etc.)" (Kant 1968, p. 162).

Let us turn now to the pertinent questions: How does the death of Christ save us? And is faith really a superstitious thing, an illusory substitute for moral transformation? In short, how should the atonement be understood?

There are several theories of the atonement, but three have been especially prominent in the history of theology. Each of these is reflected in Gibson's film. Indeed, it is clear that Gibson has done his homework in this regard and that he has succeeded in portraying a view of atonement that is a creative synthesis of the three views. As such, the film makes an interesting theological statement as well as an artistic one. Let us consider the three theories in turn.

The first theory, sometimes recognized as the classic view because it was popular with many Church Fathers, construes the atonement as a great conquest that Christ won over the forces of sin, death, and the devil. Let us call this the *Christ as Victor View*. This view emphasizes that humanity has been captive to Satan since the fall, and consequently subject to death and sin. Christ, as the "second Adam," overcame all this by succeeding precisely where the first Adam failed. Whereas the first Adam yielded to the temptations of Satan, and fell into disobedience, Christ lived a perfect life, resisting every temptation. In the Garden of Eden, the first Adam mistrusted God, but in the Garden of Gethsemane Christ maintained total trust in God, despite the trial of a much more severe temptation. Even in the face of great suffering and death he prays for the Father's will to be done, not his own. Satan's every attempt to break him, to cause a breach in his relationship with his Father, failed miserably. In so defeating Satan, Christ broke his power over humanity and released us from his bondage.

Some of the Church Fathers who took this view, such as Origen (184–254) and Gregory of Nyssa (335–398), even saw Christ as a ransom paid to Satan. The life of Christ was the payment God made to win the release of captive humans. This debt was thought to be owed to Satan since he had won the right to control the human race by successfully tempting them to evil and disobedience. However, Satan was utterly foiled in this transaction because he did not see how things would finally turn out. In a famous metaphor, Saint Augustine (354–430) pictured the cross as a mousetrap, baited with the blood of Christ! Satan took the bait, not realizing that death could not defeat Christ.

The Christ as Victor View, sometimes also called the "Dramatic View," is, appropriately enough, portrayed in dramatic fashion in Gibson's film. The opening scene with Satan in the garden is only the first of several eerie scenes where the devil and other demonic figures play prominent roles. With striking artistic flair, Gibson foreshadows Satan's defeat when a serpent crawls out of his garment and slithers up to Christ as he kneels on the ground in prayer. After showing his resolve to do his Father's will, however difficult, Christ emphatically crushes the serpent's head with his heel, recalling the first prophecy of redemption in Genesis 3:15.

Satan's sinister presence is also evident when Christ is being scourged and crucified. He mills around in the watching crowd, and in one scene, holds a monster child who smiles maliciously. This hints at the notion of Christ as ransom since Satan appears to take pleasure in Christ's suffering and death, perhaps believing that will be the end of him. But Christ's ultimate victory is not merely in his perfect obedience, vital as that is, but in his resurrection. Although the resurrection is depicted only briefly in the film, it is crucial to the atonement since death was the original penalty for sin. Only when the power of death is broken can the power of sin be broken. Christ's resurrection demonstrated that in overcoming death, he had also decisively defeated sin and freed us from its power over us. This is foreshadowed when Satan is shown to be frustrated and enraged immediately after the death of Christ, perhaps indicating his awareness that he had not defeated Christ after all.

Another significant scene depicting Christ as the triumphant victor occurs in the brief allusion to the Jewish Passover meal, a meal that celebrated God's action to liberate the Jews from their bondage to Egypt. During the meal, a child asks the traditional question, "Why is this night different from other nights?" The answer given is that "we were slaves, but we are slaves no longer." In the film this is alluded to when Mary, the mother of Jesus, is shown suddenly waking up on the night Christ was arrested. She asks Mary Magdalene why this night is different, and Mary Magdalene answers that they are slaves no longer. This clearly suggests that just as God, through Moses, delivered his children from slavery to Pharaoh, so now through Christ he is breaking the bonds of slavery to sin and Satan, a more desperate form of bondage to an even more ruthless oppressor.

A second prominent view of the atonement, famously defended by the great medieval philosopher and theologian Saint Anselm (1033–1109), is the *Satisfaction Theory*. This view differs significantly from that of those Church Fathers who saw the death of Christ as a ransom paid to Satan. On the Satisfaction Theory, God himself is owed a debt because of human sin. As a being of infinite worth and goodness, God deserves total obedience and honor from his creatures. Consequently, sin is infinitely serious and racks up an infinite debt, a debt that humans do not begin to have the resources to repay. Moreover, Anselm argued, God cannot simply forgive our sins without requiring some sort of satisfaction. He cannot rightly compromise his dignity and honor. If we are to be forgiven and restored to God, someone must pay, on humanity's behalf, the infinite debt of honor that is owed to him.

This is why God became man according to Anselm. As man he was able to satisfy the debt humanity owed to God. As God, he had something of infinite worth to offer. His life of perfect obedience was offered as a sacrifice to God, thereby allowing God to forgive us while also vindicating his honor.

In a subtle variation, the Satisfaction Theory has also been understood in terms of divine justice, as distinct from honor. Sin deserves punishment, the argument goes, and as a perfectly just being, God cannot simply forgo this punishment. On this interpretation of the theory, Christ bore the punishment for human sin, so human beings can be forgiven without God compromising his perfect justice. This understanding is sometimes also referred to as the "Penal Substitution View" of the atonement, indicating that Christ was our substitute, who took our deserved penalty when he died on the cross. The notorious criminal Barabbas, who was released instead of Christ, would be a symbol for all of us, on this view. While we are guilty and Christ is innocent, he died in our place.

It is worth distinguishing, at this point, the difference between atonement and retribution. Whereas the point of retribution is essentially to punish a guilty offender with an appropriate punishment, this notion of atonement involves an innocent person willingly accepting punishment so that the truly guilty can be spared. The ultimate aim of retribution is justice, but the ultimate aim of atonement is mercy and reconciliation.

This is perhaps the most familiar view of atonement and some variation of it has been widely embraced in western theology, both Roman Catholic and Protestant. It is also the understanding of atonement most prevalent in popular preaching and devotion. Not surprisingly, this account of Christ's death is clearly featured in *The Passion of the Christ*. Indeed, an article in *Time* magazine discussing the movie said that "its graphic depiction of how Christ was killed is dramatic testimony of the director's fervent belief in this theory of atonement." This is particularly suggested by the most intense scene in the film, namely, the scourging, a prolonged scene that many viewers have found especially difficult to watch. The scene provides a shocking visual for the well known words of the prophet Isaiah with which Gibson's film begins, a favorite text, moreover, of those who advocate the penal substitution view of atonement: "He was wounded for our transgressions, he was punished for our iniquities, by his stripes we are healed" (Isaiah 53:5).

Furthermore, the director subtly suggests this view in a scene full of symbolic significance, the only one in the movie where Gibson himself appears, albeit rather indirectly. When Christ is being crucified, Gibson's hand holds the nail that is driven into Christ's hand. Thereby, Gibson depicts the conviction that we—all of us—are responsible for putting Christ to death. It is our sins that he bore, it is in our stead that he died, and because of that we can be forgiven and escape the penalty that we deserve.

The third influential theory of atonement, known as the *Moral Influence Theory*, comes from another famous medieval philosopher and theologian, Peter Abelard (1079–1142). The core of Abelard's view is that the passion of Christ was a powerful exhibition of God's overwhelming love for us designed to elicit our love in return. So long as the fear of God's wrath hangs over us, this view insists, we are not free to love him. The cross is a stunning display of God's heart of love that lifts the fear of wrath and enables us to love him and experience moral and spiritual transformation in the process.

This theory of atonement is suggested by the characters in the film who are transformed by the power of Christ's love. Four that come readily to mind are Mary Magdalene, the thief on the cross who died alongside Christ, Simon of Cyrene who was forced to help carry the cross, and the Roman soldier who fell to his knees when he pierced Christ with his spear and the blood flowed from his side.

Mary's transformation is suggested as she is mopping up Christ's blood after his scourging and there is a flashback to the incident where a group of Jewish leaders wanted to stone her for adultery. Christ intervenes with the challenge that the one who is without sin should cast the first stone. (Apparently Gibson identifies Mary with the woman taken in adultery in John's Gospel). Instead of wrath, she is offered forgiveness and love, and as she mops up Christ's blood, she is returning that love.

Similarly, the scene with the thief on the cross is a striking statement that the death of Christ is a stunning revelation of God's love for all who have eyes to see. As the Jewish leaders mock Christ by telling him to come down that they might see and believe, he prays to the Father for their forgiveness. While one of the thieves joins in the mockery, the other rebukes him, pointing out that Christ was praying for him. Christ would be just in condemning him, he recognizes, but instead Christ prays for his forgiveness. As the scene concludes, the first thief has his eyes plucked out by birds, symbolizing the spiritual blindness of any who could not see the love of God so obviously blazing forth in their midst. It was not in coming down from the cross, but in willingly staying on it that God's love was so unmistakably displayed.

Likewise, Simon is changed by his encounter with Christ. At first he protests against having to carry the cross, saying he is an innocent man forced to carry the cross of a criminal. But as he and Christ carry the cross together and he observes how Christ bears his suffering, Simon's attitude turns around completely. He becomes angry with the soldiers for their cruelty and begins to defend Christ. By the end of the walk, it is clear he has come to admire Christ, if not love him. He leaves regretfully only after being chased away by the Roman soldiers. Finally, one of these soldiers is compelled to fall to his knees in an apparent act of worship.

But Does It Really Make Sense?

The doctrine of atonement is rife with philosophical implications and obviously raises numerous questions. Just as each of the three theories presented above can claim illustrious advocates in the history of philosophy and theology, so each of them has notable critics. Indeed, the debate is very much alive in our time, and *The Passion* has done much to bring these issues to the attention of the broader culture. Fortunately, for those interested in further exploration, the doctrine of atonement has received considerable attention from contemporary philosophers of religion, and each of the main theories has been defended in recent literature by one or more respected philosophers. Next, I identify one of the central issues raised by each of the theories, and briefly indicate how it might be addressed.

First, the Christ as Victor view has been often criticized insofar as it includes the idea that Christ was a ransom given to the devil. It is morally absurd, critics charge, to think that Satan might have some sort of moral claim on human beings, and that God would respect his wishes by giving him Christ. Charles Taliaferro, a contemporary defender of the ransom theory, notes that there are several replies that can be offered to such criticisms:

> One is that paying Satan the requested ransom is an almost fortuitous event, for Satan was requesting the very thing that would destroy him. . . . Early Church fathers went on to note the irony of this overcoming of Satan for it seemed to bring out the ultimate absurdity and self-destructive nature of evil. The fool digs a ditch to capture another and falls into it himself. There is irony especially as Christ gains our freedom precisely by the means by which the devil was seeking our final destruction. (Taliaferro 1988, pp. 86–87)

Here it is important to emphasize the self-destructiveness of evil, a central theme in philosophy and theology. Taliaferro illustrates this with the example of a captor who demands gold kryptonite in exchange for the lives of his captives, not suspecting the gold kryptonite will rob him of his power. There is much more to his argument than this brief quote can convey, but the point for now is that even the more difficult aspects of this theory of atonement are not without interesting and plausible lines of defense.

Next, let us turn to the Satisfaction Theory. A common objection to it, as represented by the quote from Kant above, is that belief in atonement is a means to evade moral responsibility, a dubious attempt to avoid the requirement to become truly righteous. This sort of criticism is especially aimed at penal substitution theories, whose adherents sometimes suggest that Christ's sacrificial obedience to God exempts them from the need to be obedient and holy themselves.

In response to this, it can be pointed out that thoughtful defenders of satisfaction theories of atonement, represented by such contemporary thinkers as Philip Quinn and Richard Swinburne, construe the atonement in such a way that faith in it is not a matter of mere intellectual assent that is morally indifferent. Rather, it is a response of genuine gratitude that involves sincere repentance of our sins. Swinburne, who defends what he calls the sacrifice version of this theory, holds that Christ, by giving up his perfect life, makes available the sacrifice, but it is we who must offer it if that sacrifice is be effective. He explains this as follows: "Christ's laid-down life is there made available for sacrifice, like a ram caught in a thicket. Any man who is humble and serious enough about his sin to recognize what is the proper reparation and penance for it may use the costly gift which another has made available for him to offer as his sacrifice" (Swinburne 1989, p. 153).

To plead the atonement in this fashion is obviously not a matter of being flippant about one's sins. On Swinburne's account, atonement requires repentance and apology on our end. Christ has done the costly work of reparation by offering to God the perfect obedience and worship we owed him. He has done the necessary repair work, as it were, in response to the damage we have done with our sins. But this work of reparation is not personally effective in our lives until we sincerely acknowledge our wrong and distance ourselves from it. We cannot simultaneously plead the atonement of Christ and be content to be the kind of persons whose sins required such a costly sacrifice.

It is worth reflecting, in this connection, on the remarkable phenomenon of how so many viewers of *The Passion of the Christ* have been affected in their personal lives. There are numerous accounts of persons seeking forgiveness for various wrongs, restoring marriages and other relationships, and even confessing to crimes. Some of these stories have been told in a television documentary called "Miracles of the Passion." Jody Eldred, the executive producer of this program, visited websites where such stories were reported and found over 70,000 such accounts of lives who were touched by the film. This is an interesting piece of data from the information age confirming that genuine faith in the atonement is a morally transforming reality, not an alternative to moral transformation.

That brings us to the Moral Influence Theory. The strength of this view is that it provides a psychologically intelligible account of how the death of Christ transforms us and changes us in such a way that we can be restored to a loving relationship with God. Its weakness, however, is that it does not so easily account for how the death of Christ removes the guilt of our past sins. Indeed, critics charge that this view does not really grasp either God's holy demands or the seriousness of our failure to meet them. It suggests that all we need is spiritual illumination and inspiration, and if this is so, any sufficiently impressive martyr could have provided it. There is no obvious need for the Son of God Himself to become incarnate and die for us. To put it another way, this theory focuses entirely on the *subjective* elements of how the atonement changes us personally, to the neglect of the traditional emphases on the *objective* elements, in particular Christ's work to pay the penalty for our sin and secure our forgiveness.

Philip Quinn, who has recently defended a version of penal substitution, has also taken up the mantle of defending the Moral Influence Theory of Peter Abelard. He contends that in fact Abelard endorses penal substitution, although this was not his primary emphasis. As he puts it, Abelard was a "hierarchical pluralist" who offered an account of the atonement that has a "dominant motif to which others are subordinated" (Quinn 1993,

p. 291). This suggests that many criticisms of the Moral Influence Theory are misguided insofar as they pit that theory against the Satisfaction Theory, as if they were competing accounts or were somehow incompatible.

The larger lesson here is that perhaps any satisfactory account of the atonement will include elements of all three of these major theories. The debates will no doubt continue as to which theory should be dominant, but any proposal that does not address both the objective and the subjective aspects of the atonement will not capture the vital dimensions of what faith in the atonement involves. This is not to deny that some claims of the different theories may be incompatible with claims of other theories. For instance, *some* ways of construing the ransom theory may be inconsistent with *some* accounts of penal substitution. But the point remains that there are ways of including central concerns of all three theories that are mutually compatible and enriching. What Gibson has done with artistic creativity can also be done with theological coherence and integrity.

All of this shows how *The Passion of the Christ* has stimulated our minds as it has stirred our hearts. In doing so, it has demonstrated afresh that philosophy at its best is reflection on matters that matter. What moves us to care is what moves us to seek understanding. And for that we should all be grateful.

SOURCES

Colin Gunton. 1992. The Sacrifice and the Sacrifices: From Metaphor to Transcendental? In Ronald J. Feenstra and Cornelius Plantinga, Jr., eds., *Trinity, Incarnation, and Atonement* (Notre Dame: University of Notre Dame Press).

Immanuel Kant. 1968. *Religion within the Limits of Reason Alone.* Translated by Theodore M. Greene and Hoyt H. Hudson. New York: Harper.

Philip Quinn. 1993. Abelard on Atonement: Nothing Unintelligible, Arbitrary, Illogical, or Immoral about It. In Eleanore Stump, ed., *Reasoned Faith* (Ithaca: Cornell University Press.)

Eleanore Stump. 1992. Atonement and Justification. In Ronald J. Feenstra and Cornelius Plantinga, Jr., eds., *Trinity, Incarnation, and Atonement* (Notre Dame: University of Notre Dame Press).

Richard Swinburne. 1989. *Responsibility and Atonement.* Oxford: Clarendon Press.

Charles Tarliaferro. 1988. A Narnian Theory of the Atonement. *Scottish Journal of Theology* 41, pp. 75–92.

Jerry L. Walls. 2002. *Heaven: The Logic of Eternal Joy*. New York: Oxford University Press. See especially Chapter 2.

QUESTIONS FOR DISCUSSION

1. Can one believe in the atonement of Jesus and also believe there are other ways to be united with God?

2. Why is the resurrection important for the atonement?

3. Do you believe Christ's atonement can save us even if we are not morally transformed by it?

4. Which theory of atonement makes the most sense to you? Why?

5. How does the atonement relate to other central teachings of the Christian religion, such as Incarnation and Trinity?

4

The Focus of *The Passion* Puts the Person of Jesus Out of Focus

CHARLES TALIAFERRO

It hardly seems fair to complain that a movie entitled *The Passion of the Christ* gives too much attention to the passion of the Christ. This is particularly true because Mel Gibson's movie takes on board more than the passion; there are some flashbacks to a charming, humorous scene of Jesus jesting with his mother and to a scene in which Jesus forgives and protects a woman charged with adultery, and the movie ends with the resurrection. Even so, Gibson's giving center stage to the intense, relentless violence of the passion does raise a philosophical worry about whether the passion ultimately threatens to eclipse the nature and value of the person Christ who underwent the passion. Many (though not all) Christian theologians see *Christ's whole life* as redemptive: Christ's birth, youth, coming of age, baptism, nonviolent teaching, healing, and resurrection as well as the passion and death by crucifixion. By focusing almost exclusively on the trauma of the passion, has Gibson given us a portrait of suffering that is so riveting and absorbing that we naturally lose sight of the broader context of the life of Christ?

There is also the following related worry: Does Gibson's portrayal of Christ's submission to unjustified torture wind up giving excessive pre-eminence to the value of redemptive suffering? In the film, it appears that the principal work of redemption is accomplished in the passion itself, whereas other theological treatments see the resurrection as just as vital as the passion.

In this chapter I explore these questions and consider the positive contribution of theologies that give greater priority to the resurrection, but I must add at the outset that my chief goal is not to unleash a series of objections to the movie itself. My intent is more to raise questions and then to suggest ways in which experiencing this significant movie may be put in a helpful, expanded setting.

A Prelude on the Philosophy of Persons

Many ethicists and political philosophers in the twentieth century have lamented the way in which enormous harms have been brought about for the sake of impersonal, abstract ideals. Losing sight of, or just simply denying, the goodness of concrete individual persons has been at the core of the worst atrocities in recent history, as documented in Jonathan Glover's superb book, *Humanity: A Moral History of the Twentieth Century*. This has led a number of philosophers who have come to be known as *personalists* to adopt a view which recognizes the fundamental value of persons themselves. For personalists, persons are valuable in themselves and not because persons can be happy or flourish, exercise reason, have desires and so on. By their lights, to value a person because a person can be happy (or to experience or do something in particular) is to elevate the value of something that is less than a person as a whole. Persons are more than any one state of mind or activity; they are capable of an inexhaustible array of feelings, thoughts, and actions, and are not to be valued only because they are good for some overriding purpose.

These philosophers believe that locating the value of persons in some specific, singular aspect of their nature involves a failure to recognize the transcendent overflowing worth of persons themselves. By elevating some aspect of personal life like happiness as a basic value, one winds up relegating the concept of a person to some kind of vehicle or container that is worthy of regard because it can include happiness. Personalists see the person as a fundamental, irreducible good.

Personalism may seem odd with its insistence on valuing persons rather than the state or activity of persons, but you may gain sympathy for it when you take seriously the enormity of harm done to persons in light of impersonal ideals and values.

In *Humanity*, Glover writes convincingly about the dangerous consequences of a dehumanized, abstract ethic that fails to take seriously the reality of other persons who are as real and valuable as oneself. Even the best ideals, like justice and charity, have been distorted and used to great harm. Personalists have sought to combat such harm by keeping before us a robust, concrete concept of the good of persons.

An example of harm that results from not seeing the good of concrete individual persons is the persecution of Jews carried out at different times by so-called Christians. This example is particularly fitting here because some religious leaders have worried that the release of Gibson's movie might be a catalyst to anti-Semitic violence, much in the way that in the High Middle Ages in Europe Jewish communities would be subject to great violence during the Easter season when the passion of Christ was re-enacted.

The modern movement of personalism grew out of a concern that if persons are valued for some other "greater" reason than being a person—whether it be religious, political or economic—then individual persons would inevitably be sacrificed in light of these "greater," impersonal values. Although a wide range of philosophers have been classified as personalists from Martin Buber (1878–1965) to Max Scheler (1874–1928), there was a distinctive, important school of personalism that flourished at Boston University in the twentieth century and included B.P. Bowne (1847–1910), E.S. Brightman (1844–1932) and P. Bertocci (1910–1989). This movement influenced the great civil rights leader Martin Luther King, Jr.

Focussing More on the Passion than the Person?

Why should anyone think that Gibson's movie risks a subordination of the person of Christ to the passion he underwent? The worry lies, in part, in the very nature of torture itself. Victims of torture report that one of the most grave injuries that one may experience is a complete collapse of one's personal identity. A principal aim of a great deal of torture, whether the torture is physical or principally psychological is to destroy a person's ability to think coherently about him or herself as a whole, integrated, healthy individual. Now, in the movie, Christ is not annihilated through the torment. He retains his identity and, when you get to the resurrection, one may even see him more as a survivor than only as a victim. In fact, his endurance of the sustained whipping, laceration, and immense loss of blood, testifies to an almost supernatural endurance of the person. Still, the brutality of the beating and the haunting ripping apart of his flesh, inevitably (at least for me) shatters my grasp of the breadth and redeeming scope of Christ's life as a whole, including the resurrection.

In a sense, there is so much violent bloodshed that the movie becomes about violent bloodshed. Rather than think of Christ as a whole, integrated life of healing, teaching and so on, it is the focused, mesmerizing torment that so consumes our attention that all else seems peripheral and decentralized. The cosmic, all absorbing point of view of the movie is Christ's innocent endurance of the unjustified infliction of inhumane violence. The result is what many studies of violence have recorded in victims of traumatic violence: a loss or obscuring of peripheral vision. Under severe threat, a human (and many animals) will lose his or her broader visual capacities, sometimes seeing things as though through a tunnel. My worry here is not that *The Passion of the Christ* somehow discredits the person Christ, but that the intense focus of the film displaces a regard for Christ's life as a whole. The combined graphic torment, bloodshed, and grueling punishment is so gigantic and shocking that it edges to one side an appreciation of Christ's whole life, teaching, and resurrection.

In defense of the movie, it should be pointed out that any good, cinematic portrayal of intense agony is likely to focus its audience on the horror at hand. Would the movie be better if it were re-worked to show the birth and life of Christ as a preface or, like *The Lord of the Rings*, there was a sequence of three movies? This seems too much to expect. It seems unavoidable that in witnessing a re-enactment of the passion, one see the person Christ as shattered and brutalized. It would be odd if, for example, there was immense, endless bloodshed in a movie about the life of Gandhi, but it seems that a movie about Jesus cannot avoid taking seriously the violence that was unleashed in his torture and crucifixion.

Fair enough. Perhaps it is enough of a reply to my worry that the film still makes good sense when accompanied with the suggestion that shell-shocked viewers might like to know something more about Jesus's nonviolent love, healing, and so on. But even if the movie comes with a warning label, it still poses a danger I want to highlight.

Let me shift gears at this point and outline a positive reason for seeing the passion in the context of the full life and resurrection of Christ. Then I make the case that the movie, with its singular focus, does indeed have some troubling implications.

Resurrection and Reconciliation

Consider a case where there has been some wrong and there is need for reconciliation. Imagine Patricia and Kris are friends but Patricia betrays Kris. Reconciliation between the two might include the following steps: Patricia realizes she did wrong, feels and expresses profound remorse, intends not to do this wrong again, renounces her past error, and perhaps even does something uncalled for in presenting Kris with some gift. We might further picture Patricia suffering immensely with regret for her wrong, perhaps even undergoing punishment. The problem of restitution still remains, however. Given that we can't change the past, Patricia can never undo the fact that she committed some wrong.

This would be most dramatically obvious in a case where she was involved in some great crime, like killing Kris' child. No matter how much suffering Patricia undergoes or how many times she rescues other children, there will be no earthly way to restore the lost child. There will always be, on a merely human level, an inability to make full restoration of the good that has been destroyed. (This is true both in catastrophic cases like murder and in grievous but serious wrong-doing. Imagine I betray the confidence of my friend. Even there, I cannot reverse the wrong or somehow give her back the time she may feel she has wasted in our "friendship.")

The way the story of Patricia and Kris might intersect the Christian narrative is if we expand the context from the merely human to include the supernatural. Imagine Patricia does all that is within her power to reform and restore all past harm, albeit she cannot restore the child. But now imagine there is a person, a God-man, who is able and in fact does bring the child back from the dead, resurrecting the child in a transformed, good state. Imagine further that such a resurrection is also willed or sincerely hoped for by the wrong-doer so that Patricia, in a sense, wills along with the God-man that, indeed, the child be restored. This, I think, would be a decisive act, providing the element that will always go missing in reconciliation without the supernatural.

On this view, the resurrection of the child would be part of the atonement (at-onement) between Patricia and Kris. And it would also be part of the atonement between God and creation if we expand the story even further to see the resurrection as restoring what Patricia wrongly did against God, given that such a killing or any wrong doing may be seen as violating a life in harmony with God. Obviously, a great deal more would need to be said to fill out an account of just how the resurrection of Christ is linked with the promise of the resurrection to new life of others. My point here is simply that early Christian theology, including Biblical teaching, saw the resurrection as well as the passion as central, defining features of Christ's redeeming work (John 11:25).

When the portrait of atonement includes the resurrection, there is a natural place for joy (even laughter, as I suggest later), as the resurrection is about the making whole and transfiguration of persons. You can't rise from the dead without dying, and so the joy in the resurrection presupposes sorrow in dying and death. But there is a substantial Christian tradition that also sees the dying and death as inextricably bound up with, and leading to, the resurrection. The New Testament describes Christ as enduring the shame of the cross for "the joy set before him" (Hebrews 12:2). Christian joy was and is best seen as not *in the cross* but before and after the cross or, if you will, *through it*; God's loving power is stronger than death (Romans 8:35-39). Early Christian teaching in the Book of Acts emphasizes the profundity of Christ's dying as the Messiah, but the preaching of the primitive Church makes no sense without the resurrection.

In a sense, the teaching of the resurrection would probably carry even more wonder than the teaching of the crucifixion as that form of execution was commonplace in the ancient world. It was sometimes even regarded an entertainment. At the coliseum in Rome, criminals were often crucified during the lunch hour, which marked an intermission between the morning show of people being killed by "exposure" to wild beasts and the afternoon gladiatorial games. Christ's torture and barbaric death may have been more brutal than others, but early Christians chiefly celebrated the overcoming of this form of murder and, even more importantly, death itself. While the ancients may not have found the violence of the cross unusual, what they did find unusual and deeply attractive was the nonviolence of Christ's life and teaching, and visions of the resurrected Christ (I Peter 1:3).

Gibson's portrayal of Christ, however, with its focus on the horrors of the passion seems to place one more squarely in the suffering than in the resurrection as the key to the atonement. In another chapter in this volume, Jerry Walls outlines three different accounts of the atonement. I will not re-address each of those theories, though I will comment briefly on how Gibson's theology of the atonement can encourage an unduly pre-eminent view of the good of redemptive suffering while subordinating the indispensable value of the resurrection.

As Walls notes, my own preference is for what he calls "The Christ as Victor model" of the atonement. I think Mel Gibson's film speaks more to the Satisfaction Theory and the challenges facing that theory are at work in the movie. In the Satisfaction theory, the sacrifice that Christ makes is itself a good thing. The movie begins with a passage from Isaiah 53 in which, as many Christians have held, the prophet is referring to Christ who will be wounded and crushed for our transgressions. On many versions of the Satisfaction model, the wounding and crushing is something deserved or fitting. The suffering of Jesus is seen as a sign of love; Jesus loves the world so much that he undergoes that soul-destroying degree of degradation and defilement as a payment of the penalty or debt that we sinners owe to God.

This can lead one to value or take pleasure in the crucifixion or passion itself. This is dangerous, for what is pivotal to most Christian theology is that the cross, as an instrument of torture, and death itself are defeated by and through the love of God. Indeed, apart from the occasional Christian cult, the central Christian tradition holds that there is no pleasure, or relish, in the torment. Some Christian practices, especially for the Orthodox and Roman Catholics, include kissing the cross and this may be a symbolic or sacramental way of kissing Christ or enacting a ritual reversal of the kiss of Judas who betrayed Christ. But this is not kissing torment. If it were a veneration of torment, it would constitute theological sadism and a dangerous accommodation of violence. In a world where people have been persecuted in the name of Christ, such an accommodation must be avoided at all costs.

In an account of the atonement in an essay on C.S. Lewis's work, I suggest that Christ's work is best seen not in terms of the surrogate bearing of a penalty that we deserve, but in terms of it breaking in and rescuing persons from an entangling, evil captivity. In this model, there is a sense in which Christ takes the place of human hostages who have bound themselves to oppression, but this is to break everyone free, or to make such freedom possible, by dying and then by resurrection (Taliaferro 1988).

The personalist tradition has an important bearing on the way violence and suffering are portrayed, both in film and philosophy. Max Scheler (1874–1928) has brought to light the profound difference between those who are motivated to oppose violence because it is hateful and those who oppose it because of their love of health and wholeness. He thought of the latter as positive and life-affirming, whereas the former risks a dangerous development in which persons may become shaped and defined by the very thing they despise. Gibson certainly does not glamorize violence in *The Passion*, but its disproportionate, grievous intensity makes it hard to concentrate on positive, life-affirming values. Consider Scheler's portrait of St. Francis of Assisi's embracing poverty and his assistance of others through sickness:

> He does not love sickness and poverty, but what is *behind* them, and his help is directed *against* these evils. When Francis of Assisi kisses festering wounds and does not even kill the bugs that bite him, but leaves his body to them as a hospitable home, these acts (if seen from the outside) could be signs of perverted instincts and of a perverted valuation. But that is not actually the case. It is not a lack of nausea or a delight in the pus which makes St. Francis act in this way. He has overcome his nausea through a deeper feeling of life and vigor! This attitude is completely different from that of recent modern realism in art and literature, the exposure of social misery . . . the wallowing in the morbid . . . Those people saw something bug-like in everything that lives, whereas Francis sees the holiness of "life" even in the bug. (Scheler 1976, pp. 91, 92)

I would not describe Gibson's film as morbid or a case of modern realism depicting people as bug-like! But I do think that the more positive, Fransiscan affirmation of the holiness of life is edged out of the picture.

Tragedy and Comedy: Gibson and Tolkien

To fill out the point I have been making about seeing the passion in light of the whole of Christ's life, consider a comparison between two contemporary cinematic portraits of resurrection. It will seem strange to compare J.R.R. Tolkien's *The Lord of the Rings* with *The Passion of the Christ*, but both works involve life and death struggle, and the overcoming of deadly violence. In Tolkien's work, the wizard Gandalf engages in dramatic combat with a beast and either dies or undergoes an extraordinary purgation before he is dramatically restored or re-born with immense good power.

Gibson's portrayal of Jesus's resurrection is brief, dramatic, and elegant, but I cannot imagine Gibson's Jesus laughing after the event. And I suspect this is because both Jesus and we are literally exhausted by the horrors of the passion. The film couldn't depict Christ laughing after the resurrection because the whole center of gravity of the movie is on the mock trial and the cruel breaking of an innocent person.

With Tolkien's Gandalf, however, we might come closer to the Biblical portrait. First a word on the Bible, and then on Gandalf. The New Testament, of course, describes the agony and humiliation of the cross. But, after the resurrection, Jesus joins some people at a dinner party (Luke 24); there is even what might be described as a beach picnic with the resurrected Jesus (John 21). I can't help but think of this Jesus laughing, and I suspect Tolkien (who was, like Gibson, a practicing Catholic) modeled Gandalf on the Christ.

There is a wonderful portrayal in the book, *The Return of the King*, and in the movie version as well, of Gandalf laughing with Frodo and Sam after evil has been defeated. In the book, here is the crucial passage:

> 'A great Shadow has departed,' said Gandalf, and then he laughed, and the sound was like music, or like water in a parched land; and as he listened the thought came to Sam that he had not heard laugher, the pure sound of merriment, for days upon days without count. It fell upon his ears like the echo of all the joys he had ever known. (Tolkien 1973, p. 283)

Here is the philosophical substance of this chapter: As a personalist I am uneasy when the value of a person becomes obscured or subordinated to the good of some specific event or action. *The Passion of the Christ* is a powerful, spell-binding portrayal of Christ's last hours with brilliant merits. Meditation on the passion has a rightful place within Christian theology, and it can serve to crystalize or consummate an appreciation of Jesus's value as a person. Nonetheless, some caution is needed, for one may be so overcome by the ferocity and skin-lascerating horror of the suffering that one losses sight of the whole of Christ's life. The danger is that the appreciation of Christ as a healer and teacher of nonviolence will be eclipsed by the dread engendered by watching an innocent person who is loving and forgiving as he is made the object of horrifying, unrelieved violence.

SOURCES

Gustaf Aulen. 1940. *Christus Victor.* Translated by A.G. Hebert. London: SPCK.

Edgar Sheffeld Brightman. 1958. *Person and Reality.* Edited by Peter Bertocci. New York: Ronald Press.

T.O. Buford and H.H. Oliver. 2002. *Personalism Revisited.* New York: Rodopi.

Jonathan Glover. 2000. *Humanity: A Moral History of the Twentieth Century.* New Haven: Yale University Press.

A.C. Knudson. 1949. *The Philosophy of Personalism.* Boston: Boston University Press.

J. Macmurray. 1961. *Persons in Relation.* London: Faber.

Emmanuel Mounier. 1952. *Personalism.* New York: Grove Press.

Max Scheler. 1976. *Resentiment.* Edited by L.A. Coser, translated by W. Holdheim. New York: Schocken.

Peter Spader. 2002. *Scheler's Ethical Personalism.* New York: Fordham University Press.

Charles Taliaferro. 1988. A Narnian Theory of the Atonement. *Scottish Journal of Theology* 41 (1988), pp. 75–92.

J.R.R. Tolkien. 1973. *The Return of the King.* New York: Ballantine.

QUESTIONS FOR DISCUSSION

1. Personalist philosophers like Edgar Sheffeld Brightman claim that persons have intrinsic value or value for their own sakes and not for the sake of some other value such as happiness, reason or the satisfaction of desires. Do you think persons are valuable for their own sake? What are the implications of believing that persons have value for their own sake?

2. Arguably, suffering can lead to the shattering of one's personal identity. Can certain forms of pleasure or happiness have a similar impact?

3. This essay stresses how the life-affirming nature of the resurrecton plays an important role in redemption. Do you agree or disagree?

4. When someone does a heroic act—perhaps saving an innocent person who is threatened—we take pleasure in, and admire the act. In what ways, however, might this involve taking pleasure that there was a threat to begin with?

5. How important do you find Scheler's distinction between positive and negative moral motivation? Compare a physician who went into medicine because she hated illness with one who loved health and wholeness. What would the advantages or disadvantages be in a police officer who was drawn to law enforcement because she hated violence rather than loving peace and justice?

5
Gibson's Sublime *Passion*: In Defense of the Violence

WILLIAM IRWIN

The Passion has spurred much controversy and debate, but nearly everyone agrees that the film is difficult to watch. The violence, the blood, the gore make it too painful for most people.

Why do we willingly watch works of art that bring pain with pleasure? Aesthetics, the branch of philosophy concerned with the study of art, helps us answer this question, which has concerned philosophers since Aristotle (384–322 B.C.). To address this question and justify Gibson's depiction of violence let's consider *The Passion* in terms of three important categories: beauty, tragedy, and the sublime.

The Beautiful and the Moral

Whatever beauty is, no one could rightfully call Mel Gibson's film beautiful. Nor could anyone deny that Michelangelo's Vatican *Pietà* is beautiful. Admittedly, the subject matters of the sculpture and film are different, but there is a *Pietà* allusion in *The Passion*, as we see the bloody Jesus in the arms of a weary Mary at the foot of the cross.

Immanuel Kant (1724–1804) aside, most philosophers recognize that beauty is contextual, that knowing about the artwork and its subject matter bears on how we evaluate it. Michelangelo's *Pietà* is sad, delicate, and displays a cherry-blossom beauty, but it does not inspire thought and moral reflection. In fact the beauty of the *Pietà* distracts us from its subject matter. We do not feel moved to reflection on the suffering of Jesus and Mary. Rather we behold a sight unlike anything we have seen before, and we marvel at the artistic accomplishment.

When the beautiful connects us to the moral it tends to do so mistakenly, getting it wrong or getting it right only by accident. Still a common and psychologically persuasive notion, the ancient Greek *kalos-kagathon*, the beautiful-good, implies that the beautiful is morally good and the morally good is beautiful. But experience tells us that the beautiful is generally appreciated for itself, and when it begins to steer us toward moral judgment we need to be careful. As a beautiful face can distract us from a person's moral substance or lack thereof, so can a beautiful artwork. Knowing the subject of the artwork may heighten our appreciation for the artwork's beauty, but its beauty is unlikely to heighten our appreciation for its subject. Viewing the *Pietà* we are far less inspired to devotion than we are awed at the artistic accomplishment.

The Choice of Violence

Could *The Passion* have been beautiful? Quentin Tarantino has been wrongly acclaimed for the "exquisite and elegant violence" in films such as *Kill Bill* and *Pulp Fiction*. While the choreographed, sword-wielding violence of *Kill Bill* is spectacular, it is not beautiful and it conveys no moral truth. The crass violence of *Pulp Fiction* conveys moral truth, that redemption is possible, but lacks beauty. Gibson's choice to show the violence to tell the story of the passion precludes it being beautiful, especially if it is to succeed in directing us to moral truth. Contra Keats, truth is not beauty, nor beauty truth. *Quid est veritas?* It sometimes ain't pretty.

"It's too violent, too much blood and gore. I couldn't stand to watch it." So goes one common complaint about Gibson's film. For many Christians, *The Passion* fails to highlight the parts of Jesus's ministry that they believe are most important, his message of love and peace. The film could have been different. The violence and suffering was a choice of emphasis, not a necessity.

But Gibson did not choose to tell the story of Jesus's entire ministry with special emphasis on his passion. He chose to tell the story of the passion. So how *should* he have told that story? It is, after all, a "cruci-fiction." Aware that 'cross' and 'crucifixion' connote torture in Latin, what should we expect? Torture at the hands of Roman soldiers was far worse than what counts as torture at the hands of wayward American soldiers. So *ecce homo*, behold the man, through the sheer horror of his flogging, scourged as he is, bathed in a bouquet of blood, crowned with thorns, and made to carry his cross to the place of execution. This is the "bloody Christ" of *The Passion* not the "buddy Christ" of *Dogma*.

Some complain and conjecture that the actual scourging and flogging could not have been as severe as Gibson portrays them. Perhaps. But Scripture says that Simon of Cyrene carried the cross, so we can safely assume the scourging was sufficient to leave Jesus unable to carry it. And undoubtedly the inner agony and humiliation of the actual crucifixion were far worse than anything that film images can convey. In any case, to witness in person the bloody scourging would have been far worse than merely watching it on screen, even if the screen version surpassed the reality.

A director's choices of emphasis and perspective inevitably displease some. You can't make everybody happy and you shouldn't even try. For example, Holocaust films no matter how finely done find critics. Steven Spielberg's *Schindler's List* portrays the utter inhumanity of the concentration camps, but some complain it makes a hero of Oscar Schindler. Perhaps he was a hero, but does his heroism deserve such attention? Shouldn't Spielberg have focused attention elsewhere? Roberto Benigni's *Life Is Beautiful* is a story of boundless hope, a triumph of the spirit, a testament to resilience, but it was criticized as "Holocaust lite." Yes, Benigni and Spielberg could have made different choices, could have made different films. But the films they made are gifts to be appreciated for what they are, not to be rejected for what they could have been.

Viewers who reject *The Passion* for Gibson's choice of emphasis include in large numbers those who imagine Jesus as much like Barney the Dinosaur singing, "I love you / you love me / let's be friends / in Galilee." They choose to focus on the message of love, passing the passion, going directly to the resurrection. Of course this is not a fair description of *all* people who reject *The Passion*, and that *is* one way to tell the story. But it is not the way Gibson chose. If Jesus did not suffer for our sins and rise from the dead, then he was simply a philosopher. But Christianity holds that he was much more. Gibson's choice to graphically portray the violence of *The Passion* makes the film difficult to watch, and this is just the point.

What? A Tragedy?

Plato (428–348 B.C.) spoke against Greek tragedies and Homeric epics, finding they gave false depictions of the gods and aroused fear and pity, emotions one should avoid. Plato was right: violence can inflame "the passions." As a boy, I came out of *Rocky III* throwing punches in the air, looking to take on all comers in the parking lot. As a man, I came out of *Troy* feeling like Achilles, wanting to slay my enemies. Curiously, though, the violence of *The Passion* has no effect of that kind. It is not the "guns, lots of guns" and Kung Fu fighting of *The Matrix*. It does not incite one to violence. If anything, it leaves one numb. Plato was quick to banish the tragic poets from his ideal Republic. We should not be so quick to pan *The Passion*.

As Aristotle asked of the Greek tragedies of his day, so we may ask of *The Passion*: Why would anyone want to watch such suffering anyway? Aristotle agreed with Plato that these works of art aroused fear and pity, but, unlike Plato, Aristotle found this beneficial. Watching the tragedies produces a catharsis, a cleansing of these feelings and emotions. In fact, this cathartic effect is part of Aristotle's classic definition of tragedy in the *Poetics*.

> Tragedy, then, is a representation of an action which is serious, complete, and of a certain magnitude—in language which is garnished in various forms in its different parts in the mode of dramatic enactment, not narrative—and through the arousal of pity and fear effecting the *katharsis* of such emotions. (1449b, 24–29)

So is *The Passion* a tragedy? Not in any sense that Aristotle would recognize, not in the way *Antigone* and *Oedipus Rex* are tragedies, not in the way *Hamlet* and *King Lear* are tragedies, not at all. Consider more of what Aristotle has to say. On the proper subject matter for tragedy, he says "the poet's task is to speak not of events which have occurred, but of the kind of events which *could* occur, and are possible by the standards of probability or necessity" (1451a 38–40).

The Passion purports to tell the story of events that no matter how wildly improbable *did* occur. Aristotle argues that certain plot types are inappropriate for tragedy. Most importantly for our purposes, "good men should not be shown passing from prosperity to affliction, for this is neither fearful nor pitiful but repulsive" (1452b 34–35). And "repulsive" is precisely how some viewers find *The Passion*. Certainly it is not cleansing, cathartic. Describing the proper type of main character for tragedy, Aristotle notes that "such a man is one who is not pre-eminent in virtue and justice, and one who falls into affliction not because of evil and wickedness, but because of a certain falli-bility (*hamartia*)" (1453a 7–9). Tragedies end in death due to the fallibility of the main character. Certainly a flawless Christ cannot take such a fall.

Sublimity in the Divine

So if we don't benefit from a tragic catharsis, why do we watch *The Passion*? Why do some of us actually enjoy it? Simply watch-ing it is easy enough to explain. The film is a pop cultural phe-nomenon, a "must see." Explaining why some of us actually enjoyed the film is tougher. Perhaps the experience is sublime? But what is "the sublime"? Peter Schjedahl claims that the sub-lime is a "hopelessly jumbled philosophical notion that has had more than two centuries to start meaning something cogent and hasn't succeeded yet" (quoted in Danto 2003, p. 148). Although he overstates the case, Schjedahl appropriately highlights the confusion and chaos surrounding the idea of the sublime. Nonetheless I'd like to suggest that we can use the sublime and *The Passion* to make sense of one another.

In discussing the sublime Edmund Burke (1729–1797) points us to accounts of divine encounter in Scripture.

> But the scripture alone can supply ideas answerable to the majesty of this subject. In the scripture, wherever God is represented as appearing or speaking, everything terrible in nature is called up to heighten the awe and solemnity of the divine presence. The psalms, and the prophetical books, are crowded with instances of this kind. *The earth shook*, (says the psalmist), *the heavens also dropped at the presence of the Lord.* (Burke 1998, p. 112)

The sublime, like God, is fearful but we are not afraid of it. So what is the sublime? While early modern views on the sublime associated it with awe-inspiring, terrifying natural objects such as jagged cliffs shrouded in mist, more recent views have applied the sublime to art, helping to answer Aristotle's perennial question: Why would we voluntarily look at art that produces unpleasant emotions? Well, why would an eighty-year old man jump out of an airplane? Why would a fourteen-year old girl ride the roller coaster repeatedly? Because a thrill, a heightened sense of life, is concomitant with the fear.

Musing on movies, and revising the theories of Kant and Burke, Cynthia Freeland finds four features in the sublime. First, it involves conflict between feelings of pain and pleasure, what Burke called "rapturous terror." Second, something about the sublime object is "great" and astonishing, what Longinus (around A.D. 213–272) called the "bold and grand"–the sublime object is vast, powerful, and overwhelming. Third, the sublime "evokes ineffable and painful feelings through which a transformation occurs into pleasure and cognition." And fourth, the sublime prompts moral reflection (Freeland 1999, pp. 66–69).

While all four of Freeland's features are presented as necessary for an experience of the sublime, not every example of the cinematic sublime is an entire film. Scenes and parts of movies can be sublime. And commonly one or more of the features can be found without the others, in which case the film or scene does not produce an experience of the sublime.

The first feature, the conflict or commingling of pain and pleasure distinguishes the sublime from the beautiful. According to Kant, there is restful contemplation in the beautiful whereas there is "mental movement" or even a "vibration" in the sublime (Freeland 1999, p. 70). The experience of beauty is an escape from reality, whereas the experience of the sublime is a heightened, if contrived, confrontation with it. *The Silence of the Lambs*, like most horror movies, elicits a conflict of pain and pleasure though not an experience of the sublime. *The Passion* produces emotional conflict throughout. As Jesus is brutally beaten we want to cover our eyes, to be shielded from the pain, yet we take pleasure in knowing that the final victory will be his. Nonbelievers can also have this experience as long as they know the story from Scripture.

The second feature—greatness, power, vastness, and an overwhelming quality—is familiar in film. Think of *The Matrix* and Neo's awakening in a gooey pink pod to see himself one among countless others in the field of human batteries. The truth is almost too much to take. Think of *Troy* and the "thousand ships" gradually revealed as the camera pans to wider and wider shots. While *The Matrix* and *Troy* have sublime scenes, *The Passion* is powerful and overwhelming practically throughout. The mistreatment of the God-man is too much to take, with the indignities of being slapped, shackled, and spit upon. But even those who do not believe Jesus is God find the flogging, scourging, and fall-ridden way of the cross too much to bear. In a surreal scene one Roman soldier gives a lesson to another in "how it's done," oblivious to the suffering of the man whose flesh he impales with nine-inch nails. We just cringe.

Consider too the grotesque in *The Passion*: powerful, overwhelming, tough to stomach. Taking license with scriptural narrative, Gibson shows us the devil incarnate as an androgynous hooded figure and slithering serpent. We have no sympathy for this devil. Rather, the figure's sinister voice and appearance arouse disgust and fear, so close to Christ as it comes. As if the gore of the flogging were not enough, we see Satan as spectator, hideous child in his arms, wicked words from his forked tongue. Judas too is treated to the grotesque as madness descends on him. Children lose their innocence for virulence and chase him like the furies to his suicidal end. Too much, it is all too much to bear.

The third feature, that the sublime "evokes ineffable and painful feelings through which a transformation occurs into pleasure and cognition," links us to the suffering of Jesus. The sublime is related to the mystical via the ineffable, that to which we cannot give words. As Eric Bronson discusses in Chapter 10 of this volume, mystics often journey through great pain to reach a higher truth that the rational mind cannot comprehend and language cannot express. The experience of the mystic is ineffable, and likewise the portrayal of the suffering of Jesus engenders an ineffable response in the viewer. Sharing vicariously in the pain of Jesus, the viewer is led to the pleasure of realizing that all is not lost. Quite the contrary, everything is gained.

Thought itself is pleasurable. "All people by nature desire to know," is the first line of Aristotle's *Metaphysics*. We seek through thought the satisfaction of knowledge, true-justified-belief. Exercise of the mind, no less than the body, though sometimes painful in the process is pleasurable in its product. There are films that are not sublime though they keep us wondering and reward us with knowledge in the end, such as *The Usual Suspects* and *Snatch*. Not all knowledge is of the kind that comes at the cost of transformative suffering.

The fourth feature—the prompting of moral reflection—is the most important of all. According to Freeland, a gap or disruption in the very medium of representation evokes a deep moral response from the viewer (2004, p. 27). Whereas we rest contentedly in contemplating beauty in art, the disquiet characteristic of contemplating the cinematic sublime makes us aware it is a movie we're watching. We are pushed from sympathetic emotional reactions to deep reflective cognitions, from feelings to thoughts. Our very will to shatter the illusion of the fiction of the film becomes Gibson's tool for directing our thought. According to Kant, beauty is not in the eye of the beholder but in the object, not in our subjective belief that the *Pietà* is beautiful but in the *Pietà* itself. By contrast, Kant holds, the sublime is in us, it is our experience, but this makes the sublime no less objective. What we judge as sublime we implicitly believe others too should judge as sublime. Lots of movies, even cartoons like *The Lion King*, prompt moral reflections, sometimes even by disrupting the medium. But the disruption in *The Passion* purposefully engenders the sublime.

Consider the movie's use of Aramaic and Latin. Whatever else may be said, these languages heighten our sense of the sublime by adding to the strange and foreign quality of our experience, making us intellectually aware that this is not the familiar version of the story from memory or imagination. The subtitles engage us cognitively in a way we would not otherwise be engaged. All viewers, aside from the scarce few who know both Latin and Aramaic, get the film with subtitles and need them to follow the dialogue. The subtitles rupture the film and lead us from the emotional to the cognitive, from feeling to thought.

The visceral emotional reaction to the violence, pain, suffering, gore, and grotesque overwhelms us in such a way as to compel moral reflection. And although the film may guide us toward certain moral conclusions, we need not accept them.

It Wasn't Sublime for Me

Surely not everyone who has seen *The Passion* has found it sublime. Some will even agree that the film has all four of Freeland's features and yet insist that they did not experience *The Passion* as sublime. Fair enough. Does that mean that Freeland's account is mistaken? Not necessarily. Does that mean that sublimity is relative, that *The Passion* can be sublime for you but not for me? Not necessarily.

Watching a film safely in the theater, like watching a stormy sea safely on land, allows for an experience of the sublime. The awful and terrible sight we would run from hiding our eyes becomes the object of fascination, as pain mysteriously mingles with pleasure. Kant believed the sublime put us in touch with a truth about ourselves, that our rational nature and free will make us superior to the sublime objects of nature, like tornadoes and tidal waves, which have the power to crush us. As he puts it:

> And we like to call these objects sublime because they raise the soul's fortitude above its usual middle range and allow us to discover in ourselves an ability to resist which is of a quite different kind, and which gives us the courage [to believe] that we could be a match for nature's seeming omnipotence. (Kant 1987, p. 120)

Still, not everyone likes to watch tornadoes and tidal waves, feeling fearful even at an objectively safe distance. Such a person misses out on the experience of the sublime. The tornado is perfectly capable of affording the experience of the sublime but fear stands in the way. As Kant notes, "Just as we cannot pass judgment on the beautiful if we are seized by inclination and appetite, so we cannot pass judgment at all on the sublime in nature if we are afraid" (*ibid.*). I suspect something similar occurs in the case of *some* devout Christians viewing *The Passion*. Despite the objective safety, despite knowing "it's just a movie," fear stands in the way of experiencing the sublime of *The Passion*. We can no more insist that such people watch the film again to experience the sublime than we can insist that someone watch the thunderstorm approaching. But in both cases the experience of the sublime awaits those who leave fear at the gates.

The Violence Defended

The expectations and desires we bring to a work of art shape our reactions to it. A movie director must make choices concerning how to film and tell a story, and when the story is already well known the director's choices will inevitably disappoint some. A beautiful movie would have been an ill-suited form of expression for the passion of Jesus. To be true to the subject matter Gibson was forced to make a movie that would be difficult to watch. Thus we considered the perennial philosophical question: Why do we willingly watch works of art that bring pain with pleasure? In the case of tragedies it may be that Aristotle is right, that we experience a cleansing, a catharsis. But as we saw, the story of the passion cannot be told as a tragedy. So are the controversial blood and violence of *The Passion* simply gratuitous? No, they are justified by Gibson's attempt to deliver an experience of the sublime.

SOURCES

Aristotle. 1986. *Poetics.* Translated by Stephen Halliwell. London: Duckworth.

Edmund Burke. 1998. *A Philosophical Enquiry into the Origins of our Ideas of the Sublime and Beautiful and Other Pre-Revolutionary Writings.* Edited by David Womersley. London: Penguin.

Peg Zeglin Brand, ed. 2000. *Beauty Matters.* Bloomington: Indiana University Press.

Arthur C. Danto. 2003. *The Abuse of Beauty: Aesthetics and the Concept of Art.* Chicago: Open Court.

Cynthia Freeland. 1999. The Sublime in Cinema. In Carl Plantinga and Greg M. Smith, eds., *Passionate Views: Film, Cognition, and Emotion* (Baltimore: Johns Hopkins University Press, 1999), pp. 65–83.

————. 2004. Piercing Our Inaccessible, Inmost Parts. In Chris Townsend, ed., *The Art of Bill Viola* (London: Thames and Hudson), pp. 24–45.

Immanuel Kant. 1987. *Critique of Judgment.* Translated by Werner S. Pluhar. Indianapolis: Hackett.

Longinus. 1985. *On the Sublime.* Translated by James A. Arieti and John M. Crossett. New York: Mellen.

Plato. 1992. *Republic.* Translated by G.M.S. Grube. Indianapolis: Hackett. Especially Books II, III, and X.

QUESTIONS FOR DISCUSSION

1. Do you agree with Freeland's list of key features of the sublime?

2. What other films or scenes from films might be considered sublime according to Freeland's features?

3. Are religious subjects particularly suited to sublime treatment?

4. Why would we willingly watch horror movies? What pleasure justifies the pain?

5. Consider disgust. Why are we sometimes attracted to sights that disgust us?

6

God and Man Separated No More: Hegel Overcomes the Unhappy Consciousness of Gibson's Christianity

JAMES LAWLER

According to the theology of atonement, God the Father sent his only begotten Son into the world to atone for the sins of mankind. For God is a just God, and justice demands punishment for sin. But God is also merciful, loving. So instead of punishing humanity for its sinfulness, as we deserve, He sent a substitute, an innocent sinless being, His own Son, to be punished on our behalf. Thus the demand for justice is satisfied, and God's loving mercy for humanity is simultaneously expressed.

For this logic of atonement, the more innocent the victim, the greater is the sacrifice, and so the more sins are expiated. It follows that the harsher, the more barbaric and brutal the punishment actually inflicted, the greater is the benefit in terms of the economics of salvation, where sin is bought back and redeemed at the price it demands. How appropriate then, as the religious imagination soars on the wings of this blood-thirsty rationality, to suppose the most sadistic forms of violent torture inflicted by the most degraded specimens of human sinfulness!

And so in *The Passion of the Christ* Mel Gibson does not spare his audience one drop of blood, one sliver of flesh, in the unflinching portrait of God's love for humanity. As if the punishment described in the Gospels were not enough, we see Jesus brutalized from the moment of his arrest and then plummeting over a bridge until his chains violently break his fall. As if the scourging of Jesus with ordinary whips were not enough, Mel Gibson adds razor blades to the humanly impossible torture. Not only is Jesus nailed to the cross, but the heavy cross falls so that now flesh-rending nails instead of gentler chains break his fall.

In exemplifying this theology, *The Passion of the Christ* draws a stunning portrait of the darkest side of the human soul. It depicts all the depravity, the malice, and the meaninglessness of what the religious imagination of a certain cast understands by sin. So we see a sinister Satan lurking behind scenes in which Goodness Himself is systematically, unequivocally, thoroughly, and completely desecrated and destroyed. As the sun is covered by black storm clouds at the moment of Christ's death, evil triumphs over good, darkness shuts out the light. Or so it seems.

And yet it was all for nothing. Satan's efforts were counterproductive, so that in the end we see him screaming uncontrollably in a fit of fury and frustration. The insane frenzy of punishment produces the opposite of what was intended. Jesus rises from the dead, whole in the flesh once again, except for a stigmatized body to remind his followers that what took place was not a dream. If the film, in its exhaustive depiction of the passion of the Christ, leaves little to the imagination, its final scene is a brilliant stroke of understatement. The risen Christ sets out from his tomb with an uncanny expression of purposeful endeavor. The propitiation has been accomplished. He must now announce the achievement to his followers, so that they can bring the Good News to humankind: The sinner is no longer mired in his sin as long as he recognizes the means of his salvation, the terrible price that has been paid as his ransom from the maggoty stench of Satan's maw. Each drop of blood that was shed, which seemed only to deepen the pit of wickedness which humanity digs for itself, fills the chalice of communion with the Savior for whomever will drink of it. Although wholly sunk in unworthiness, the sinner who washes his sins in the blood of the lamb is raised to the highest heaven.

Hegel on the Death of God

In 1789, the German philosopher Georg Wilhelm Friedrich Hegel (1770–1831) entered the Protestant Seminary at Tübingen University in the German state of Württemberg with the goal of becoming a pastor or perhaps a theologian of the Lutheran Church. Under the powerful influence of the French Revolution, he and his friends and fellow seminarians, Johann Hölderlin (1770–1843) and Friedrich Schelling (1775–1854), became deeply involved in the revolutionary movements for liberating Germany from despotic government in alliance with a corrupt Church interested primarily in wealth and power. Although Hegel abandoned his initial plan of becoming a pastor for the career of a university professor, he continued throughout his life to deepen his goal of reconciling Christianity with French Enlightenment ideals of freedom, equality, and rationality.

Central to this goal was the critique of feudal and medieval ideas of hierarchical political systems and their alliance with hierarchically organized religion. Hegel understood the theological revolution of Martin Luther (1483–1546) to be a radical critique of the Church as an indispensable mediator between God and a fallen, sinful humanity. The fundamental theological justification of this order is the notion of the radical separation of Creator and creature, of God and humanity. To overcome this separation, a Savior is required to mediate between God and fallen humanity. And when that Savior returns to Heaven, the Church takes his place on earth as the indispensable means of salvation from the threat of eternal damnation. The theology of atonement thus underpins the hierarchical power of the priesthood over the laity, with all the potentiality for abuse that this implies. The greatest abuse, for Hegel, is that directed to human intelligence itself (Hegel 1974, pp. 389, 390).

It is not the degradation, but the exaltation of the human spirit, expressed in Luther's conception of the priesthood of the laity, that is in fact the deep meaning of Christianity itself. Christianity rejects the ancient notion of an unattainable deity in its astounding portrait of God becoming a human being and dying the wretched death of a criminal on the cross. In his *Lectures on The Philosophy of Religion* (1827), Hegel reflects on the Christian doctrine of "the death of God":

> "God himself is dead," it says in a Lutheran hymn, expressing an awareness that the human, the finite, the fragile, the weak, the negative are themselves moments of the divine, that they are within God himself, that finitude, negativity, otherness are not outside of God and do not, as otherness, hinder unity with God. (Hegel 1985, p. 326)

Hegel calls the Christian vision of the death of God "a monstrous, fearful picture [*Vorstellung*], which brings before the imagination the deepest abyss of cleavage" (Hegel 1985, p. 125). The cleavage or separation of God and humanity culminates in Jesus's cry from the cross: "My God, my God, why have you forsaken me?" (Mark 15:34). While suggesting the monstrous, fearful picture presented by *The Passion of the Christ*, Hegel develops an alternative interpretation to that of the theology of the atonement.

According to Hegel, the central teaching of Christianity is that Jesus is both God and man, both human and divine (Hegel 1985, p. 121). He emphasizes Jesus's statement in the Gospel: "I and the Father are one" (John 10:30). The death of Jesus must therefore be the death of God. But instead of separating Jesus as the divine God-Man from the rest of humanity, as the theology of atonement does, this doctrine serves instead to elevate humanity as a whole from its false conception of separation from God to the same oneness proclaimed by Jesus. Accused of blasphemy in asserting his oneness with God, Jesus replied: "Is it not written in your law, 'I said, you are gods?'" (John 10:34; see Psalm 82:6). He who believes in Jesus, that is, he who understands and puts into practice what Jesus teaches, knows that he too is one with the Father. And so the human being with all her weakness, all his abysmal negativity, is a "moment of the divine."

Hegel on the Relation between Reason and Faith

In an interview for *Hollywood Jesus News*, Mel Gibson affirms both the theology of atonement and the death of God:

> There is no greater hero story than this one, about the greatest love one can have, which is to lay down one's life for someone. The Passion is the biggest adventure story of all time. I think it's the biggest love-story of all time; God becoming man and men killing God. If that's not action, nothing is. . . . Christ paid the price for all our sins. (Gibson 2003)

But what does it mean to say that God died on the cross? We have two radically opposed conceptions of the death of Jesus, that of the theology of atonement which separates God and humanity, the innocent Savior and a sinful humanity, and Hegel's quite different conception that the death of Jesus is the death of God, that God too dies and so even in its abysmal sinfulness, humanity is one with God. Which conception is right? Which one offers a more philosophically intelligible conception of Christianity?

Traditionally, the problem of the relation between faith and reason has been solved by drawing a line somewhere and saying, up to this point we have the sphere of reason, and beyond this we have truths that are made accessible to us only by revelation. But if you can't make any sense of these teachings of revelation, what does it mean to believe in them? If you don't really know *what it means* to say that God has become human and dies the death of a criminal, how can you accept this idea on faith? If someone whom you regard as reliable tells you that he has seen flying saucers, you understand what he means by this and so you can accept what he says as a revelation for you. But if the revelation involves a logical contradiction, that A and not-A are one and the same, what can it mean to accept this on faith? This is what Christian doctrine appears to be saying in affirming the oneness of God and humanity, of the divine and the non-divine, in the person of Jesus.

According to Hegel, such problems of logic are not crucial to the ordinary believer. The human being is not merely a rational being, but also a being of feeling and imagination. We do not demand a rational formulation of a poem, and neither should we do so of religion. To do either is to destroy the integrity of distinctive forms of consciousness. As Hegel says above, Christianity first presents a monstrous "picture" [*Vorstellung*] of the death of God. Religious consciousness operates through images or "picture thinking" rather than through concepts. Its main appeal is not to the intellect but to the emotions. The faithful Christian *feels* the infinity of God, the melting of the finite into the infinite, of the individual personality into the All, and projects this feeling into the images portrayed visibly and tangibly by religion.

Similarly, through imagination and feeling, the Christian believer who attends a showing of *The Passion of the Christ* relives for himself the dissolution of the finite personality into the infinity of the divine by identifying with the images of the suffering and death of Jesus. Perhaps above all the film's depiction of the *Mater Dolorosa*, the sorrowing mother of Jesus, invites us to identify with the suffering Jesus through a mother's love, so anxious to avoid any harm to her child, yet compelled to accompany him helplessly on this gruesome journey. All the egoistical concerns of the separate personality dissolve in a mother's love that knows no limits. This is not a matter of doctrine about the separation of God and man and the need for a Savior, but a feeling, an experience—the experience of oneness with infinite love which Christianity tells us is the real meaning of God.

As a work of art, Mel Gibson's film invites us to *identify* with Jesus. He is the good son of his loving mother, a talented carpenter who is proud of his work, a man who sees through a hierarchical society's hypocritical condemnation of the prostitute to the beautiful soul of Mary Magdalene and thereby awakens in her the consciousness of her own real worth. Above all we identify with Jesus as a being of flesh and blood like ourselves, and so we cringe with every flailing stroke of the whip. But the theology of atonement puts Jesus on a pedestal and deifies him in a realm utterly apart from us, the audience. This theoretical *understanding* implicitly obstructs our identification with the action hero Jesus that the film wants us to *feel* and conflicts with the requirements of both art and religion.

Blaise Pascal (1623–1662), the first Christian apologist of the dawn of modern science, said: "The heart has its reasons, which reason does not know" (Pascal 1958, #277, p. 78). Pascal both contrasts the emotional sphere of the heart with the mental sphere of reason and at the same time points to another kind of rationality that is embedded in the feelings of the heart. Hegel attempts to develop just such an alternative form of rationality with a conception of dialectical reason that explores the multiform phenomena of consciousness. Dialectical reason is capable of taking us into spheres of consciousness that are off-limits to ordinary rationality with its logic of either A or not-A. Hegel's *Phenomenology of Spirit* takes us into spheres of consciousness where contradictions are rife yet meaningful, transformative impulses to growth from limited to more comprehensive perspectives (Lawler 1988).

On the Separation of Creator and Creation

From the point of view of ordinary logic, the unity of God and not-God is not comprehensible, to be sure. But so, argues Hegel, is their separation. If there is a created world outside of God, then God cannot be infinite. If there is something that is not-God—the finite, limited world of mortal creatures—then God too must be finite, and *other than* what is not Him—other than, for example, a finite human being condemned to die (Hegel 1968, par. 95, pp. 176–77).

A God outside of the world may be very large, very power-ful, far more than the world He creates, but He remains one dis-tinct finite being along side all the rest. This is how the ancient polytheists pictured their gods—bigger, more powerful than the humans they lord over, but otherwise finite beings just as we are. To say that there is only one such Over-Lord does not change the substance of the matter. Nor does it reflect the Christian notion that God is infinite. The orthodox theologian who insists on the separation of God and the world, and so the need for a external mediator and a caste of priests to save us, fails to go beyond an earlier form of religion, and fails to rise to the level of Christianity. If God is truly infinite then everything that exists is within God. So if God is infinite, it follows that "the human, the finite, the fragile, the weak, the negative, are them-selves moments of the divine" (Hegel 1985, p. 326).

The Christian teaching that God has become a human being is intimately linked to the doctrine that God is infinite. The sep-aration of Creator and creature is a projection of the narrow van-tage point of the separate ego. This was understood by the great Christian mystic and theologian, Meister Eckhart (around 1260–1328). Hegel cites with approval Eckhart's profoundly Christian teaching: "The eye with which God sees me is the eye with which I see him: my eye and his eye are the same." "If God did not exist nor would I; if I did not exist nor would he" (Hegel 1984, pp. 347–48). The same fundamentally Christian idea is at the foundation of modern Western philosophy. If Descartes begins with "I think," he goes on to show that all thinking takes place in the light of God. The rationally incomprehensible the-ology of atonement that Mel Gibson espouses harkens back instead to the fideism attributed to Tertullian (around A.D. 160–220): *Credo quia absurdum,* I believe because it is absurd.

The Unhappy Consciousness

For his consistent affirmation of the Christian doctrine that God and humanity are one, Meister Eckhart was condemned as a heretic. The theology of atonement insists on the radical separation of God and humanity, with the one exception being the God-Man, Jesus. But how can God and humanity be radically separate if even one human being can be God? Such would-be orthodox theology is not content with enunciating images for the devotional expression of feeling, but claims the status of conceptual thought for its representations. Consequently, this conceptual theology inevitably falls within the evolution of contradictory forms of consciousness explored in Hegel's *Phenomenology*. Specifically, the theology of atonement occupies the place in the evolution of consciousness that Hegel calls "The Unhappy Consciousness."

The Unhappy Consciousness is a moment or stage in the evolution of the Master-Slave dialectic that arises in Hegel's *Phenomenology* out of the standpoint of the separate ego. The ego inevitably confronts other egos in a life and death struggle. Out of fear of death, the losers in this struggle submit to the winners, and so the ego standpoint gives rise to a society of masters and slaves, of dominators and dominated, or rulers and ruled (Hegel 1977, pp. 111–19). Hegel anticipates Friedrich Nietzsche's (1844–1900) notion that Christianity is an expression of "slave morality." But for Hegel, if Jesus appeals to the slave with his blessings for the meek and the poor in spirit, he transforms this spirit of abasement with his teaching that humility of the ego is a necessary step for recognizing that beyond narrow ego-consciousness the human being is essentially divine. What dies on the cross on Mount Calvary is both God and humanity: God as the transcendent Creator regarded as separate from his creations, and the separate human individual regarded as a finite, fragile, negative being. What is resurrected from this two-fold death is the unity of God and human being as the universal truth of the unlimited power and fulfillment of the loving human community, which Jesus called the kingdom of God on earth. The true meaning of the Church is not that of a hierarchical power over the laity, but the loving community that implicitly embraces all of humanity.

But before attaining this kingdom, the human being as a finite, separate individual must recognize her nullity and descend to the depths of the Unhappy Consciousness. There God is an unreachable Beyond, and the human being is less than nothing. She is a mere worm, less than the beasts in fact for being truly bestial, like the human-looking brutes in *The Passion of the Christ* who laugh as they flay the helpless flesh of Jesus. What is the real meaning of sin, Hegel asks, if not the separation of the self as a finite ego from all the rest of reality, from Infinite Being. Such separation or "cleavage" produces the knowledge of good and evil, the world of duality and separation (Hegel 1987, pp. 740–41). The finite, separate ego boasts of its truth and power as the center of the universe, its lord and master. But a *world* of such egos unleashes what Thomas Hobbes (1588–1679) calls "a war of all against all" and what Hegel calls "the life-and-death struggle." The world of separate egos is a reign of murder in which each ego attempts to triumph over every other ego. Inevitably some egos do triumph over others, producing the world of masters and slaves. This world is epitomized by the Roman slave empire, into which was born the babe of Bethlehem.

The ultimate truth implicit in the master-slave dialectic is the illusory nature of the separate ego. The slave, both because of her abasement before the master and the achievement of her creative work, is much closer to this truth than the master, who glories in his separate individuality with all the displays of pomp and circumstance that the spoils of conquest and the creative efforts of his slaves can produce. The pathetic weakness of the master, in contrast to the dignity of the slave, is seen in the contrast that *The Passion of the Christ* draws between the Roman Governor, Pontius Pilate, and simple yet courageous Simon of Cyrene. Simon is a kind of Everyman, naturally reluctant to be dragooned into an awful job with no pay and no glory, but soon siding with the oppressed that he is too. Hang in there, friend, he tells Jesus; it will all be over soon.

The slave mentality nevertheless has some devices for avoiding the lesson of the essential nullity of the separate and separating ego consciousness. Stoic philosophy teaches that true freedom is freedom of thought and such freedom is attainable even for the individual in shackles. But Skeptical philosophy, which dialectically follows on the heals of Stoicism in the

Phenomenology, undermines the pretenses of such abstract rationality, showing that to every would-be universal truth affirmed by the Stoic an opposite truth is just as convincingly defensible. Through a relentless skepticism not only has the physical being of the slave been reduced to a state of impotence, but so has his mind, the abstract reasoning of the separate ego. The truth, which seemed to be within the grasp of such consciousness, recedes into "an unattainable beyond," while the individual is left to contemplate in both body and soul her essential nothingness (Hegel 1977, p. 131).

Jesus as Sinful Human Being

This anguish over the nothingness of the separate ego is depicted in *The Passion of the Christ* both in Jesus's agonized plea in the Garden of Gethsemane that he be spared the coming trial, and more completely in his despairing cry from the cross: "My God, my God, why have you forsaken me?" Here we are furthest from the conception of a deified Jesus who is radically different from ordinary humanity. How is this completely human anguish compatible with the doctrine of the God-Man, separate from the rest of us? Another artist, inspired by another conception of Christianity, would linger over this moment, as Hegel does in his lectures, in which Jesus plumbs the depths of human despair. Hegel's interpretation radically departs from the theology of atonement. Jesus saves sinners only by being one of them.

In plumbing the depths of the radical separateness of the finite ego, Jesus embodied human sinfulness to its fullest extent. The deep spiritual meaning of the atonement is at-one-ment: the reconciliation of the human and the divine through the death of the separate self. It is not that Jesus, as a separate deified individual, takes on the sins of others and sacrifices himself for them, but that he himself fully embodied human sinfulness, in other words human finitude and separation, to the extent of dying the infamous death of a criminal on the cross. In the context of Roman civilization Jesus was indeed a criminal for his teaching of the oneness of God and humanity, profoundly contradicting the hierarchical authority of the Roman slave-state. Hence, it was *his own* sinfulness that was "expiated" through his death (Hegel 1985, pp. 128–29).

In the anguish of death, Jesus comprehended the Unhappy Consciousness of the separate ego and so initiated a new stage in which human consciousness grasps its true nature. Having taken the all-too-human form of ego consciousness to its logical conclusion in an ignominious death, he died to death itself, and so rose from this death in the transformed existence of the radiance of Spirit. In the final scene of *The Passion of the Christ*, this Spirit is identified with Jesus alone. For Hegel, however, the resurrected Spirit is primarily that of the revolutionary new human community that has overcome the Unhappy Consciousness.

The resurrection of Jesus brings out the full meaning of his death. The death of God is at the same time the death of death, for Spirit is precisely that inner bond within each human being that unites with others and so survives the death of the finite separate self. Hegel defines Spirit [*Geist*] as the overcoming of the separate ego: "'I' that is 'We,' and 'We' that is 'I'" (Hegel 1977, p. 110). The "I" that confronts all the separate "I"s in a life-and-death struggle must die to this separation to rise to the level of Spirit. This full meaning of the human Spirit as the overcoming of the separation of the ego and the Unhappy Consciousness to which it leads is the goal of the *Phenomenology*, a goal that is implicitly realized in the form of feeling in the religious experience of the death of Jesus.

The Calvary of Absolute Spirit

It remains to recognize this achievement in an adequate conceptual form by overcoming all remaining limited understandings and forms of experience. So at the conclusion of the *Phenomenology*, Hegel calls the preceding stages of consciousness the "Calvary of Absolute Spirit" (Hegel 1977, p. 808). The *Phenomenology* as a whole, with its successive stages of the evolution of limited forms of human consciousness driven by contradiction, constitutes the full unfolding of the meaning of the crucifixion of Jesus.

By placing the burden of universal human self-transformation exclusively on the shoulders of the separate God-Man Jesus, the theology of atonement remains fixated at the stage of the Unhappy Consciousness. In holding that the individual must affirm his own essential nothingness before an almighty Beyond, and so requires a mediator to save him, this theology ultimately fixes the sinner in his sin, and establishes him as incapable of real redemption. But no one can perform the transformation of consciousness that saves us from the nullity of the isolated ego for anyone else. Against the superficial theology of atonement, the teachings of Jesus, consistently expressed in his death and resurrection, present in religious form, at the level of feeling and picture thinking or parables, what conceptual philosophy shows to be the fundamental meaning of the human spirit (Hegel 1985, p. 128).

The Passion of the Christ concludes with the resurrected Jesus setting out to announce his message. But what is this message; what is the Good News? That humans are abject sinners incapable of saving themselves, or that the human spirit is indeed indestructible, and that we must all reach beyond our own separate ego-identification, like the two Marys and Simon, and recognize the reflection of divinity in each human being? *The Passion of the Christ,* insofar as it embodies the theology of separation, wants to perpetuate the first view of the radical human abasement of the Unhappy Consciousness, but in its fidelity to the Gospel account, which includes heroes and heroines as well as villains, it implicitly challenges this theology.

Hegel's own treatment of the passion of the Christ does not end with the death and resurrection of Jesus, but continues with the story of the new human community founded on the recognition of the Holy Spirit as an I that is a We and a We that is an I. This is the Kingdom of Heaven, which Jesus likens to a mustard seed. It starts as the tiniest of seeds and multiplies and spreads until it becomes a home for all of humanity. Hegel stresses the words of Jesus that he must go away, or die, so that the Comforter, the Holy Spirit, can descend on his followers (Hegel 1985, p. 222; John 16:7). Otherwise they would be tempted to turn the individual Jesus into a separate deity, and establish separatist communities of believers depending on whether or not they accept this new god—instead of recognizing the divine where it belongs, in themselves as human beings, bound together in spirit, in love. Jesus therefore really has to die, to leave the scene, Hegel says, for his teachings to be truly understood. For his teaching is not about himself as a special being, but about what is special in all of us.

Just as it is not necessary for us today to repeat all the illusion and suffering of slave society in concrete forms to grasp the

lessons of this history, so we do not have to be nailed to the
cross to die to the separate ego. The historical Jesus performed
this exemplary act in the flesh. But each human being must
repeat this death in spirit, and so be reborn in the awareness of
our oneness with universal Spirit, of the oneness of the individual with all humanity, with All That Is. The kingdom of God on
earth is present here and now for those who understand the
meaning of the evolution of human experience. This, Hegel brilliantly shows, is the deep meaning of Christianity.

For Jesus, we are all sons and daughters of God. And so the
one prayer that he taught begins with the words, "Our Father."
As in Jesus's parable of the prodigal son (Luke 15:11–32), as separate human egos we get lost in the worldly pursuit of riotous
living, until we are reduced to a state of despair. The Father
allows his Son, the expression of Himself in ordinary human
ego-consciousness, to go into the world to have experiences of
limitedness, want and conflict, anguish and despair. For only in
this way can our intrinsic divinity be truly experienced; only by
overcoming the illusory state of non-divinity, can the divine
essence of each individual be fully appreciated.

And so, we human beings live our lives of noisy or quiet des-
peration in our various forms of isolation from the Infinity of
Being. The Father knows that such a life leads inevitably to the
crucifixion of the ego, but gives Himself, in the form of the Son,
in the form of ego-centered human life, to this experience. The
inevitable abandonment, impoverishment, and spiritual death to
which this experience leads is not the end of the story, however.
The Son, abandoning the abandonment, returns to the Father in
the unity of the Holy Spirit, reborn in the experience of his
inalienable truth as a being inseparable from all other beings,
one with the All, an I that is a We and a We that is an I. In this
way Hegel explains the meaning of the Christian doctrine of the
Trinity, which is also the theoretical meaning of the Passion of
the Christ (Hegel 1985, pp. 327–28).

Jesus says that whatever we do to the least of his brothers
and sisters we do to him (Matthew 25:40), for there is no separation between Jesus and the most wretched human being. It
is Hegel's thought, not the theology of atonement, that gives
full meaning to the words of Jesus: "He who believes in me,
the works that I do he will do also; and greater works than
these . . ." (John 14:12).

In today's world of global economic unification, doctrines that promote religious exclusivity, like the theology of atonement, exacerbate the dangers of violence and the threats of war. According to Hegel, the God that rules over an unworthy humanity from a lofty heaven is the reflection of a human world of masters and slaves, rulers and ruled. The God of Christianity instead is one with the wretched of the earth, dying the death of a criminal, so that even the lowliest human beings can discover that the kingdom of heaven is within them, but only when they are willing to join together across separating political and religious borders to create a world that is worthy of us. Is it not written in the Scriptures that Jesus said to his critics and enemies: You are gods?

SOURCES

Georg Wilhelm Friedrich Hegel. 1968. *The Logic of Hegel*. Oxford: Oxford University Press.

————. 1974. *Lectures on the History of Philosophy*. Volume Three. New York: Humanities Press.

————. 1977. *The Phenomenology of Spirit*. Translated by A.V. Miller. Oxford: Oxford University Press.

————. 1984. *Lectures on the Philosophy of Religion*. Volume I, edited by Peter C. Hodgson. Berkeley: University of California Press.

————. 1985. *Lectures on the Philosophy of Religion*. Volume III, edited by Peter C. Hodgson. Berkeley: University of California Press.

————. 1987. *Lectures on the Philosophy of Religion*. Volume II, edited by Peter C. Hodgson. Berkeley: University of California Press.

Mel Gibson. 2003. Interview. April 23rd. http://www.hollywoodjesus. com/newsletter053.htm.

James Lawler. 2002. We Are (the) One! Kant Explains How to Manipulate the Matrix. In William Irwin, ed., *The Matrix and Philosophy* (Chicago: Open Court), pp. 138–152.

James Lawler and Vladimir Shtinov. 1988. Hegel's Method of Doing Philosophy Historically: A Reply. In Peter Hare, ed., *Doing Philosophy Historically* (Buffalo: Prometheus), pp. 267–280.

Vincent A. McCarthy. 1986. *A Quest for a Philosophical Jesus: Christianity and Philosophy in Rousseau, Kant, Hegel, and Schelling*. Macon: Mercer University Press.

Blaise Pascal. 1958. *Pascal's Pensées*. New York: Dutton.

QUESTIONS FOR DISCUSSION

1. How does the theology of atonement conflict with the artistic requirement of emotional identification with Jesus? What changes would you make in the film if you were to adopt Hegel's theology?

2. Which conception of Christianity described in this article gives a better account of the following: 1) To those who call him a blasphemer, Jesus quotes Scripture saying "you (meaning ordinary human beings) are gods"; 2) the parable of the prodigal son; 3) the parable of the kingdom of heaven as like a mustard seed; 4) Jesus's saying that if we understand and practice his teachings we will be able to do more than he did; 5) Jesus's cry from the cross that God has forsaken him.

3. Does the theology of atonement lend support to religious institutions as power structures liable to abuse and corruption? How does Hegel's alternative conception of Christianity counteract such hierarchical structures of religion?

4. What's the difference between a conception of religion as consisting of dogmas about God in which one should believe, and a conception of religion as consisting in emotional experience of God?

5. Explain the apparent conflict between faith and reason. How does Hegel overcome this conflict in his interpretation of Christianity?

II

Is *The Passion* Anti-Semitic?

7

Passions of the Christ: Do Jews and Christians See the Same Film?

THOMAS E. WARTENBERG

Shortly after the release of Mel Gibson's *The Passion of the Christ*, I served as the moderator for a panel discussion at Mount Holyoke College, the liberal arts college where I teach philosophy and film studies. The panel organizer consulted with me about whom to have on the panel because I am Jewish and play a central role in the College's Film Studies Program. The diverse panel we assembled was composed of a New Testament historian, a scholar of Jewish mysticism, the College's Protestant Minister, the Catholic Chaplain to the College, and a film historian. The panel went as anyone who has seen the film might expect.

First, the historian criticized the film because of its historical inaccuracies. He argued that such criticism was very important because the film presents itself, and will be taken by many viewers, as the truth about Jesus's life. But, he argued, the Gospels themselves reflect the specific concern to make Christianity appealing to the large numbers of Romans who were joining the faith in the century after Jesus's death. Because the leader of this growing religion was both Jewish and killed by the Romans, Pilate's role in the crucifixion was whitewashed in all of the Gospels. That Gibson went even farther than the Gospels themselves by portraying Pilate as a tormented soul while having the Jewish leaders appear petty and spiteful was, for the New Testament historian, truly appalling, especially when viewed in light of the current global climate of religious warfare.

Next came the scholar of Jewish mysticism, who wanted to explain the anxieties and concerns that the film had raised for Jews. Although Gibson has said that he intended to show that all of us are sinners and therefore guilty of Jesus's death, that is not the message our scholar got from the film. A group of Jewish rabbis and members of the Jewish community are the ones who demand Jesus's death by crucifixion from a Roman proconsul who is portrayed as deeply troubled by it and who only very reluctantly bows to the Jews' pressure. Stressing the importance of the world climate today, in which anti-Semitism is on the rise in many quarters, the scholar argued that the film is likely to inflame those fires just at a time when we should be doing our best to augment the Jewish-Christian dialogues that have stemmed the spread of anti-Semitism.

The Protestant minister agreed that the film is anti-Semitic, but that was not her central worry. To her, it represented a real distortion of the message of a man who had deeply affected her life. She told the audience that Jesus's message was that we had to embrace those on the margins, whom no one cared about or wanted to love. This message is the real gift of Jesus to the world, she said, and it is completely missing from Gibson's film, which focuses exclusively on his torment. Although the crucifixion is important, it has to be seen in the broader context of Jesus's teachings, virtually none of which is given prominence in the film.

The Catholic College Chaplain emphasized the Church's complicity in the murder and torture of Jews over the centuries through its propagation of the questionable moral idea of collective guilt, an idea that the Church has been combating since at least 1962. In her eyes, the film does a disservice to the Catholic Church and harms the dialogue between Catholics and Jews. She pointed out that U.S. Catholic Bishops had issued a statement emphasizing the importance of maintaining the dialogue between Catholics and Jews, rather than taking any step backwards, let alone a giant one, as this film is.

The last speaker on the panel was the College's film scholar who approached the film very differently. She saw the film in light of previous attempts to bring Jesus to the screen. Her claim was that Jesus's body had always presented filmmakers with a problem, because it inevitably registered contemporary bodily styles at the same time that it was supposed to be historical.

From her point of view, Gibson had succeeded in doing what he attempted to do: tell Jesus's story on the screen in a way that is not inherently a parody. He did it by making that body virtually unrecognizable as contemporary by having it beaten thoroughly from virtually the beginning of the film.

After these presentations, I made a few comments and the discussion was turned over to the audience, composed mostly of students. I found remarkable the number of students who quite openly said with great conviction that *The Passion* had tremendous religious significance for them. One of them said that she had seen the film three times with three different groups of friends and all of them had their faith not merely renewed, but actually ignited for the first time. All of the students said that they didn't perceive the film as anti-Semitic because it isn't a movie about Jews at all but about Jesus and his suffering. They also admitted that the film made them realize that they were responsible for Jesus's death, as was each of us.

I left that discussion puzzled that the same work could produce such widely divergent responses. It seemed as if the people I had been listening to had watched very different films. Some saw it as historically inaccurate and a real threat to Jewish-Christian relations; others considered it an abasement of the true message of Jesus's life and death; and still for others it was a remarkable document of faith that captures the essence of their religious belief. And, of course, there may be many other ways in which audiences reacted to the film that did not get expressed that afternoon.

In order to register this wide divergence of viewer response to Gibson's film, I will talk of a number of different "films" that audiences "saw," using the terms figuratively. Of all these films, I want to focus on just two. The first is the film that people like myself and some of the other panelists had seen. It is a film that is deeply anti-Semitic and portrays sadism to an almost unbearable extent, a film that is hard to reconcile with the message of Christianity as I understand it. The second is the film that many Catholics and some other Christians—among them many students in the audience at Mount Holyoke—saw, a film of unparalleled spiritual significance that taught them the real meaning of their faith in a way nothing previously had done.

I was genuinely puzzled about the enormous discrepancy between these two films and have thought about it a great deal.

How can people have such radically different experiences of a single work of art? Aside from my concern about the film itself—what I saw as its anti-Semitism and the effect that this might have on Jewish people the world over, for example—it was a more abstract issue that kept gnawing at me: I couldn't understand how viewers of the same film could have experiences that appeared so completely to contradict one another. Perplexed, I had to figure out how this could be.

Why Different Responses?

One reason why the divergent responses to the film troubled me is that I am not a postmodernist. Adherents of that ideology think that it is only natural for people with different backgrounds, assumptions, and commitments to interpret artworks differently. At its most extreme, a postmodernist affirms the multiplicity of meanings that a work—a "text" in their parlance—has for every viewer.

I have no doubt that there is some truth to postmodernism, but I had always thought that interpreting works of art required me to think that there is a single meaning of a work that I am uncovering when I interpret it. Although we may react to certain features of a work differently because of our own particular identity as viewers—our "subject positions"—I still adhere to the idea that we can get others to accept the validity of our reactions once we explain what it is that makes us react as we do.

However, what struck me the moment I left the theater on the night before the discussion—I had put off viewing the film until the last moment, dissuaded by the press coverage—was my inability to understand how anyone could consider this film to be spiritually uplifting in any sense. To me, the repeated scenes of Jesus's suffering—especially during the very long procession to Golgotha—portray rather the enormous brutality and sadism of which human beings in general are capable or, at least, that of the Roman soldiers at the time. Even though I know that it would make a difference if I thought that the body being abused was God's body, I was thoroughly perplexed about how seeing people taking pleasure in its destruction could yield a spiritual message. Indeed, to me this overly long sequence was its own parody, for each new abuse seemed laid on only to prolong the sequence and show that no stone could be left unthrown, no flesh left intact, no indignity unsuffered.

Slowly an idea dawned on me about these two, highly divergent responses to the film. The reason there were two films—on the one hand, an anti-Semitic tract made by the son of a Holocaust denier that Jews and others like me saw and, on the other, a deeply spiritual portrayal of the agony of the Christ that moved a certain segment of the Christian community—is that the film itself is divided and contains each of these other films in it.

To explain what I mean, I'll say that *The Passion of the Condemnation* is the film up to the point where Jesus is condemned by Pilate and *The Passion of the Crucifixion* is the remainder of the film culminating in a very short sequence depicting Christ's return to life. One audience of the film—let me call them "Jews," without meaning to prejudice the case— focus on what is depicted in *The Passion of the Condemnation* while another audience of the film—let me call them "true believers"—respond most fully to *The Passion of the Crucifixion*.

Although the narrative of *The Passion* is an amalgam of the four Gospels and is thus familiar material, *The Passion of the Condemnation* focuses on the quasi-legal processes that led to Jesus being condemned to death. In Gibson's version, the Jewish community as a whole is responsible for this. They apprehend him in the woods as a result of Judas's betrayal and then, in the film's version, subject his body to its first round of torture—events not mentioned in any of the Gospels—as they bring him into a Jewish court. After he is condemned by the court, Jesus is brought before Pilate and the head rabbis ask that he be crucified, a request that Pilate finds unjustified and excessive. In these scenes, the film depicts a humane and thoughtful, if troubled and pressured leader—Pilate—succumbing to the vengeful, sadistic crowd of Jews that demands Jesus's crucifixion. Even then, Pilate accepts this outcome only after repeated failed attempts to find other solutions, including appealing to Herod and having Jesus cruelly beaten.

At this point, I think most viewers understand the film to be presenting the Jewish community as a whole, though its leaders especially, as responsible for Jesus's death. The Roman soldiers are already depicted as sadistic goons whose delight in Jesus's torture appalls us, but we are meant to be even more repelled by the Jews' failure to be satisfied with the destruction of Jesus's body by the Romans, by what we see as their adamant and irrational demand that he be killed by crucifixion.

One thing that bothers Jews is that Gibson's version of events exonerates Pilate of any responsibility for Jesus's death, by using the flashback, among other cinematic techniques. Pilate begins to wash his hands and this action leads to a perceptually similar scene in which Jesus is washing his hands before that Passover Seder which has become known as the Last Supper. (For those that may not know, this is one of the traditional acts of the celebration of Passover.) When we return to Pilate, he says that he has washed his hands of Jesus's blood and the Jews respond that his death will now be on them alone.

It is notable that the last phrase from Matthew 27:25 ("The blood be on us, and on our children.") is not translated onto the subtitles of the American version of the film because test audiences found it upsetting! Despite Gibson's avowal that the film is an expression of his faith, financial considerations do play a role in what we see on the screen and, indeed, in the entire controversy about the film. However, at least in some versions of the film the phrase is translated.

The Jews' supposed acknowledgment of their guilt for Jesus's death has been an ongoing spur to anti-Semitism. Its acceptance by many centuries of Christians resulted in countless assaults on Jews and untold suffering by them. It's no wonder, then, that at this point Jewish audiences have had enough of the film. In it they see a depiction of Jesus's conviction and sentencing that emphasizes the most anti-Semitic aspects of the Christian tradition. For those who have this response, this is essential to the film: its pointed emphasis and expansion of the anti-Semitic aspects of the Gospel's version of Jesus's condemnation.

However, Gibson is not by any means done with us. We have yet to sit through *The Passion of the Crucifixion*, a film that is more gory and unrelenting in its depiction of gore than *The Passion of the Condemnation*. The entire journey to Golgotha, the nailing of Jesus to the cross, and the suffering throughout are extended scenes of a body being brutalized well beyond any possible point of tolerance. But Jesus, as Gibson presents him, has extraordinary powers of endurance and he—or his body—just takes more and more abuse until he finally dies upon the cross. The process takes more than two hours in the film.

Sitting through *The Passion of the Crucifixion* is an ordeal, even for a non-believer. But for those who think that they are witnessing, albeit in fictional form, their God being tortured, brutalized, and, finally, killed, I imagine this must be a truly agonizing and yet purifying experience. My proposal is that this film—*The Passion of the Crucifixion*—so overwhelms *The Passion of the Condemnation* for true believers that it and it alone constitutes the film for them. They focus on and think the film is about the horrendous suffering that Jesus chose to endure in order to save them and everyone else. How can they see any other film? The earlier scenes of the various trials and machinations of *The Passion of the Condemnation* are just so much stage setting for the real issue at hand: Jesus's sacrifice.

The reason, then, for the discrepancies in people's experiences of *The Passion* is that different audiences focus on different aspects of the film. Jews will naturally be sensitive to the film's tendentious portrayal of the events leading up to Jesus being sentenced to death by crucifixion, while true believers will naturally focus on their God's acceptance of all the suffering, humiliation, and pain that the film depicts with such intensity. These, then, are the two *Passions of the Christ* that form the center of our interest.

Fiction as History

If, as I have claimed, it is possible for audiences to see two different "films" while watching the same set of images and sounds, does this mean that I think both of these films—one a vicious anti-Semitic tract and the other a profoundly religious movie—are equally valid when treated as interpretations of *The Passion* as a whole? In fact, I do not. Although I understand why those whom I have called true believers might find *The Passion* to be a source of faith, I think that they have been manipulated by Mel Gibson, for they think that they have seen an accurate re-creation of Jesus's apprehension, conviction, suffering, and death. In fact, what they have seen is a highly slanted version of those events, one that Biblical scholars regard as riddled with error. Why, then, can *The Passion* be so convincing to these viewers?

The film relies on an important property of films that has received extensive discussion among philosophers: its basis in photography. Beginning with the French film theorist and journalist, André Bazin, film scholars have been struck by the medium's ability to capture reality accurately. For these thinkers, photography is distinguished from all other arts by its automaticity, its ability to present us with a world that is, in some sense, not mediated by the consciousness of a human being. Once a photographer presses the shutter, the world is imprinted on his film no matter what he happens to think or desire.

This is significant because it gives films a verisimilitude that all the other arts lack. When we look at a painting, we may be impressed by how much it looks like the object it depicts, but we remain aware that what we see depends upon the painter's decisions about what to include and exclude. We would never dream of using a painting of someone as conclusive evidence in a trial because we realize that what is shown in a painting is crucially mediated by the beliefs and desires of its painter.

Things are different with photographs. We believe that they give us good evidence about what happened at, say, a crime scene—so long as they have not been doctored. And, even then, we believe that the negative tells the truth. Indeed, many of our legal procedures are based upon just this belief.

A film benefits from the verisimilitude of photography. Viewers have a tendency to trust that what they are seeing is real, even when they know it isn't. Although analogue photography has become compromised by the advent of digital imaging, generally viewers still retain their faith in the realism of the medium.

Film makers have sometimes used the viewers' trust in a film's verisimilitude to present a work of fiction as historical truth. A prime example is D.W. Griffith's classic 1915 film, *The Birth of a Nation*. The nation referred to in the film's title is the Ku Klux Klan and the film attempts to vindicate the Klan as necessary for defending whites against marauding blacks in the aftermath of the Civil War. To get audiences to accept his claim, Griffith made a film that was self-consciously styled to appear to be a work of authentic history.

For example, throughout Griffith's masterful presentation of the Civil War, he stops the action and inserts a still tableau that he presents as a copy of a famous photograph of the War, even including information about where and when it was shot, and by whom. The effect is to make audiences believe that they are seeing a completely accurate recreation of the historical epoch of the Civil War and its aftermath.

In fact, however, *The Birth*'s narrative offers a highly skewed version of the historical period it portrays, relying on rumor and fabrication in the service of its ideological goal. It uses its apparent verisimilitude in re-presenting the events of the Civil War to subtly lead audiences into accepting the rest of its narrative—including its presentation of black men as sexual predators of white women—as if it were also gospel truth, so to speak.

At the time of its release, *The Birth of a Nation* was subject to protests by various black organizations that were offended by its racism. Although many white viewers had trouble understanding this charge then, it is hard to imagine a viewer now who would take the film to be historically accurate. One reason is that we are no longer susceptible to Griffith's cinematic strategies for creating the illusion of verisimilitude.

I suggest that Mel Gibson's *The Passion of the Christ* relies on a very similar cinematic strategy to that of Griffith's racist masterpiece, and with similar results. Gibson goes to great lengths to make the film seem realistic. A central strategy is the explicit portrayal of violence, intending that the film not be seen as a romanticized portrait of Jesus's martyrdom. This is why Gibson focuses so explicitly on many cruel events and why the film shows, in excruciating detail, the effects of violence on Jesus's body as a repeated object of torture. Why else do we need to see Jesus's skin literally ripped from his body and then stuck in the teeth of the torture instrument with which he was beaten?

I can understand how true believers might wind up thinking that what they are seeing is a virtual recreation of the events of Jesus's passion. The realism that Gibson employs in showing Jesus's tortured body can easily lead one to assume that what one is seeing *in the film's narrative* is equally realistic. But just as viewers who accepted *The Birth*'s racist narrative about the Klu Klux Klan were duped by that film's realism into accepting its version of the Reconstruction Era, so too, I suggest, are viewers of *The Passion* who come away thinking that they have learned the truth about what took place in Jerusalem one spring so long ago.

Forging Bonds

This is my proposal, then. It is not an interpretation of the film or an interrogation of its anti-Semitism or anything like that. My aim has been to understand how *The Passion of the Christ* can produce such different responses in different viewers, depending on their religious or ethnic affiliations. It is important that everyone who is interested in this film think about this question so that the film not result in an increasing polarization between people. Too often, when Jews feel they have been victimized, their very response to that victimization alienates others even more, bringing about increased anti-Semitism rather than a greater awareness of its perils. I have tried to explain not only why the film upsets Jews but also, and equally importantly, why some Christians find it spiritually compelling. In closing, I ask those who share that second response to consider why some of this film's audiences might react so differently, rather than simply dismissing them or regarding them as having missed the film's point. For, as I have argued, there are more *Passions of the Christ* than it might seem on a first viewing.

SOURCES

André Bazin. 1971. *What Is Cinema?* Berkeley: University of California Press.

Thomas Cripps. 1977. *Slow Fade to Black: The Negro in American Film, 1900–1942.* Oxford: Oxford University Press.

Thomas E. Wartenberg. 1999. *Unlikely Couples: Movie Romance as Social Criticism.* Boulder: Westview.

———. 2001a. Film and Representation. In Ananta C. Sukla, ed., *Representation and the Arts* (Westport: Praeger), pp. 210–220.

———. 2001b. Humanizing the Beast: *King Kong* and the Representation of Black Male Sexuality. In Daniel Bernardi, ed., *Classic Whiteness: Race and the Studio System* (Minneapolis: University of Minnesota Press), pp. 157–177.

QUESTIONS FOR DISCUSSION

1. Do you think *The Passion of the Christ* is anti-Semitic? Why or why not?

2. Does knowing that many people take a point of view opposed to yours affect your own view?

3. Do you think that there can be multiple interpretations of a film? What about the possibility that these different interpretations contradict one another?

4. Do films deserve a special status as works of art in virtue of their basis in photography?

5. Do you agree with the author's contention that viewers who found the film spiritually compelling did so because of the film's realistic portrayal of violence?

8

The Passion as a Political Weapon: Anti-Semitism and Gibson's Use of the Gospels

PAUL KURTZ

The Passion of the Christ is not simply a movie but a political club; at least it is being so used against secularists by leading conservative Christians. TV pundit Bill O'Reilly clearly understands that Mel Gibson's film is a weapon in the cultural war now being waged in America between traditional religionists and secular protagonists—such as the *New York Times*, Frank Rich, Andy Rooney, and the predominant "cultural elite." Newt Gingrich chortled that the movie may be "the most important cultural event" of the century. James Dobson of *Focus on the Family* and a bevy of preachers herald it as "the greatest film ever made."

Busloads of devoted churchgoers were brought daily to view the film, which portrays the arrest, trial, crucifixion, and death of Jesus with graphic brutality. It is used to stir sympathy for Jesus, who, half naked, suffers violent sadomasochistic whippings at the hands of his persecutors; and it has engendered hostility to Jews, secularists, and separationists who have dared to question Gibson's allegedly scripturally accurate account.

The Passion of the Christ reinforces a reality secularists dare not overlook: more than ever before, the Bible has become a powerful political force in America. The Religious Right is pulling no punches in order to defeat secularism and, it hopes, transform the United States into a God-fearing country that salutes "one nation under God" and opposes gay marriages and the "liberal agenda." The interjection of religion into the public square (which in fact was never empty) by powerful religious and political forces has ominous implications. James Madison, framer of the Constitution, rightfully worried about factions disrupting civil society, and religious factions can be the most fractious.

Movies are a powerful medium. Film series including *Star Wars, The Lord of the Rings, Harry Potter, Star Trek, The Terminator,* and *The Matrix* all draw upon fantasy; and these have proved to be highly entertaining, captivating, and huge box office hits. *The Passion of the Christ,* however, is more than that, for it lays down a gauntlet challenging basic democratic secular values. It also presents fantasy as fact, and for the unaware and the credulous, this is more than an exercise in poetic license; it is artistic and historical dishonesty.

A Distorted Version of the Bible

According to Mel Gibson, *The Passion of the Christ* is "a true and faithful rendition of the Gospels." This is hardly the case. For there are numerous occasions when it presents material not found in the New Testament, and when it does, it distorts the Biblical account. Gibson uses poetic license with abandon. Commentators have pointed out that Gibson distorts the character of Pontius Pilate, making him seem to be a tolerant, benevolent, and fair-minded judge—when independent non-Christian historical texts indicate that he was a mean-spirited political opportunist. The film also portrays Pilate's wife Claudia as a kind of heroine. She is sympathetic to Jesus and thinks his punishment is unjust; there is some basis for that in the Bible. But Gibson goes beyond this in his portrayal, for Claudia acts kindly to Mary, the mother of Jesus, and Mary Magdalene at one point in the film, approaching them with a gift of linen cloths. Gibson has Mary use them to wipe pools of blood from the spot where Jesus was flogged by the Romans. Nowhere are these scenes found in any of the four Gospels. Church historian Elaine Pagels has said that it is "unthinkable" that Jewish women would have sought or received any sympathy or succor from the Romans.

Nor do the Gospels provide any support for the severe beatings inflicted on Jesus by the Jewish soldiers and guards who arrest him in the Garden of Gethsemane prior to those inflicted by the Romans. In one gruesome scene, as Jewish troops bring Jesus back to Jerusalem heavily bound, they constantly beat him and at one point, even throw him off a bridge. There is no account of this in the Gospels. It is tossed in to underscore the brutality of the captors.

All the Gospels say is that a large crowd sent by the priests came to the garden to arrest Jesus. There was a scuffle and Jesus told his disciples to lay down their swords. (Here as elsewhere, Jesus does not seem to be a part of his own cultural and religious Jewish milieu; both he and his followers are consistently characterized as renegades and "other" than their social environment.) Matthew 26:57 states: "Jesus was led off under arrest to the house of Caiaphas the High Priest." Mark 14:53 reads: "Then they led Jesus away to the High Priest's house." Luke 22:54: "Then they arrested Him and led Him away." John's version in 18:12: "The troops with their commander and the Jewish police, now arrested Him and secured Him. They took Him first to Annas . . . the father-in-law of Caiaphas."

If Jesus's abuse by the Jewish guards did not come from the Scriptures, from where did Gibson borrow it? From the supposed revelations of a Catholic nun and mystic, Anne Catherine Emmerich (1774–1824). Indeed, much of *The Passion* is taken from Emmerich's book first published in 1833, known in English as *The Dolorous Passion of Our Lord Jesus Christ*. A current edition proudly asserts on its jacket that it is "the classic account of Divine Revelation that inspired" the Mel Gibson motion picture.

Emmerich, a passionate devotee of the practice of meditating on the "sacred wounds of Jesus," described how after Jesus was arrested, he was tightly bound, constantly struck, dragged, and made to walk with bare feet on jagged rocks. Let us focus on a bridge, which they soon reached, and which Gibson depicts in the film. Emmerich states, "I saw our Lord fall twice before He reached the bridge, and these falls were caused entirely by the barbarous manner in which the soldiers dragged Him; but when they were half over the bridge they gave full vent to their brutal inclinations, and struck Jesus with such violence that they threw Him off the bridge into the water. . . . If God had not preserved Him, He must have been killed by this fall" (Emmerich 2003, p. 71).

I refer here to this scene only to show that Gibson went far beyond the texts of the Gospels and inserted non-Scriptural events mostly drawn from Emmerich. Remember that these are the subjective visions of a psychic-mystic rendered over 1800 years after the events they concern. I went to see the movie a second time to see if any credit line is given to the Emmerich book at the end of the film. I could find none, a glaring omission.

A good deal of the focus of *The Passion of the Christ* is on the flogging (scourging) of Jesus. Two Gospels state simply that Pilate "had Jesus flogged and handed over to be crucified" (Matthew 27:26, Mark 15:15). John's description agrees (19:1–2): "Pilate now took Jesus and had Him flogged." Luke's account (23:16) has Pilate saying: "I therefore propose to let Him off with a flogging."

What the Gospels state as a matter-of-fact and without narrative elaboration is luridly expanded by Emmerich: First they used "a species of thorny stick covered with knots and splinters. The blows from these sticks tore His flesh to pieces; his blood spouted out" (Emmerich 2003, p. 135). Then she describes the use of scourges "composed of small chains, or straps covered with iron hooks, which penetrated to the bone and tore off large pieces of flesh at every blow" (p. 135). Moreover, nowhere do the Gospels describe who watched the flogging. Emmerich states that "a Jewish mob gathered at a distance." Gibson has the high priests watching the brutal flogging (with a feminine incarnation of Satan looking on with them). Nowhere is this described in the Bible. Gibson thus goes far beyond the New Testament account, implying that the Jews and their leaders were accomplices in the brutal beatings of Jesus.

The New Testament account next states that the high priests and crowd in the square before Pilate called for the crucifixion of Jesus, and when given the choice, selected Barabbas to be freed rather than Jesus. This is fully depicted in Gibson's *Passion*.

The film, however, is silent about the fact that Jesus, his mother Mary, Peter, James, and the other disciples and supporters in the crowds were themselves Jews. In the depiction of Emmerich and Gibson, the Jews come off as the main enemies of Jesus, provoking the Romans not only to crucify him, but to torture him and inflict maximum suffering. I think the point in the film is even more anti-Jewish: it's that Pilate tries to placate the Jews with the beatings, but they won't be satisfied—some real blood-thirstiness here!

Is *The Passion of the Christ* anti-Semitic? Yes, flagrantly so, in my judgment. *The Passion* repeats the description of the Jews portrayed in medieval art and Passion Plays, which provoked in no small measure anti-Semitic pogroms and persecutions suffered by the "Christ killers" for centuries. Much has been said about the fact that Mel Gibson's eighty-five-year-old father Hutton Gibson is a Holocaust denier. He has been quoted as saying that Vatican II was "a Mason plot backed by the Jews." Mel Gibson removed from the subtitles of the original version of his film the statement from Matthew (27:25–26): "The blood be on us, and on our children," though apparently it remains in the spoken Aramaic text.

To his credit, Pope John Paul II in 2000 made an historic apology, declaring that the Jews of today cannot be held responsible for the death of Christ. Still, *The Passion* debuts at a time when anti-Semitism is growing worldwide, especially in Europe and throughout the Islamic world.

According to Scripture (especially the Gospel of John), Christ died on the cross because God sent His only begotten Son to die for our sins; thus, all sinners are responsible, not simply the Jews of ancient Israel. Mel Gibson has himself blamed all sinners for the crucifixion. If this is the case, the crucifixion of Christ had to happen, and was for that matter foretold by Him.

Why God was willing to allow His only beloved Son to suffer a horrible death is difficult to fathom, but according to Christian apologetics it was preordained so that those who believed in Christ could be saved. Thus it was God—not the Jews alone or the Romans—who was responsible for the crucifixion of Jesus. One might even say that if this was part of a divine plan, the Jews should get the credit for carrying it out.

Is the Biblical Account Reliable?

Is the story of Jesus as described in the New Testament—in this case of his trial, crucifixion, and death (let alone his birth, ministry, and resurrection)—an accurate account of historical events? I doubt it. This negative appraisal is drawn from careful, scholarly, and scientific examination of the New Testament account.

The key point is the fact that the authors of the Gospels were not themselves eyewitnesses to the events described in these documents. If Jesus died about the year 30 C.E. (this is conjectural, since some even question whether he ever lived), the

Gospel according to Mark was probably written in the 70s of the first century; Matthew and Luke in the 80s; and John anywhere from 90 to 100 C.E. They were thus written some forty to seventy years after the death of Jesus. (For convenience I identify the Gospels by the names they received from later church tradition. No one knows the names of the actual authors of these Gospels, which were originally anonymous documents.)

The Gospels are based on an oral tradition, derived at best from second- and third-hand testimony assembled by the early band of Jewish Christians and including anecdotal accounts, ill-attributed sayings, stories, and parables. The Gospels' claims are not independently corroborated by impartial observers—all the more reason why some skepticism about their factual truth is required. They were not written as history or biography *per se*—and the authors did not use the methods of careful, historical scholarship. Rather, they were, according to Biblical scholar Randel Helms, written by missionary propagandists for the faith, interested in proclaiming the "good news" and in endeavoring to attract and convert others to Christianity. Hence, the Gospels should not be taken as literally true, but rather as a form of special pleading for a new ideological-moral-theological faith.

In writing the Gospels the authors evidently looked back to the Old Testament and found passages that were suggestive of a Messiah who would appear, who was born of a young woman (or a virgin), and could trace his lineage back to David—which is why Matthew and Luke made such a fuss about having Jesus born in Bethlehem. Accordingly, the Gospels should be read as works of literary art, spun out of the creative imagination, in order to fulfill passionate yearnings for salvation. They are the most influential fictional works to dominate Western culture throughout its history. Whether there is any core of truth to them is questionable; for it is difficult to verify the actual facts, particularly since there is no mention of Jesus or of his miraculous healings in any extant non-Christian literature from the same time-period.

Tradition has it that Mark heard about Jesus from Peter. Eusebius (260–339 C.E.) is one source for this claim, but Eusebius wrote some three centuries after the death of Jesus. In any case, Matthew and Luke most likely base their accounts on Mark. The three synoptic Gospels are similar, though they contradict each other on a number of significant events. Scholars believe that Matthew and Luke both drew upon Mark and upon another literary source (Q, or in German *Quelle*, meaning "source") that has been lost.

Another historical fact to bear in mind is that the Gospels were written after a protracted war between the Romans and the Jews (66–74 c.e.), which saw the destruction of Jerusalem and of the Temple (70 c.e.). Hundreds of thousands of Jews were killed in these wars and were dispersed throughout the Mediterranean world. Jerusalem was eventually leveled in 135 c.e. The synoptic Gospels were influenced by the political conditions at the times of the various authors who wrote the Gospels, not during the years of Jesus. John's Gospel, written somewhat later, reflected the continuing growth of Christianity in his day. The other book attributed to John, Revelation, which is so influential today, predicts the apocalyptic end of the world, the Rapture, and the Second Coming of Jesus. This book in the view of many scholars reflects the ruminations of a disturbed personality. We have no reliable evidence that these events will occur in the future, yet hundreds of millions of people today are convinced that they will—on the basis of sheer faith.

Let's consider another part of the historical context in the latter part of the first century, when most of the New Testament was composed. Two Jewish sects contended for dominance. First was Rabbinic Judaism, which followed the Torah with all its commandments and rituals (including circumcision and dietary laws). Drawing on the Old Testament, Rabbinic Judaism held that the Jews were the "chosen people." Once slaves in Egypt, they had escaped to the Promised Land of Palestine. Someday after the Diaspora the Jews would be returned to Israel, and the Temple would be rebuilt. The second sect was early Jewish Christianity, which attempted to appeal not only to Jews but to pagans in the Roman Empire. It could do so effectively only by breaking with Rabbinic Judaism. This is the reason for increasing negative references in the Gospels to "the Jews" (especially in John), blaming them for the crucifixion of Jesus. Christianity was able to make great strides in recruiting converts and competing with non-Jewish sects, such as the Mithraic religion. But it could only do so by disassociating itself from Rabbinic Judaism. It developed a more universal message, which, incidentally, was already implicit in the letters of Paul (written some fifteen to twenty years after the crucifixion of

Jesus): The new Christians did not need to be circumcised nor to practice the dietary laws.

Thus, the Biblical texts drawn on in *The Passion of the Christ* should not be read literally as diatribes against the Jews *per se*, but rather as the record of a dispute among two Jewish sects competing for ascendancy: traditional and Christianized Judaism.

If one reads the four Gospels side-by-side, as I have done numerous times, one finds many omissions. Evidently their writers never knew Jesus in his own lifetime. Each Gospel was crafted *post hoc* to satisfy the immediate practical needs of the new Christian churches then developing. They were contrived by human beings who were motivated by the transcendental temptation to believe in Christ as the Son of God and the Savior of mankind. The Gospels thus are historically unreliable, and insofar as *The Passion of the Christ* used them the film is also historically unrealiable. But Gibson goes even beyond the Gospels, as I have indicated.

The Establishment of Christianity

I submit that there are two important inferences to draw from this analysis: First, the union of a religious creed with political power can be extremely destructive, especially when that creed is supported by the power of the state or the Empire. It was the conversion of the Emperor Constantine (around 312 C.E.) that led to the establishment of Christianity as the official religion of the Roman Empire, some three centuries after the crucifixion of Jesus.

The "Nicene Creed," which was the product of the Council of Nicaea (convened in 325 C.E.), said that Jesus was crucified under Pontius Pilate. It also declared Jesus the divine son of God "in one substance" with the Father. The decision which books should be included in the New Testament was political, determined by the vote of the bishops attending the council of Nicaea. At this and other church councils, various apocryphal books revered by particular Christian communities were omitted from the canonical Scriptures. So much for historic objectivity.

The Emperor Julian (331–363 C.E.), a nephew of Constantine and a student of philosophy, became skeptical of Christianity and was prepared to disestablish the Christian church, which he probably would have done had he not been murdered, most likely by a Christian soldier in his army. In any case, Christianity prevailed and the great Hellenic-Roman civilization of the ancient world eventually went into decline. But this occurred in no small measure because of political factors: the grafting of the Bible with the sword, and the establishment of an absolutist Christian creed, intolerant of all other faiths that disagreed, and willing to use any methods to stamp out heresy.

By the fifth century more and more of the inhabitants of the Roman Empire became members of Christian churches, which replaced pagan religions. Christianity reigned supreme across Europe, North Africa, and the Middle East. The latter two were overrun by the Muslims in the seventh and eighth centuries, but feudal Europe remained stolidly Christian as it entered into the so-called Dark Ages. Only with the Renaissance, the Reformation, and the development of science and the democratic revolutions of our time was the hegemony of Christianity weakened. The secularization of modern society brought in its wake naturalistic ideas and humanist values.

The union of religion and political power has generated terrible religious conflicts historically, pitting Catholics against Protestants, opposing Jihadists versus Crusaders, and triggering constant wars among Christians, Jews, Muslims, Hindus, and others. God save us from God-intoxicated legions which have the power to enforce their convictions on those who disagree! All the more reason to laud the wisdom of the authors of the American Constitution who enacted the Bill of Rights, including the First Amendment, prohibiting the establishment of a religion.

Freedom of Inquiry

The second inference to be drawn is that the origins of the Christian legend have for too long lain unexamined, buried by the sands of time. The New Testament was taken by believers as given, and no one was permitted to question its sacred doctrines allegedly based on revelations from On High. But skepticism is called for—the same skepticism that should also be applied to the alleged revelations by Moses on Mount Sinai and other prophets of the Old Testament. Orthodox Jews who accept the legend of a "chosen people" and the promise that God gave Israel to the Jews likewise base this conviction on uncorroborated testimony.

Today, thanks to the tools of historical scholarship, Biblical criticism, and science developed in the past two centuries, we can undertake sophisticated scholarly and scientific inquiries. These tools enable us to use circumstantial evidence, archaeology, linguistic analysis, and textual criticism to authenticate or disconfirm the veracity of ancient literary documents. Regrettably, the general public is almost totally unaware of this important research. Similarly for the revelations of Muhammad and the origins of Islam in the Qur'an. Since they are similarly uncorroborated by independent eyewitnesses, they rest on similarly questionable foundations. There is again a rich literature of skeptical scrutiny. But most scholars are fearful of expressing their dissenting conclusion.

The so-called books of Abraham—the Old and New Testaments, and the Qur'an—need to be scrutinized by rational and scientific analyses. And the results of these inquiries need to leave the academy and be read and digested more widely. Unfortunately, freedom of inquiry had rarely been applied to the foundations of the "sacred texts." Indeed, until recently severe punishment of religious dissenters was the norm in many parts of the world.

Given the tremendous box office success of Mel Gibson's film, there are bound to be other Jesus movies produced—for Jesus sells in America! *The Passion of the Christ* unfortunately may add to intolerance of dissenters; and this may severely endanger the fragility of social peace. It may further help to undermine the First Amendment's prohibition of the establishment of religion, which has been the mainstay of American democracy. This indeed is the most worrisome fallout that the Gibson film is likely to produce.*

---

* This chapter first appeared, with slight differences, in *Free Inquiry*.

SOURCES

John Dominic Crossan. 1995. *Who Killed Jesus? Exposing the Roots of Anti-Semitism in the Gospel Story of the Death of Jesus.* San Francisco: Harper.

Anne Catherine Emmerich. 2003. *The Dolorous Passion of Our Lord Jesus Christ.* Translated by Klemens Maria Brentano. El Sobrante: North Bay Books.

Randel Helms. 1988. *Gospel Fictions.* Amherst: Prometheus.

R. Joseph Hoffmann. 1984. *Jesus Outside the Gospels.* Amherst: Prometheus.

Paul Kurtz. 1991. *Transcendental Temptation: A Critique of Religion and the Paranormal.* Amherst: Prometheus.

G.A. Wells. 1980. *Did Jesus Exist?* Amherst: Prometheus.

QUESTIONS FOR DISCUSSION

1. In what ways can one construe *The Passion of the Christ* as anti-Semitic?

2. How historically reliable are the Gospels?

3. Is Gibson's film historically accurate?

4. How does the use of Emmerich's visionary book affect the understanding of Gibson's film?

5. Is what ways could one argue that Gibson's film is socially dangerous?

9

Is *The Passion of the Christ* Racist? Due Process, Responsibility, and Punishment

J. ANGELO CORLETT

The Passion of the Christ is a moving depiction of the last days of Jesus of Nazareth, who is believed by many to be the Messiah prophesied by the Jewish Scriptures. *The Passion* is to films about the death of Jesus what *Saving Private Ryan* is to movies about the storming of the beach at Normandy. Never before has the death of Jesus been dramatized so vividly. Never has the torture that was his experience been brought to life for viewers to appreciate, however uncomfortably.

The film raises several ethical issues related to suicide, betrayal, freedom of religious expression, political separation of church and state, racism, due process, responsibility, and punishment. In this chapter, I focus mostly on those involving racism, due process, responsibility, and punishment.

Racism and *The Passion of the Christ*

Is *The Passion of the Christ* anti-Semitic and racist? Many believe it to be so, perhaps motivated by the idea that no Jewish person can do great wrong, or by the notion that anything that portrays any Jew in a negative light is anti-Semitic, or by a fear that anything even resembling anti-Semitism today might well bring wrath upon Jewish persons that might rival Hitler's genocidal acts, or by the attitude that Jews are a divinely chosen people and in their special relationship to God should never be treated "unfairly" even in works of art, or by some other implausible

view. But is this movie in fact racist in its portrayal of Jews? I
take it that what is typically meant by viewers of the film who
ask this kind of question is whether or not Jewish persons are
depicted throughout the film as "responsible" for the killing of
Jesus, which was on any plausible account unjust and even evil.

Let us assume for the sake of discussion that the Christian
Scriptures (mostly the Gospels of Matthew, Mark, Luke, and
John) are reasonably accurate in what they state about the life
and death of Jesus. And let us also grant that most of what is
depicted in the film is reasonably faithful to these records. One
could still quibble over certain details, such as whether the
placement of the nails on Jesus's hand (rather than the wrists)
in the crucifixion is historically accurate, or whether or not Satan
really did appear as portrayed in the film, or whether or not certain women are presented as being overly weak, or whether or
not the languages spoken by the characters in the film match the
ones that were most likely spoken, and so on. But all in all, the
film seems to fit well with a common-sense but sensitive reading of the Christian Scriptures. These other details, while of
interest to those of us who have serious concerns regarding historical accuracy, do not play a significant role in an ethical evaluation of some of the major issues raised by the film. The
concentration on such details functions as a smoke screen
which covers the real ethical issues the film raises in its attempt
to tell the story of Jesus's death.

So let us return to the original question: Is *The Passion of
the Christ* anti-Semitic and racist? There are at least two important questions to consider here. First, we might ask whether the
content or message of the film is anti-Semitic and racist. Here
we would be asking whether, say, the director or scriptwriters
of the film intend to send an anti-Semitic message to viewers,
for whatever reasons. I am in no position to judge this question, as I do not lay any claim to the director's or scriptwriters'
intentions or views. So I leave it for others to explore, hope-
fully with fairness.

Second, might the film inflame the passions of some who will
hate the Jewish High Priest (Caiaphas) so badly for his role in the
violent killing of Jesus that they unthinkingly generalize their
hatred to all Jews? This is definitely a possibility. Works of art typically engage audiences to think profoundly about their subject
matters, but at times the emotions are aroused so as to leave ratio-

nality behind. However, that this is likely to happen is insufficient reason to think that the film itself (either intentionally or not) portrays *all* Jewish people negatively or unfairly. Indeed, the film depicts some Jewish religious leaders as disagreeing vehemently with the majority of their colleagues (including Caiaphas) arguing that Jesus was innocent of the charges of blasphemy and threatening to destroy the Temple, and that he should be left alone.

Just as important is the depiction in the film of various mixed reactions to Jesus as he was forced to carry his cross through the streets of Jerusalem, where some onlookers jeered him while others cheered him. In fact, one of the heroes of the film is Simon of Cyrene, the humble Jewish man who helped carry Jesus's cross when Jesus himself could carry it no further. He also stood up for Jesus, courageously scolding the Roman soldiers who were abusing him both verbally and physically along the way. Nor should we forget that the characters that are portrayed most positively in the film (Mary, the mother of Jesus, and Jesus) were themselves Jews.

So there is clearly a balance of sorts in how Jews are depicted in the film. Some of the leaders in the Sanhedrin and their supporters, along with the brutal Temple guards, are depicted as being very bad indeed, whereas other members of the Sanhedrin, along with many humble Jews, are quite supportive of Jesus. If the Gospels are accurate in these matters, the former were evil, while the latter were good, morally speaking.

There is no anti-Semitism in this film detectable by an open mind and a plausible understanding of the nature and function of racism. Jews today ought to feel a sense of deserved pride in that many of their forebears were among the dissidents regarding the unethical treatment of Jesus, while the remainder of us ought not to condemn all Jews for what only a few cowards did. The evils committed by Caiaphas and his gang of supporters were not done because they were Jewish, but because of their own lack of moral character. As *The Passion* implies, Jews as a group are not to be blamed for the death of Jesus. Instead, those particular individuals who were most involved with Jesus's unjust execution are to be blamed for it.

If *The Passion* does display anti-Semitism and racism, perhaps it is in its portrayal of what some would argue is Jewish self-hatred in the way some of the most influential Jews of that time and place sought to destroy one of the greatest (and

Jewish) liberators of human history. However, further argument and analysis would be required to establish this claim.

Was Jesus Given Due Process?

Jesus is provided only a semblance of due process in the film. The most powerful Jewish high priests plotted against him, and they held their own "hearing" of this allegedly "blasphemous" prophet before the Sanhedrin. Jesus was accused of both destroying the Temple and falsely claiming to be the Messiah prophesied in the Jewish Scriptures. Rather than bloody their own hands, the majority of high priests sought to have Roman government officials find him guilty and put to death. They eventually succeeded in having Jesus condemned, though the Romans found no sign of Jesus's guilt. And when the Jewish leaders and their supporters were offered a choice between letting Jesus go free versus having Barabbas, a convicted killer, do so, the leaders and their followers chose the latter.

Perhaps it was Jesus's harsh preaching about the moral hypocrisy of those Jewish leaders ("Woe unto you, scribes and Pharisees, hypocrites!" Matthew 23:23) that led them to despise Jesus. Perhaps it was the fact that Jesus's life and teachings to the multitudes threatened their entire way of life. Perhaps it was Jesus's cleansing of the Temple, a flagrant challenge to the authority of Jewish religious leaders. Perhaps they feared that Jesus would spark a violent and futile uprising against the Romans. Whatever the reason, they are vividly portrayed in the film as hating him so much that they demanded his crucifixion. And this for preaching a religious message that was in certain ways antithetical to the lives, message, and power structure of the Jewish religious authorities of the time.

Even if Jesus's words inflamed the passions of some, such that they were incited (perhaps unintentionally) to overthrow the Roman government or even the Jewish religious leadership in Jerusalem, it is unclear that the punishment inflicted on him was just or proportional to the damage that his words may have caused. Some scholars argue that Jesus was indeed a revolutionary, and was deemed such by Jewish religious authorities. This explains, they claim, why Jesus's reply to Pilate's question, "Are you the king of the Jews?" (Mark 15:2; Matthew 27:11; and Luke 23:3), appeared somewhat evasive: "You have said so"

(Mark 15:3) or "Do you say this of your own accord, or did others say it to you about me?" (John 18:34). After all, one of Jesus's followers Simon, was a member of a sect called "the Zealots," that advocated violent resistance to Roman rule (Luke 6:15; Acts 1:13). Indeed, if the Romans perceived Jesus as a potential revolutionary, Pilate might have been swayed by Jewish religious authorities to silence him. But even if Roman and Jewish governing authorities saw Jesus as a threat to their power, this does not justify their putting him to death, and so violently!

Those of us who prize freedom of conscience and expression, as protected by the First Amendment to the United States Constitution, find the treatment of Jesus nothing short of morally blasphemous and evil. This is precisely why freedom of expression ought to be protected by a total separation of religion and state. Recall that Jesus himself is reported to have argued that people ought to render unto Ceasar what is Ceasar's and unto God what is God's. As depicted in *The Passion*, such a policy would have allowed the Roman government to tell those Jewish religious leaders to go to hell. For *any* religion that cannot cope with the freedom of expression of its adult members is a religion not worth having. When due process and fundamental human rights are violated as badly as they were in the case of Jesus, it is high time to question the very morality of those individuals and institutions directly responsible for the resultant evil. We would want to argue similarly if Moses, Mohammed, or Bertrand Russell were treated as Jesus is depicted as having been treated in Gibson's film.

Due process of law and freedom of expression are correctly regarded as basic human rights, and their violation—which the high priests in question carried out—cannot be permitted. Morally speaking, we can only hope that there is a just and fair God and that those most responsible for the unjust death of Jesus will receive precisely the treatment that Jesus received, but for eternity.

Was Jesus given due process? We have scant information about Jewish criminal procedure in Jesus's lifetime. But scholars have pointed out that many procedures that were in place two centuries later were not followed in Jesus's trial before the Sanhedrin. Certainly the trial itself left itself open to manipulation by forces of evil which in this case led to an innocent person's death. Morever, due process was clearly violated when, as depicted in the film, Jesus was beaten by Temple guards immediately after his arrest and on the way to his hearing before the Sanhedrin. However, even if Jesus did violate some religious norm, this would not entail that he was guilty of any moral wrongdoing—clearly these are not the same. For he might well have been on the side of truth in protesting an unjust religious norm. The evidence could not rightly convict Jesus even on religious grounds, so a policy that permitted Roman officials to free one convict each year allowed Jesus's detractors to exchange his death for the liberty of a killer. Legal justice? Perhaps. Ethical? Absolutely not! The plotting against Jesus by the High Priest Caiaphas is a case of religion gone evil. Any self-respecting Jews today would do well to disavow such evil so as not to allow anyone to think for even a moment that they support it.

In short, according to the Christian Scriptures, certain Jewish high priests were primarily responsible for the death of Jesus. If this is true, and Jesus was innocent of the charges brought against him, then the Jewish leaders in question bear the responsibility for the death of an innocent person, and are thus guilty of evil. This makes it all the more obvious that religious Jewish leaders today ought to disassociate themselves from the evil that was caused by some of their religious forebears.

This is not to say that "the Jews ought to apologize for killing Jesus." Genuine apologies can only be made by those who do wrong, or by those who truly represent them. And apologies can be genuinely accepted only by victims of wrongdoers, or those who truly represent the victims. Jews would need to apologize to Christians only if they as a whole still identified with the attitude of the high priests who were responsible for Jesus's death. This is why the matter of disassociation is important. The failure of contemporary Jews to disassociate themselves from what happened to Jesus would lead many to think, rightly or wrongly, that Jews today align themselves with the moral evil of unjustly having Jesus put to death. In such a case, today's Jews would not be apologizing for the death of Jesus caused by some of their forebears, as they cannot sensibly apologize for something they themselves did not do. Rather, they would be disassociating themselves from that evil act so in order to remove any question as to whether or not they support what was done to Jesus by Caiaphas and his cowardly crew. We are often responsible for our failures to act, not just for our actions and attempted actions.

It is incumbent on us to disavow, symbolically or otherwise, evils if for no other reason than to show the world that we take a stand against injustice wherever it raises its ugly head. It can also serve as a way of affirming our support for the person who was treated unjustly as well as demonstrating our solidarity with the communities with which the victim identified.

Did the Punishment of Jesus "Fit the Crime"?

This leads us to the issue of punishment. *The Passion of the Christ* depicts the death of Jesus in a most painful manner, and graphically so. Does the torturous and bloody death of Jesus imply anything one way or another about the justifiability of punishment—specifically capital punishment? Does the brutality that Jesus endured suggest that such punishment is inhumane and ought never to be practiced by a reasonably just society.

One principle of punishment might be that those who unjustly punish others ought themselves to be made to suffer the very same kind(s) of punishment that others suffered unjustly. This would imply that many of the Jewish high priests should have been made to suffer the most horrendous forms of inhumanity. Perhaps there is a God who will be sufficiently just to make their proper suffering a reality in an afterlife. Consider Adolf Hitler, who did not remain alive to be tried and, if convicted, suffer what he genuinely deserved for his crimes against humanity. Some evildoers appear to escape justice in this life. But if there is a way to suffer at the hands of a just God, they will perhaps get what they deserve after all. I say "perhaps," as it might turn out that God wrongfully forgives those who deserve harsh punishment. In which case, the universe is much better-off without a God. There is no room in a just world (or a world in which many are attempting to be just) for an unjust God.

But Jesus's unjust death does not imply that punishment itself, or severity in punishment, is necessarily unjust. What made Jesus's punishment wrong was not that it was harsh, or that it led to his death. Rather, it was that Jesus was, as far as we know, completely innocent of anything that would have justified such punishment, or any punishment at all. One need not be an avid Christian to believe that this is so. The torture and death of Jesus imply nothing that would suggest that harsh punishment or capital punishment is unjust, unless, of course, it is administered to those who are undeserving. For there is a principle, The Unjust Punishment Principle, that suggests that those who unjustly punish others (or have others punished unjustly) ought to be made to suffer the harm they wrought on those innocents. In the case where someone is made to suffer torture (like crucifixion) or even death unjustly, those most responsible for the unjust punishment ought themselves to be punished in the same ways. This principle in turn assumes a principle of proportional punishment, as well as principles of responsibility for harmful wrongdoing that constitute a plausible conception of desert. How do we know what someone deserves? We know what someone deserves by calculating, however imprecisely, their responsibility for wrongful harm to others coupled with the degree to which they made another suffer harm. This ensures against both over-punishing and under-punishing wrongdoers.

In short, even if it were true that blasphemy is morally wrong and that Jesus was a blasphemer, what moral right did anyone, even the leaders of the Jewish religious community, have to punish him at all, much less with torture and death? The most that reason would permit would be censorship in the Jewish religious community of which Jesus was a part, or perhaps expulsion from it, or perhaps even a Temple fine. But the punishment administered to Jesus by Roman soldiers, pressed ardently and incessantly by Caiaphas and his evil cohorts, was an unambiguous violation of the moral principle of proportionality in punishment. Apparently, even though Jewish religious norms permitted the stoning to death of blasphemers, Caiaphas was himself too cowardly to kill Jesus, or to have it done directly by members of his own religious community. This is understandable, however, since it is often the most hypocritical among us who attempt to hide their evils by getting others to carry out their foul deeds.

Against the Death Penalty?

Can the unjust execution of Jesus ground an argument against the morality of the death penalty itself, as some think? The answer to this question is "no." Abuse does not negate proper use. More specifically, the unjust punishment of Jesus (or anyone else, for that matter) never nullified morally the proper punishment of persons, namely, those who deserve punishment.

Jesus's execution was unjust because he was innocent of having wrongfully inflicted any severe harm on others; he did not deserve to be punished. That capital punishment was unjustly administered to Jesus in no way implies that capital punishment *per se* is morally unjust. Surely the Jewish religious leaders who were responsible for the unjust punishment of Jesus deserved the most painful and bloody of deaths, and they serve as counter-examples to the simplistic claim that capital punishment *per se* is morally wrong. They, along with Hitler, Andrew Jackson, and a host of others, are among the most evil humans on record.

In sum, *The Passion of the Christ* is not anti-Semitic or racist in any recognizable way. But I can understand how a viewer who does not pay proper attention to the details of the film might wrongly blame all Jews for the unjust death of Jesus. Since one ought not to blame artists for their audiences' misunderstandings of their work, neither this film nor its director ought to be blamed for any anti-Semitism and racism that result from the lack of due diligence of audiences. Jesus was accorded due process, at least to some extent, although due process was violated in the sense that he was treated as being guilty until proven innocent. Those who are arrested, whether Jesus in ancient Jerusalem or African-Americans in the U.S. today, ought always to be treated as though they are innocent until they are, by way of proper due process, found guilty beyond a reasonable doubt (criminal courts) or by the preponderance of the evidence (civil courts).

Finally, does the abuse of Jesus count against capital punishment? Not unless the way he was treated, however unjustly, counts against various other stages and forms of punishment as well. Fault should not be found in the way Jesus was punished after such meager due process. Rather, blame should accrue to those who punished him unjustly. One lesson we learn from reconsidering the life and death of Jesus, as *The Passion of the Christ* does, is that religion itself does not hold the highest form of truth and justice. It is reason, and reason alone, that is capable of correcting those forms of religion that are so badly in need of reform.*

---

* This essay is dedicated to my friend and former mentor, Joel Feinberg, who taught me to reason openly and without fear of finding truth and error wherever they might be.

SOURCES

J. Angelo Corlett. 2003. *Race, Racism, and Reparations.* Ithaca: Cornell
     University Press.
————. 2004. *Responsibility and Punishment.* Second edition.
     Dordrecht: Kluwer.
Joel Feinberg. 1970. *Doing and Deserving.* Princeton: Princeton
     University Press.
————. 1980. *Rights, Justice, and the Bounds of Liberty.* Princeton:
     Princeton University Press.
————. 1992. *Freedom and Fulfillment.* Princeton: Princeton
     University Press.
————. 2003. *Problems at the Roots of Law.* Oxford: Oxford University
     Press.

QUESTIONS FOR DISCUSSION

1. Is just any criticism of a person truly racist? What *is* racism?

2. What *really is* anti-Semitism?

3. What sorts of rights ought to be upheld during due process,
   and why?

4. Can religious or political leadership *always* be trusted? Why
   or why not?

5. Can imposing the death penalty *ever* be the right thing to do,
   morally?

10

The Passion of the Jew: Jesus in the Jewish Mystical Tradition

ERIC BRONSON

My soul thirsts for God, for the living God.

—Psalm 42:3

Who can forget the haunting opening to Mel Gibson's *The Passion of the Christ*? Moviegoers are at once transported to a misty, moonlit night in the olive grove, as the camera slowly zooms in to the back of a shivering Jesus, his body convulsing to the sound of his own heavy breathing. The dialogue begins with the awakening of the disciples to Jesus's inner torments. "I don't want them to see me like this," he painfully tells Peter. Then Jesus sets out alone again, this time to face down the snake of Satan in a scene fraught with spiritual aching. While the snake scene is not taken from the New Testament, the suffering in Gethsemane is familiar to most Christians. There Jesus's soul is "overwhelmed with sorrow to the point of death," (Matthew 26:38, Mark 14:34), and because of his anguish, "he prayed more earnestly, and his sweat was like drops of blood falling to the ground" (Luke 22:44).

Why all this suffering? Many critics of the *Passion* have argued that throughout the movie, Gibson focuses too much on pain and torture, and not enough on developing the more redemptive and life-affirming aspects of Christianity. In his review for *The New York Times*, critic A.O. Scott stated that the *Passion* "is so relentlessly focused on the savagery of Jesus's final hours that this film seems to arise less from love than from wrath." This criticism may hold some weight, but before a final judgment is reached, one must keep in mind that Gibson is heavily influenced by a tradition of mystical Scriptural interpretation. One thing not made clear in the movie is that, like the New Testament, Christian mysticism springs from Judaism and Jewish mysticism, which has long emphasized inner pain and turmoil in the tortuous journey to find God. Placing Jesus in the Jewish mystical tradition may help us understand the primary role of suffering in Gibson's interpretation of Jesus's life and death.

First of all, we need to continuously remind ourselves that Jesus was Jewish. Although his faith isn't in any serious dispute, Jesus's religious conviction has caused a tremendous amount of discomfort for both Jews and Christians around the world. Jews often downplay Jesus's Judaism. Even though it is an unofficial Jewish tradition to memorize a list of hundreds of celebrities that have at least an ounce of Jewish blood, Jesus rarely gets mentioned. Jewish comedians have long poked fun at the Jewish naming ritual. Think of Adam Sandler's "Hannukah Song" in which the three stooges, Captain Kirk, and even baseball player Rod Carew ("he converted") are credited for their Jewishness. With such a time-honored practice, one would expect that Jews would freely list Jesus as one of their own. If Jews still heap praise on singer-songwriter Bob Dylan, who denied his faith, and comedian Woody Allen, whose personal ethics is not exactly borrowed from a Jewish context, why not acknowledge Jesus?

Christians also have issues with Jesus's past. As we know, Jesus acted as a rabbi who prayed in synagogues and studied the Torah. His last supper was a celebration of the Passover, commemorating the Jewish exodus out of Egypt and the journey into the land of Israel. After his death, many of his disciples continued to pray in the holy Temple of Jerusalem, the center of Jewish life. Yet, throughout Western and Eastern Europe, Jews have at times been discriminated against, persecuted, and even murdered by Christians for sharing the same religion as Jesus. How can this be?

I suspect that like most religious divides, the conflicts have more to do with politics and economics than they have to do with theology, because the more we dig into Jesus's life, the more he is revealed as an important Jewish figure in a dynamic religious outpost at the fringes of the Roman Empire. Breaking away from the Jewish power structure of his day, Jesus followed a long line of Jewish mystics who challenged the established hierarchy, while holding on to their roots.

By emphasizing Jesus's mysticism and suffering, Gibson ends up focusing on the very characteristics that make Jesus appear *more* Jewish. To understand Jesus's mysticism, however, we need a better understanding of mysticism and its relationship to philosophy. Only then can we determine what makes Jesus a mystic, and one who understands his important place in the Jewish tradition.

Philosophy and Mysticism

Before Jesus, it was Socrates (470–399 B.C.) who publicly questioned the leading officials of his day, combating their undeveloped ideas with his rational argumentation. Through dialogue and debate, Socrates learned and taught *philosophy*, literally "love of wisdom" in Greek. Over two thousand years later, Western philosophy still follows in the legacy of the Ancient Greek philosopher.

But while Socrates often sought truth through rational argument, he also admitted that loving wisdom is a dangerous path, and loving anything is ultimately a "sort of madness." In Plato's two greatest dialogues on love, *Symposium* and *Phaedrus*, Socrates speaks of a wisdom that is not learned from books or schooling. Such mysterious wisdom involves a vision of true beauty that is only transmitted to a person who has learned to love. As Socrates explains in the *Symposium*, through love such wisdom "bursts upon him that wondrous vision which is the very soul of the beauty he has toiled so long for. It is an everlasting loveliness which neither comes nor goes, which neither flowers nor fades" (210e–211a). In the *Phaedrus*, Socrates makes it clear that people who experience such rare visions of beauty will have a deeper understanding of the world, even while all the world thinks they have gone mad. And, of course, they have gone mad since mundane experiences of beauty cause them to act differently from the common people. A true lover experiences "a shuddering and a measure of that awe which the vision inspired, and then reverence as at the sight of god. . . . Next, with the passing of the shudder, a strange sweating and fever seizes him" (251a). Socrates, then, gives us two different paths to attaining wisdom: the path of sober analysis and the shudders of the heart that come neither from words nor thoughts.

The idea that wisdom can be imparted through irrational means had a lasting impact on Muslim, Jewish, and Christian thinkers in the Middle Ages. Between the eleventh and thirteenth centuries, philosophers such as Al-Gazali (1058–1111), Moses Maimonides (1138–1204), and Thomas Aquinas (1224/6–1274) all agreed that the rational emphasis of philosophy was insufficient for getting close to God. While philosophy might help prepare the path for the truth-seeking novice, these philosophers argued that books are poor substitutes for direct experiences of God's revelations. And such revelations often flew in the face of some of the best laid theories in Western philosophy. Similar to Socrates's descriptions of love, philosophers of the Middle Ages hinted at divine visions of beauty that would shake even the most profound thinker out of his carefully planned arguments.

Since the Middle Ages, philosophers have had a difficult time reconciling the way of reasoned questioning with the mystical path of immediate experience. One of the most impressive attempts at confronting this problem was made by the American William James (1842–1910). In his seminal work, *The Varieties of Religious Experience*, James attributes four primary characteristics to mystical experiences. In the first place, they defy all rational understanding. Mystics can never adequately convey to others the full exchange that takes place. The nature of the experience is ineffable. If you want to understand what happens, "you have to be there." According to James, the second characteristic of mystical experiences is that they convey truths that the rational mind is unable to comprehend, although one is made wiser through them. The third and fourth features are the fleeting nature of the experiences and the passivity of the person having them. The last point, though, is somewhat misleading. Mystics may not be active participants during their mystical encounters, but many have reported traveling rigorous roads of inner pain and struggle in order to open themselves to their possibility.

Using James's perceptive account, let us understand mysticism as *the belief that a higher truth (divine Wisdom, in Western religions) can be accessed not through book learning, but through a painful inner journey that leads to a short-lived, direct experience that defies all rationality.* Philosophy is no stranger to the torments of the soul, but it does require the kind of rational investigation and explanation that precludes its use of mysticism. While philosophers such as Socrates have at times acknowledged the possibility of mystical encounters, such encounters are usually mentioned as the exceptions to the rule. Rather than relying on direct experience, contemporary Western philosophy requires proofs and logical discourse, involving a rational thrust that distinguishes it from mysticism. As James and the Medieval philosophers argue, philosophy and mysticism may simply be two different paths to the same goal.

With this new definition, we can better understand Gibson's portrayal of Jesus in *The Passion*. Most scenes in the movie are not mystical, though there are a number of touching "other worldly" moments that show Mary's love for her son. In *The Passion*, Mary seems to exude love so strongly that Jesus is made aware of his mother whenever she is near. Remember the beautiful scene after Jesus is tortured by Pilate's guards and sent to the dungeon. Mary is seen walking along the Temple grounds, feeling for her son with an almost sixth sense. She then drops to the ground and lovingly moves her hand over the floorboards. Jesus, below, lifts his head in gentle understanding. Stirring as this scene is, if true, it wouldn't qualify as a mystical experience by our above definition because there is not a direct experience with God or a higher being.

Now let's compare the mother-son scene with the opening of *The Passion*. After battling his inner demons, Jesus briefly experience a vision of God that changes him in non-rational ways. His renewed sense of peace and higher wisdom baffle his disciples, as Jesus willingly puts his life in the hands of his enemies. Here, Gibson makes the clearest connection between Jesus's life and the mystical life as espoused by philosophers and theologians throughout the ages. While many other scenes show the powerful love between Jesus and Mary, the opening scene most clearly portrays the mystical love between Jesus and God.

Mysticism and Philosophy in the Hebrew Bible

Gibson focuses on the suffering of Jesus to highlight the mystical nature of Jesus's crucifixion. Of course, Jesus wasn't the first mystic to preach in the Promised Land. Tension between philosophy and mysticism is already evident in the Hebrew Bible. The author of The Song of Songs discusses a bride waiting for the groom as a metaphor for our longing to be physically touched by God.

> Thou that dwellest in the gardens,
> The companions hearken for thy voice:
> 'Cause me to hear it.' (8:13)

For thousands of years, both mystics and philosophers have hearkened for His voice. But does one hear God's voice through rational questions or irrational experiences?

From the Tower of Babel to the wise men in the Book of Job, mortals who speak of knowing God's wisdom are continuously thwarted. "Wisdom cries aloud in the street," we are told in the Book of Proverbs (1:20), but the average person cannot hear it. Even the wisest among us are laid low. "For in much wisdom is much vexation; / And he that increaseth knowledge increaseth sorrow" (Ecclesiastes 1:18). On the one hand, God's wisdom is everywhere; on the other hand when people try to find it, they invariably run adrift. Some wise men such as King Solomon are blessed by God in part because they pursue logical questioning. But other Old Testament prophets are blessed so much that they directly receive visions of God. Through these rare divine visions, select Jews are able at once to grasp the higher truths and thereby be changed forever.

Before Jesus's time, the land of Israel was rife with mystics and philosophers. In the Old Testament, however, it is the mystics who most often get closer to God. Moses, for example, didn't learn his ethical code from a textbook, but from a direct experience with God. He walked up Mount Sinai, despite "the thunderings, and the lightnings, and the voice of the horn, and the mountain smoking" to receive the Ten Commandments (Exodus 20:15). Moses's experience has all the marks of mysticism. It was, likely, a relatively short-lived experience that conveyed messages of truth to a passive listener. And like all mystical experiences, the effect that the divine words had on Moses cannot be explained. All the text says is that the skin on Moses's face "sent forth beams" (Exodus 34:29, 34:35). What Moses saw and heard might be explained, but its effect on

Moses's soul cannot be described. We know there are beams in Moses's face, but what took place inside Moses's soul to cause such a light is "known" only to the one who has experienced it.

Daniel is another figure in the Jewish tradition who directly experienced the divinity. According to the Hebrew Bible, Daniel became an important adviser to King Nebuchadnezzar, because of the wisdom that God gave him through visions and dreams in the night. His most powerful vision is of the "ancient of days" sitting on a throne.

> His raiment was as white snow,
> And the hair of his head like pure wool;
> His throne was fiery flames,
> And the wheels thereof burning fire. (Daniel 7:9)

To the throne comes "one like unto a son of man," who is given dominion over all the earth. Again, in Daniel's account, the mystic's voice speaks loudest, and wisdom is imparted through this brief vision. As with Moses, while Daniel can relate the specifics of the experience, the essence of the experience is ineffable. He is incapable of rationally describing the effect it had on his soul. All the reader gets is that Daniel's spirit is "pained." What took place inside the Old Testament prophet? The inner change is shrouded in mystery typical of mysticism. "As for me Daniel, my thoughts much affrighted me, and my countenance was changed in me; but I kept the matter in my heart" (7:28).

Mysticism in the Time of Jesus

These mystical encounters of the Old Testament had a lasting impact on Jews like Jesus. The *Dead Sea Scrolls*, for example, point to a Jewish community in Qumran (150 B.C–A.D. 68) that lived in some seclusion around the time when Jesus was preaching in Galilee. Apparently the desert commune spoke of the Holy Spirit entering anointed individuals directly, and kept a number of copies of the mystical Book of Daniel deep within their caves.

The New Testament links the Jewish prophet Elijah with the mystical John the Baptist. In the Old Testament, Elijah is so blessed, he gets a one-of-a-kind escort to heaven. In the Book of 2 Kings, we learn that a chariot comes down from heaven with horses of fire to carry Elijah with them. The vision of Elijah's chariot becomes an important theme in later Jewish mysticism. In the Old Testament, Ezekiel picks up the chariot theme. In his vision, "the appearance of the likeness of the glory of the Lord" is on a throne brought down by chariot to speak with Ezekiel. It is this throne that Daniel sees in his mystical vision. It should come as no surprise that John the Baptist dressed like Elijah, performed his cleansing rituals at the place where Elijah was carried off to heaven in a chariot, and is frequently likened to Elijah. "He is the Elijah who was to come," Jesus claims of John (Matthew 11:14). John speaks as the voice of the wilderness, preaching the possibility of direct contact with God for all those who are physically and spiritually purified. For bringing God closer to the people of the desert, John's reputation as a mystic grows. He is much "more than a prophet" (Luke 7:26).

In the time of Jesus other Jewish mystics also experienced God on intimate terms. The Mishnah, written not long after the death of Jesus and the burning of the Temple, tells a story of Honi the Circle-Drawer. Honi got his name by allegedly drawing a circle and informing God that he wouldn't leave the circle until the Father of the world caused rain to end the drought. It began to rain lightly, but Honi insisted on more. Then it started raining violently and Honi was still not satisfied, asking instead for "rain of good will." Finally, God made it rain in a way that was pleasing to Honi. One amazed onlooker likened Honi to a spoiled child, who wanted his father to give him everything. "For you [Honi] make demands before the Omnipresent so he does what you want, like a son who makes demands on his father so he does what he wants" (Mishnah Taanit 3:8). Honi's story is just one of many examples in Jewish lore of mystics and prophets who speak to God in familial terms.

Jesus the Jewish Mystic

Jewish mysticism has long preached an intimate, immediate relationship with the world's creator. In both Old and New Testaments, God is seen as a father close to his kin, and the mystic's suffering is like the discipline a father metes out to his children. In Gibson's *Passion*, we continuously hear Jesus refer to God as *Abba*, Aramaic for papa. By emphasizing the Father,

Jesus the Son continues the Jewish practice of treating one's direct experience with God as a family affair. When Jesus refers to God as *Abba*, he places himself within that Jewish context.

According to the New Testament, Jesus also has direct experiences with God, the Father. Gibson begins and ends *The Passion* with Jesus speaking to God on intimate terms. From Jesus's pleading with God to take the cup away from him, to his anguished final cry on the cross, Jesus appeals to God like a distraught child appeals to his loving dad. Throughout the movie, Gibson seems particularly drawn to this intimate relationship so typical of Jewish mystical tradition.

One of the most vivid mystical experiences in the New Testament, however, is the transfiguration (not shown in Gibson's *Passion*). Disciples describe Jesus speaking with Old Testament prophets Moses and Elijah. True to the tradition of Jewish mysticism the participant is changed in ways that defy rationality. The disciples note how Jesus's face "shone like the sun, and his clothes became as white as the light" (Matthew 17:2). Through their own mystical vision, the disciples learned directly from God that Jesus is the Son, and "fell facedown to the ground, terrified." Better than any other story in the New Testament, the transfiguration connects Jesus to the tradition of Jewish mysticism. By placing Jesus alongside Moses and Elijah, Jesus is directly linked to two prophets who figure prominently in the annals of Jewish mysticism.

Gibson connects Jesus to Elijah's chariot mysticism more directly. In *The Passion*, the High Priest Caiaphas says to Jesus skeptically, "Some say you're Elijah. But he was carried off to heaven in a chariot." In the New Testament, *Merkavah*, or Jewish chariot-throne mysticism, is a recurring theme in Jesus's visions. He sees himself sitting at "the right hand of the mighty God" (Luke 22:68) "and coming down on the clouds of heaven" (Matthew 26:64, Mark 14:62). Such visions of the chariot-throne are well-trodden chapters in the lore of Jewish mysticism since the time of the prophet Elijah.

There is also an element of inner turmoil that is common to most documented mystical experiences. While mystics may come to taste God's glory, they do so only after many desperate failures. The mystics' path to a higher reality is rarely easy. "Cry and wail, son of man," God tells Ezekiel (21:17), for it is through the trembling of the soul that God is experienced. Paul of the

New Testament reminds us that joining ourselves with God involves "great endurance; in troubles, hardships and distresses; in beatings, imprisonments and riots; in hard work, sleepless nights and hunger" (2 Corinthians 6:4). And Paul should know. He received his "secret wisdom" from a flash of light and a mystical vision of his own that left him blind and unable to eat or drink for three days (1 Corinthians 1:7, Acts 9:9).

Though Moses faithfully spent forty years wandering the desert, he was still denied entrance to the Promised Land. John the Baptist was beheaded. Jesus was crucified. Such are often the fates of Jewish mystics.

Mysticism After Jesus

For many Jews of Palestine, it wasn't Jesus's crucifixion, but the destruction of the Temple in Jerusalem in A.D. 70 that became the defining test of their faith. Forced to scatter across Europe and Asia, the Jewish people lost their centralized power structure. To compensate for this loss, many contemporary historians argue that mysticism disappeared from Judaism for hundreds of years in place of the more rigid and legalistic rabbinic literature. But if we are to understand Jewish mysticism as the belief that through suffering one can experience God directly in a way that defies all rationality, then we'll see it alive and well after the Jews' banishment from the Holy Land. The idea that God is everywhere is pervasive in the Mishnah and the Talmud—books that still constitute the backbone of modern-day Judaism. God's word comes to Jews through the Torah. But the Torah is more than simply the first five books of Moses; Torah is a way of life. Anyone can experience God by living Torah in simple day-to-day activities. So we get stories such as the one in the Talmud about a disciple hiding out in a bathroom to listen for God's word in a mundane exchange between a rabbi and a bathroom attendant.

In the first few hundred years after Jesus's death, the Jewish God had become so familiar to the Jewish mystic that He is sometimes even stripped of his awe-inspiring powers. One classic story in the Talmud recounts an argument between Rabbi Eliezer and Rabbi Joshua regarding Jewish law. Eliezer summons God who weighs in on the side of Eliezer. But even God's own voice is not good enough for Joshua. "Torah is no longer in Heaven," Joshua boldly proclaims. "God has given it to men." God can only smile after having been on the losing side of the argument. In these Talmudic stories we don't get the same soul-wrenching transformation that we saw with Moses and Daniel, and later with Jesus and Paul, but the intimacy between man and God that is so important in mysticism is also a hallmark of the rabbinic literature in later centuries.

Jewish mysticism sees its most potent revival in the twelfth and thirteenth centuries with the publication of the Book of Zohar in Spain, and other works that come to be known simply as the Kabbalah. These mystical works talk of learning God's inner meaning through a secret combination and rearrangement of Hebrew words in the Torah, of quiet prayers that bring one closer to God's mysterious chariot, and of divine sparks that cry within the human body, begging to be released and restored in God. And just like the dynamic and dangerous times of first-century Israel, the mystical ideal of finding God through non-rational channels was seen as a threat to the authorities. Many Jewish mystics were killed by the Spanish Inquisition, as they were by the Roman Empire over one thousand years earlier.

In more recent times, the Hassidic movement of Eastern Europe introduced a more joyous piety to Jewish mysticism. As the movement flourished in the eighteenth and nineteenth centuries, Hassidic mystics argued that the Kabbalah's divine sparks could lead to a "cleaving" to God that brings enduring joy to those blessed enough to experience it. Still, all is not light and easy. There's an old Hassidic story of Rabbi Firkes who yearns to learn the mystical secrets of God. When he is publicly insulted for his ambition, he cries a flood of tears. Only in the deep recesses of his anguish does the rabbi experience God, and within the tears of his soul, he finds inner peace and lasting hope.

Quid est Veritas?

Mysticism, and its emphasis on personal suffering, always seems to flower in turbulent times. Since 9/11, more Americans see life as fragile, much like the Jews saw their own lives in the chaotic days of Jesus. In such times, many people look to mystics, more so than to philosophers, for truth. Today, the Kabbalah Centre in Los Angeles opens its doors to celebrities such as Madonna,

Demi Moore, Paris Hilton, and Britney Spears. In such a climate of spiritual upheaval, it's hardly surprising that Mel Gibson's mystical interpretation in *The Passion* has received such widespread attention. History teaches us that when people are bombarded with stories of intolerance and prospects of death, they turn to more direct paths of becoming united with God.

Is this turn toward mysticism a good thing? Should we instead encourage the steady hand of philosophy over the non-rational, individualistic pursuit of a higher being? Which truth is more valuable? In Gibson's *Passion*, this question is raised in an exchange between Pontius Pilate and his wife. The scene takes place after Pilate has already interrogated Jesus in private. During the questioning of the prisoner, Pilate asks Jesus if he is a king. Jesus answers cryptically: "Everyone on the side of truth listens to me." Later, Pilate, still confused, goes on to raise the age-old philosophical question: "*Quid est veritas?*" What is truth? There's no reason to suspect Pilate is a truth-seeking philosopher, but he does have a bit of the pragmatist in him. Pilate has orders to follow and a family to consider. He considers Jesus's words, but they appear illogical.

Though Pilate's wife is hardly mentioned in the New Testament, Gibson has her play the role of the mystic in *The Passion*. "What is truth?" Pilate repeats to his wife in the movie. Knowing that her husband is too rational to grasp higher truths, she responds mystically, "If you will not hear the truth, no one can tell you."

What, then, is the truth, and how can we find it? In *The Passion*, Gibson seems to side with Pilate's wife. By adding the exchange (not found in the New Testament), Gibson makes a special effort to favor the mystical path of attaining truth. Let's not crucify him for that. In some of the other chapters of this volume, we saw just how much Gibson is influenced by Christian mystic Anne Catherine Emmerich (1774–1824). But whether he chooses to acknowledge it or not, Gibson also stands within thousands of years of Jewish mystical tradition when he champions the painful, irrational journey to find God. It's a tradition that still fascinates people of all religions, from the hills of Hollywood to the silent shores of the Galilee.*

* Thanks to Aryn Martin and Gail Sheena for their help with New Testament interpretations.

SOURCES

Bruce Chilton. 2000. *Rabbi Jesus: An Intimate Biography*. New York: Doubleday.

William James. 1997. *The Varieties of Religious Experience*. New York: Simon and Schuster.

Gershom Scholem. 1961. *Major Trends in Jewish Mysticism*. New York: Schocken.

Adin Steinsaltz. 1976. *The Essential Talmud*. Translated by Chaya Galai. New York: Basic Books.

Geza Vermes. 1974. *Jesus the Jew: A Historian's Reading of the Gospels*. New York: Macmillan.

QUESTIONS FOR DISCUSSION

1. Which aspects of Judaism does Jesus follow?

2. Why were purification rites and baptisms so important to the ancient Jews?

3. During the time of Jesus, Jews were sharply divided on the future of their faith. Are Muslims going through similar rifts today?

4. Is Mel Gibson a mystic?

5. How does mysticism differ from philosophy?

III

What Is the Truth?

11
Pilate's Question: What Is Truth?

WILLIAM IRWIN

If *The Passion of the Christ* asks one clearly philosophical question it is: *Quid est veritas?* What is truth? Indeed philosophers have "a passion for truth." Certainly Socrates (470–399 B.C.) did. His dialectical method involved asking questions and exposing false answers by providing counterexamples, prompting further questions and answers. So in this chapter I'll consider *The Passion* in light of the question and the question in light of *The Passion*.

A word of warning though, this chapter does not attempt to deliver a "final answer" to the question "What is truth?" Rather, like a nervous contestant on *Who Wants to Be a Millionaire?*, the chapter tells you everything I know about the topic off the top of my head. The theories described all have more sophisticated versions. My apologies to their advocates. This is just a starter's kit. Thinking things through with me perhaps you'll find the answer yourself, though. If you do, give me a hint.

"Truth Is Just Another Fiction": Relativism

Gibson's genial Pilate seems intent on finding a way to get Jesus off the hook, or rather spare him from the cross. But the guy just won't help himself. In the midst of interrogation Gibson's Jesus, faithful to Scripture (John 18:37), informs Pilate that "[e]veryone on the side of truth listens to me." A vexed Pilate remarks later, "What is truth?" He might as well say "What the hell is this guy talking about?"

Pilate does not think of truth as something real and ideal. Pilate is a relativist. As they say in West Virginia, "it's all relative." Pilate knows no absolute standard of truth. It's true for him that executing Jesus is ultimately what is best, even if it's not true for his wife Claudia.

Gibson's Pilate is a sympathetic character. Though he is a bad guy, the audience can see where he's coming from. Most young people have learned the valuable lesson of tolerance that not everyone acts and believes as they do. But too many have learned it too well, drawing from it the unwarranted conclusion that everyone is right in the way they think, act, and believe. It's true for some Muslim societies that female circumcision makes women better wives, but it isn't true for American society. Truth is relative. It depends on the society, sometimes it even depends on the person.

Unfortunately this textbook example of bad reasoning is reinforced and justified by some intellectuals and academics who call themselves *postmodernists*. As Jean Baudrillard, a leading postmodernist, explains:

> [N]obody really believes in the real . . . [O]ur belief in reality and evidence is . . . obscene. Truth is what should be laughed at. One may dream of a culture where everyone bursts into laughter when someone says: this is true, this is real . . .

Although it sounds a lot like the relativism that dates to Pilate and back much further still, Postmodernism claims to be something new, you know, like the emperor's clothes. The postmodern view of truth has its roots in the philosophy of Friedrich Nietzsche (1844–1900) who asks, "Supposing truth is a woman— what then?" (1966, p. 2). The idea is that there is no essential truth, certainly none that we can hope to apprehend anyway, just ways of seeing things. "There is only a perspective seeing, only a perspective knowing," Nietzsche claims (1969, p. 119). What then are we to do? Well, as Billy Joel sang, "The most she will do / is throw shadows at you / But she's always a woman to me." The answer is to get as good a perspective on the woman as you can and reconcile yourself to it. Men are foolish and doomed to be hurt if they think there is anything more to it than that.

Misogyny aside, there is just no reason to accept the pessimistic conclusion of Nietzsche and the "truthless people," postmodernists. Surely there must be criteria by which we can decide what is true.

"Truth Is Out There": Correspondence

The criterion for deciding whether a proposition is true or false is an essential concern of epistemology, the branch of philosophy that deals with knowledge. From the time of Plato (around 428–347 B.C.), without challenge until the middle of the twentieth century, knowledge was defined as true, justified belief. Clearly, to properly make use of this definition of knowledge one must have a way of telling whether or not a proposition is true.

The oldest and most commonsense criterion of truth is given by the Correspondence Theory of Truth, which in its simplest form states: a proposition is true if and only if it corresponds to the way things actually are. For example, we know that "Erwin's cat is alive" is true if and only if Erwin's cat *is* alive. If the cat is dead, the proposition is false. *The X-Files* made famous the claim, "The truth is out there." If we change this mantra to "the proof is out there," we have a version of the Correspondence Theory. The proposition is true, because the facts "out there" match what it claims.

"Jesus is God incarnate" is a proposition Christians believe to be true. But what proof, what evidence, corresponds to this proposition, showing it to be true? Like the Jesus of the Gospels, Gibson's Jesus does not give us the proverbial smoking gun, at least not prior to the resurrection. Prior to his resurrection Jesus gave clues as to his divine identity, but he did not provide any proof that would be accepted by all independently of faith. Gibson's Caiaphas and bad thief employ the Correspondence Theory when they goad Jesus to come down off the cross if he is really who he says he is. Even post-resurrection the Jesus of Scripture does not appear to Caiaphas, Pilate, or others who might admit they had it wrong all along, that this Jesus was more than he even claimed outright, that he was and is divine. Jesus's appearance to Paul on the road to Damascus and the radical conversion that resulted provides some corresponding evidence, but the testimony of a single eyewitness is always subject to some doubt. If we take Paul seriously, we must accept his word on faith, at least in part.

The Correspondence Theory is a good one, yet sometimes we just don't have enough evidence to rationally decide if a statement someone makes is true or false. If however, like Mulder and Scully, we keep after it we might eventually discover the facts that prove there is a government conspiracy with the invading aliens or that Jesus was indeed God incarnate. But it is only a might.

And there is another problem. Consider the simple proposition "Erwin's cat is alive." I might say that I see the cat playing with its ball and so I know it is alive. But this evidence is based on other beliefs, such as "Dead cats don't play with balls," which is based on other beliefs, such as "Dead cats are unable to move by their own power," which is based on other beliefs *ad infinitum* and *ad nauseam*. The problem with correspondence is that it artificially isolates claims and beliefs, but they do not exist as discrete units. They are parts of a web in which each part depends on the others.

"Truth Matters": Coherence

Recognizing the inadequacy of the Correspondence Theory of Truth, the Coherence Theory in its simplest form claims: a proposition is true if and only if it coheres, or is consistent, with propositions we already know to be true. For example, if we know that the killer did it in the study with a lead pipe, and we know that Colonel Mustard was in the kitchen at the time, the proposition "Colonel Mustard is the killer," must be false. The proposition does not cohere with, does not fit–and in fact contradicts—other propositions that we know to be true.

In *The Passion* Gibson's Simon seems to employ the Coherence Theory. At first highly reluctant to carry the cross, Simon grows to embrace the task as he witnesses Jesus's divine perseverance. Simon overcomes his doubts and fear and appears to put together the evidence to support the belief that Jesus is no ordinary convict.

The Christian philosopher Richard Swinburne in *The Resurrection of God Incarnate* does not present a lone piece of evidence that "Jesus is God incarnate." Rather he presents an array of evidence, which coheres to make a compelling case for the truth of Jesus being divine. In contrast though,

Biblical scholar G.A. Wells in *Can We Trust the New Testament?* assembles a body of coherent evidence against the divinity of Jesus. So there is coherent evidence to support the truth of the claim, "Jesus is God incarnate" and coherent evidence to support the truth of the contradictory claim, "Jesus is *not* God incarnate." But both claims cannot be true. Only one or the other can. So how can coherent evidence be the mark of truth? The fact is that the Coherence Theory gives us a necessary but not a sufficient condition for truth. If a proposition does not cohere with the evidence we have, it cannot be true, but just because the proposition does cohere with the evidence does not guarantee it is true. Recall that George Costanza of *Seinfeld* fame was infamous for coherent fabrications—none of them true—often to convince someone that he was an architect or employed by the likes of Vandelay Industries. Coherence is necessary, needed, but it is not sufficient, not enough for truth.

"Hey, It Works": Pragmatism

From the school of folk wisdom that tells us "if it ain't broke don't fix it," comes the Pragmatic Theory of Truth. Gibson's Pilate was a pragmatist in some sense of the word. He did what he thought would work out best for himself politically. Relatively few people seemed to care about Jesus's welfare, and an angry mob wanted him executed. For the sake of preserving the peace and his own neck, Gibson's Pilate reluctantly gave the order for execution.

But let's not confuse Pilate's pragmatism with the school of philosophy known as American Pragmatism and its Pragmatic Theory of Truth. William James (1842–1910) revised and defended the pragmatic theory in complex ways throughout his writings. In its simplest form the Pragmatic Theory holds: a proposition is true if it works. Broadly speaking, James argued that belief in the claim, "God exists," works. It makes life better, easier, and more meaningful. In that sense then it is true that God exists. More specifically we might argue that "Jesus is God incarnate" is true because it works, making life better, easier, and more meaningful.

The pragmatic conception of truth is well-suited to religion in that holding on faith that something is true can help to make it true. A salesman who believes he will make a sale at his next appointment will exude the confidence that will help win over the client, and he will envision the right things to do and say to close the deal. Similarly we might think that God does not restrict our freedom by making too much about him too obvious, but rather that he invites our participation through belief. In this way, believing in God helps to make God work in our lives, helps to make Him "true."

Gibson's Pilate is not just pragmatic, he seems to use the Pragmatic Theory of Truth in offering to free Jesus or Barabbas in recognition of the Passover celebration. If freeing Jesus in this way works to calm the angry crowd, Pilate seems to reason, then it would be true that it was good to free Jesus. But Pilate's plan backfires as the mob shouts to free Gibson's Hanna Barbera Barabbas.

Thwarted expectations aside, there is a problem with the Pragmatic Theory. False things also work. Sailors found that navigating by the night sky worked perfectly well when they believed that the earth was at the center of the universe. Of course it turns out that their belief was false—it never was true—even though it worked. In light of this, William James must admit, as he does, that just because a belief works does not make it true if it turns out there is no corresponding reality.

Worn out by the consideration of conflicting and ineffective criteria for truth, we might begin to think we are barking up the wrong tree. Perhaps a more serious problem with the criteria is that although they may help us decide *that* something is true, they do not answer the question "What *is* truth?" This is a question not of epistemology, not a matter concerning knowledge, but of metaphysics, a concern about the nature of reality. When I ask: What *is* a bird? a metaphysical answer would be: "A bird is a warm-blooded, egg-laying, vertebrate with fore-limbs modified into wings." That would tell me what a bird *is*. Of course most people *know* a bird when they see one even if they can't give a good definition of the word 'bird.' The criteria for truth are like criteria for picking out birds, looking for things that fly, have beaks, sit in nests, sing songs, *yada yada yada*. Since we generally know birds and know truth when we see them, let's turn away from the criteria and toward the very nature of truth as actually posed by the question, "What *is* truth?"

"Truth Is Stranger than Fiction": Disclosure

Prior to the passion Jesus had said to Thomas, "I am the way, and the truth, and the life" (John 14:6). As the God of the Old Testament identified himself with Being when He said to Moses, "I am who am," Jesus identifies himself with Truth. Jesus tells Thomas he is "the Truth" and more obliquely tells Pilate "Everyone on the side of truth listens to me" (John 18:37). Presumably the phrase "everyone on the side of truth" refers to everyone on the side of God the Father, who also presumably is "the Truth" since he is one with Jesus.

A seeming mistake in *The Passion*: Gibson's Jesus speaks Latin to Pilate. Though as God Jesus would be able to speak Latin or any other language, as the human son of a carpenter from Nazareth it would be highly unlikely that he would speak Latin. As the governor of Jerusalem, Pilate, on the other hand, would presumably speak both Latin and Aramaic. So why doesn't Gibson's Jesus speak in Aramaic to Pilate? Is this a mistake, an oversight, on Gibson's part? I doubt it.

Both Scripture and Gibson have Jesus silent in the face of the question, "What is truth?" Considered in Latin—*Quid est veritas?*—the question may reveal why he was silent. The question contains its own answer. Perhaps truth is a puzzle—like the jumble game in the comics section of the newspaper—that discloses itself if looked at properly. "Anagram" is the technical name for a word jumble. More precisely, an anagram is a word or phrase spelled by rearranging the letters of another word or phrase. *The Da Vinci Code* with its clues in the form of anagrams in the search for the Holy Grail has awakened the ancient interest in anagrams and their reputed power to reveal the truth. And who can forget "red rum" from *The Shining*?

"*Quid est veritas?*" turns out to be an anagram for "*Est qui vir adest.*" In translation, the Latin for "What is truth?" turns out to be an anagram for "It is the man who is before you." So Pilate has anagrammatically answered his own question. Consider too that "President Clinton of the U.S.A." is an anagram for "To copulate he finds interns." But of course this isn't true. We all know that he did not have sexual relations with *that woman*. After all, it depends on what the meaning of 'is' *is*. Given this evidence perhaps anagrams have tremendous prophetic power, or perhaps they are complete nonsense. You decide.

Of course the Gospels were not written in Latin but in Greek. Interestingly, the Greek word for truth is *aletheia* (αληθεια) which literally, etymologically means "uncovering or disclosure." So in identifying himself with truth, Jesus identifies himself with disclosure. As Mark Wrathall argues in Chapter 2 of this book, disclosure is about pointing to or showing a new way to look at the world, not offering criteria. The German philosopher Martin Heidegger (1889–1976) argues that already by the time of Plato the Greeks had become insensitive to the literal meaning of *aletheia* and had adopted the Correspondence Theory of Truth. Heidegger believes that to understand what truth *is* we must retrieve the ancient understanding of truth as disclosure.

"Truth is beauty, beauty truth." The notion of truth as disclosure finds sympathy with Keats's sentiment. In *Truth and Method*, Hans-Georg Gadamer (1900–2002), Heidegger's most famous student, likens our experience of truth to our experience of the beautiful. Both seize us and take us in their thrall. As he puts it:

> What we encounter in the experience of the beautiful and in understanding the meaning of tradition really has something of the truth of play about it. In understanding we are drawn into an event of truth and arrive, as it were, too late, if we want to know what we are supposed to believe. (Gadamer 1989, p. 490)

As Paul would confirm, the suddenness with which truth strikes us is well described by the biblical motif of the thief in the night. "For you yourselves know perfectly that the day of the Lord shall come just like a thief in the night" (1 Thessalonians 5:2). Gibson's Claudia, Pilate's wife, is certainly open to disclosure. Convinced as she is by truth disclosed in her dreams, she acts on them and counsels her husband, though to no avail.

But truth as disclosure is not beyond criticism. What we think is disclosed truth may be false. Christianity holds that "Jesus is God incarnate" is revealed, disclosed truth, whereas Islam holds that "[t]here is only one God and Muhammad is his prophet" is the revealed, disclosed truth. These claims are inconsistent with one another, so at least one must be false. Perhaps disclosure describes what the experience of truth is sometimes like, though it is neither a necessary nor a sufficient condition for truth. We are left then with faith, taking a leap, believing what one fallibly perceives to be disclosed. So in giving your "final answer" go with your gut, your first instinct.

Truth and Interpretation

So I'd be a lousy "phone-a-friend lifeline." I couldn't give you a good final answer to the question, "What is truth?" Instead, please accept these nice consolation prizes in the form of further questions to keep in mind while reading the next two chapters in which Jorge Gracia and Cynthia Freeland focus attention on the nature of interpretation and Gibson's take on the two Marys. Is Gibson's film a true interpretation? Were Mary, the mother of Jesus, and Mary Magdalene caring, supportive, nurturers? Or were they more active in the ministry of Jesus? Was Pilate such a genial man, essentially coerced by Jewish authorities? Was Claudia so sympathetic? Does Gibson give us the truth about Jesus? Was he *the* Truth? Did he ever really say, "I am the way, and the truth, and the life"? Are the Gospels themselves interpretations of earlier sources?

Don't like these questions? Then don't read any more. "You can't handle the truth!"

SOURCES

Jean Baudrillard. 2004. Radical Thought. Translated by Francois Debrix. Accessed online at http://www.uta.edu/english/apt/collab/texts/radical.html on February 11th, 2004.

David Detmer. 2003. *Challenging Postmodernism: Philosophy and the Politics of Truth*. Amherst: Humanity Books.

Hans-Georg Gadamer. 1989. *Truth and Method*. Second Edition. Translated by Joel Weinsheimer and Donald G. Marshall. New York: Continuum.

Martin Heidegger. 1962a. *Being and Time*. Translated by John Macquarrie and Edward Robinson. San Francisco: Harper Collins.

————. 1962b. Plato's Doctrine of Truth. In William Barrett and Henry D. Aiken, eds., *Philosophy in the Twentieth Century*, Volume 3 (New York: Random House), pp. 251–270.

William Irwin. 2001. A Critique of Hermeneutic Truth as Disclosure. *International Studies in Philosophy* 33 (2001), pp. 63–75.

William James. 1997. *The Meaning of Truth*. Amherst: Prometheus.

Jean-François Lyotard. 1984. *The Postmodern Condition: A Report on Knowledge*. Translated by Geoff Bennington and Brian Massumi. Minneapolis: University of Minnesota Press.

Friedrich Nietzsche. 1966. *Beyond Good and Evil*. Translated by Walter Kaufmann. New York: Random House.

————. 1969. *On the Genealogy of Morals*. Translated by Walter Kaufmann and R.J. Hollingdale. New York: Random House.

Betrand Russell. 1998. *The Problems of Philosophy*. Second Edition. Oxford: Oxford University Press.

Richard Swinburne. 2003. *The Resurrection of God Incarnate*. Oxford: Clarendon.

G.A. Wells. 2004. *Can We Trust the New Testament? Thoughts on the Reliability of Early Christian Testimony*. Chicago: Open Court.

QUESTIONS FOR DISCUSSION

1. Which criterion for truth do you find most effective?

2. Can the Correspondence Theory be used to give a metaphysical answer to the question, what is truth?

3. Against the Coherence Theory, can you think of a belief you hold that does not depend on any other beliefs?

4. Why is truth so important to us?

5. Can the Pragmatic Theory of Truth justify a lie?

12

How Can We Know What God Truly Means? Gibson's Take on Scripture

JORGE J.E. GRACIA

Mel Gibson's *The Passion of the Christ* is one of the most controversial films ever to have hit the screen. Much of the polemic surrounding it is based on judgments about its fidelity to the Gospels. Some critics believe that Gibson has betrayed the divine message revealed in the Scriptures, whereas his supporters hold that he has gotten to the essence of that message. Who's right?

The task of philosophy is to clarify and judge impartially. Can it do it in this case? One way in which it can help is by sorting out the issues involved in the interpretation of Scriptures. This is a central and constant topic in the philosophy of religion. It can be illustrated by the challenge faced by Gibson in filming the last hours of Christ based on the account of them presented in the four Gospels.

Is *The Passion of the Christ* Faithful to the Bible?

The criticism of many who fault the film for not following the Scriptures faithfully comes from two sides. For some, the Biblical text is the Word of God, and you are not supposed to mess with what God has told us. The liberties that Gibson takes in the film damn it. For others who do not view the Biblical text as the Word of God, Gibson's elaborations are also damning, for they convey an anti-democratic, anti-Semitic message based on superstition and fanaticism. On the other hand, many of those who praise the film point out that the important thing about the movie is the Christian message it conveys. They feel that Gibson has some room to interpret what the Scriptures say, as long as the divine message is effectively presented.

This is a classic case of disagreement based on the use of different criteria: Audience expectations determine final judgment. The issue that has to be addressed in order to understand the nature of the disagreement is more basic than the issue that appears to be at stake on the surface. Once we understand the bases of the deeper disagreement, then we can see whether there is a way of resolving it.

In the context of *The Passion*, however, matters are more complicated than one would expect. It is one thing to talk about film interpretations of Bram Stoker's *Dracula*, for example, and another to deal with a film interpretation of what many believe to be God's revelation. In the first case, little rides on the outcome. Does it really matter, except to a minuscule group of scholars or cultists whether Warhol or Coppola are right in their interpretation of Stoker? Most of us are not disturbed when Warhol pokes fun at Dracula or when Coppola makes him a romantic hero. In the case of Scriptures, however, the meaning of the text stands at the very center of many people's lives, and the correct understanding of the significance of Jesus is considered paramount. To poke fun at Christ is blasphemy and to distort his message is anathema. The reason: What can be more important than the question of the correct understanding of God's revelation? Even a non-believer cannot but realize the importance of having the right interpretation. Just think of this: If in fact it is true, as Christians claim, that the Bible contains God's message to humanity, what could be more important for a human being than figuring out what that message is? Everything else pales by comparison. God is supposed to be the creator and sustainer of the world, nothing occurs without his permission and co-operation, and he oversees that everything works for ends he has in mind, according to his providence. He is the Supreme Boss. So, if the Bible tells us what he wants us to know, we better listen, or else we might get fired, perhaps literally.

This brings me to the general issue of concern here: How should a text that is regarded as a revelation from God be interpreted? In the present context, the issue translates into the question: How should the Biblical texts that describe the passion of Christ be interpreted in a film? The answers to these questions will provide the basis for judging the value of *The Passion of the Christ*. If Gibson's movie is a legitimate interpretation of the Biblical text, then its value is clear, but if it is not, then its detractors win. Let me begin with the challenge that Gibson faced in making the movie and how he met it.

Gibson's Challenge

Gibson's challenge was to produce an accurate and effective film interpretation of the passages of the Christian Scriptures that deal with the passion of Christ: accurate in the sense of being faithful to the Gospels' accounts, and effective in conveying the divine message to those who see the film. He encountered several initial difficulties. Some of these have to do with the differences in medium between films and a written text, some have to do with the incompleteness of the four accounts that the Gospels give of the passion of Christ, and still others concern differences found in those accounts. Here I will consider only difficulties of the first two sorts because they, more than the third, challenged Gibson.

The differences in medium are significant. A film is composed of visual images of real people and objects accompanied by a sound track of background noise, music, and voices. A written text usually consists of abstract signs arranged in certain ways so they can convey meaning. Films do leave something to the imagination of viewers, of course. In a film we are presented with a picture of how things are, but images can be suggestive, although not as much as a written text. Imagination plays a much larger role in texts. We do not at all see, but rather are told, what is happening. In response to suggestions from the text, we construct images in our mind. This leaves more room for readers to develop images that correspond to their understandings. Indeed, to some extent the images will depend on what readers know prior to their acquaintance with the text. For someone who has never been to Palestine, a description of the terrain where Jesus walked might suggest something very different than it would do to someone who has been there or who has seen pictures of it. Because a film must present us with definite pictures, Gibson had to create definite images in response to the text, thus giving us his interpretation.

A text can be silent in areas where a film has to be explicit, such as clothing, location and landscape, the physical appearance of the characters in the narrative, and gestures and facial expressions, to name just a few. There is practically no indication in the Scriptural passages describing Christ's passion of the clothing worn by Jesus, the Apostles, or any of the people that surrounded him. In many other films about Christ, he is presented as dressed in white clothes that look not just new, but as if they had just come out of the laundromat. But Gibson chose to dress Christ in garments of natural colors that appear worn and dusty.

There are few references in the Scriptures to the landscape where the events of the passion took place. Even the place of the crucifixion is disputed by scholars. How urban was the site? Was it dry and dusty or rich with vegetation? How high was the promontory where Christ is supposed to have been crucified? Even if the precise location were known, two thousand years have elapsed, and we would have no assurance that today the place looks anything like what it looked when Christ was there. But a landscape is needed for a film, and Gibson provides us with one, although it is not in Palestine, but Italy.

Another important area where the Scriptural text gives little guidance concerns the gestures and facial expressions of the players in the story. Yet, these are extremely important, not only because they are part of communication, but also because they convey moods. The same words accompanied by a shrug of the shoulders mean something very different. An ironic tone contradicts an affirmation. And the direction of a gaze can alter the audiene of a message. Indeed, in the Last Supper, when Christ speaks to the Apostles, at one point Gibson makes him look directly at the camera. In this way Christ seems to be speaking to those watching the film, whereas in the story he is talking to those sharing the meal with him.

Perhaps most important of all is the physical appearance of the characters in the story, particularly Christ. How many films about Christ have been produced in which he looks like the northern European ideal for a male: blond, blue-eyed, tall, and with the cheekbone structure of an Anglo-Saxon? Yet, the reality must have been different. The Biblical text tells us hardly anything about Christ's appearance. Was he tall or short? Did he have blue or brown eyes? What color and consistency was his hair? Was he handsome or ugly, muscular or scrawny? Had he lost any teeth by the time of the passion? Were his teeth straight or crooked, stained or perfectly white? Gibson had to make choices. He portrays Jesus as a handsome, tall, and muscular man, with dark hair and eyes, a tanned complexion, and a fairly long face.

The relative short nature of films—even of a relatively long one like *The Passion*—and the limited section of the Gospels with which this move is concerned—merely the description of events from the moment Christ is apprehended until he dies and comes back to life—pose another problem. Much needs to be filled in to make the movie intelligible. Characters have to be developed (Satan, Jesus's mother), some context to Jesus's life has to be provided (the prior life of Jesus, the means whereby he earned his living), and the relations among other persons in the movie (Pilate to his wife Claudia, Jesus's mother and Mary Magdalene). Things are happening all around the events of the passion and a movie would not appear credible, or even make sense, if some of this context were not presented.

Gibson accomplishes this by adding scenes to the film that are not part of the Gospel narratives concerned with the passion, often as flashbacks. Some of these are based on other biblical texts, such as the exchange between Christ and the Apostles or about his work as a carpenter. But others have no Scriptural bases, such as the exchange between Mary and Jesus in which she orders him to wash his hands before coming in to eat, or the scene toward the end of the movie in which Satan is seen having a fit of rage.

The violence and cruelty that Christ suffers in *The Passion* is a good example of an area where Gibson elaborated well beyond what the Scriptures say. The pertinent Scriptural passages merely point to the fact that Jesus was flogged and abused (Matthew 27:26; Luke 23:16; Mark 15:15; John 19:1–2). But the movie dwells in excruciating detail on these abuses, including their effect on Jesus. After his arrest, one of Christ's eyes is swollen shut, and the flogging leaves his ribs exposed. These images have prompted accusations that *The Passion* is a religious version of *Lethal Weapon*.

Films also have a powerful way of affecting the understanding and the mood of viewers through the sound track. The text of the Gospels has no sound. There is no music, no background noise, and most often readers do not utter the sounds of the words they read. Written texts are silent in this sense. The understanding and mood these texts produce on readers is generally the product of an understanding of their context. But films can create a mood through the use of music, and the music in Gibson's film has a powerful impact on the audience. From the very beginning, it is both eerie and foreboding, creating a sense of doom and the momentous importance of the events taking place. Its Middle Eastern allusions and the echoes of Chant suggest authenticity and spirituality.

There is another interesting sound factor in Gibson's film that is missing in texts: the languages spoken in the film. We hear Jesus and his Apostles speaking Aramaic and Pontius Pilate and the Romans speaking Latin. The differences between the two languages are substantial and they are perceived differently by different audiences. To someone whose native tongue is a Romance language, Aramaic sounds rough, confusing, and uncouth, whereas Latin sounds smooth, clear, and sophisticated.

In short, Gibson faced a serious challenge in the making of *The Passion:* To provide a film account of Christ's ordeal based on the Gospels that is accurate and effective. Yet, as we have seen, for much that he had to do, he had little guidance, or no guidance at all, from the Biblical text. Still, he tried to meet the challenge. The question is: On what basis?

Different Ways of Knowing What God Truly Means

There are several common ways of interpreting the Scriptures. They break down into two groups. Some assume that the Scriptures are the Word of God and, therefore, that an interpreter's function is to find out what God means. What is it that God wishes to communicate through the text he has given to humanity? A second way looks at the Scriptures as just another historical record without any religious significance except for those who believe in them. The Christian Scriptures are the texts that Christians believe to be the Word of God. The task of interpreters, then, is to try to figure out what the texts mean either to their historical audiences or to Christians in general, rather than what God means through them.

If one takes the second approach, sociological, historical, and linguistic data should be the means to understand the Scriptures. However, if one takes the first approach and assumes that the Scriptures reveal God's wishes for humanity, then the question of how to understand them becomes something more than a matter of scholarly inquiry. Why? Because an element of faith, a supernatural factor absent from the other accounts, plays a decisive role in interpretation.

The Passion is an interpretation that assumes the Biblical text is the Word of God. We know this not only because Gibson is on record as being a believer, but also because the film takes the Scriptures at their face value. The film does not put the story in the context of what Christians believe now or believed then. It is not a report on the beliefs of a group of persons, as for example, we might report concerning ancient Greeks. The film presents the story narrated in the Gospels as what it claims to be, the story of the Messiah. As an interpretation, the task of the film is to make plain to us what God wished to say through the Scriptures. But how can it accomplish this? Several ways recur in the history of Scriptural interpretation: personal intuition, authority, the Scriptural text alone, historical scholarship, or tradition.

Personal intuition determines what God wishes for us to know based on the interpreters' own understanding of the text or on a personal revelation they have from God. A good example of this is found in the famous scene in the garden described in the *Confessions*, when Augustine (354–430), in torment over his spiritual life, hears a child say, "Take and read." In response he opens the Scriptures on Romans 13:13, which he interprets as a divine message for his personal situation. Many Christians regularly use this method to cope with their daily lives and find answers to personal problems, but some seek to extend the applicability of the message to others.

This method has the advantage of immediacy for interpreters. Those who use it are convinced that they are right because it is directly present to them. But there are also disadvantages, for this approach assumes that an individual person has some privileged connection with God and it fails to provide confirmation except at a personal level. How can we know that someone's particular understanding of the Scriptures reflects what God truly means? And how can we settle disagreements between two conflicting individual views of it? In our context, this would entail Gibson's take on the Scriptures based on his own intuition of what God has said. And indeed, he plugs into the film some things for which there is no evidence beyond his own perspective. An example is the introduction of the devil in the flogging scene, another is the demon like children that haunt Judas before he hangs himself.

Authority is another source of claims of interpretative legitimacy. It consists in the acceptance of the legitimacy of a person or group of persons to provide interpretations of the Scriptures. The validity of the interpretation is, therefore, unquestionable. This position has been frequently asserted in Christianity, although different Christian denominations identify different sources of authority. Among those most frequently cited are church councils, particular congregations, groups of elders, individual leaders, and those who hold determinate offices.

The main advantage of this view is that the interpretations provided or sanctioned by the authority do not come into question, although questions do arise concerning the legitimacy of a particular authority. Gibson is a Catholic and it is evident in *The Passion* that he accepts certain interpretations of the Scriptures that are based on the authority claimed by the Catholic Church. For example, he gives a very prominent role to Jesus's mother in the film, whereas she only appears briefly at the foot of the cross in one of the Gospels. Moreover, he accepts that Christ did not have any brothers, something that comes through clearly when the film provides glimpses of the child Jesus. (The New Testament does refer to Jesus's brothers, but the Catholic Church, unlike Protestants, maintains that Mary remained a virgin her entire life.) Under normal circumstances, domestic scenes would present the child playing with his brothers, as a part of a larger family. But the film's shots of the child Jesus are always of him and Mary alone. Indeed, even his father Joseph is absent.

Gibson also appears to rely heavily on the visions of two nuns, the German Anne Catherine Emmerich (1774–1824) and the Spanish María de Agreda (1602–1665). From one or the other of the accounts of Christ's passion by the first or of Mary's life by the second, he borrows the view that Jesus's arm was dislodged in order to line it up with pre-drilled holes in the cross, the scene in which Christ is thrown over a bridge, the turning over of the cross, and many other details. Indeed, Philip A.

Cunningham argues that the film is "so dependent on her [Emmerich] that it could have been titled *The Passion According to Emmerich*."

Another way used to interpret the Scriptures emphasizes the texts themselves as the source for their interpretation. The Scriptures speak for themselves, and in cases in which a particular text is not clear, other Scriptural texts can be used to enlighten us about its meaning. Some take the view that only the Scriptures are authoritative and only the Scriptures can tell us what God truly means through them. But others accept the authority of the Scriptures while allowing other sources in their interpretation. For both, Scriptural interpretations have to be as faithful to the text of the Scriptures as possible.

The problems with this approach arise particularly when the Scriptures themselves are regarded as the only source of Scriptural understanding. The interpretive method that Martin Luther (1483–1546) called *sola Scriptura* (only the Scriptures) is fraught with difficulties. Perhaps the most vexing is that the Scriptures are silent on many key points of doctrine. The doctrine of the Trinity, for example, is not explicitly stated anywhere in the Bible. Its formulation by the early Christian community was an attempt to make sense of various Scriptural statements about God, Christ, and the Holy Spirit. *The Passion* illustrates well some of the inadequacies of this approach. For instance, although Gibson tried to be faithful to the languages spoken at the time of Christ, he made choices for which there is no Scriptural support. In the film, Pontius Pilate speaks Latin with various people, including Christ, but did he actually do so? Latin was not a commonly spoken language at the time in Palestine. Moreover, the Gospels are written in Greek, not Latin. So this is a reconstruction based on what Gibson and his advisers think makes sense, considering that Pilate was a Roman. Something similar can be said about the use of Aramaic rather than Greek in the film.

Historical scholarship characterizes another approach: perhaps we can figure out God's message by putting the words of the Scriptures in their historical context, and using the tools supplied by sociology, history, textual criticism, linguistic studies, and other related disciplines. After all, it seems essential that before we determine what a Biblical text says, we understand the language in which it is written and the meaning of the words it uses in their historical context. This information is available to us only through scholarship. Indeed, for philosophers such as Martin Kusch and Volker Peckhaus, the key to the interpretation of texts, including religious ones, lies in their social context–whence the name "sociologism" or "contextualism" often given to their approach.

It's quite clear that Gibson helped himself to this source. He dressed his characters, including Christ, in historically accurate clothing; the buildings that appear on the film, again, seem to be historically accurate; and the actors were taught to speak the ancient languages correctly. Much that the film adds in order to complete the picture presented in the Scriptures can be traced to information provided by various disciplines of learning about the period. Yet, this information is neutral when it comes to God and religious belief. Scholarship cannot tell us what God means, but only what the people who were writing the Gospels believed he meant. This way of interpreting the Scriptures, then, also fails when used exclusively to try to understand what God truly means.

The last position I wish to consider identifies tradition as the context in which the Scriptures should be interpreted. At the outset, tradition makes considerable sense, for the Scriptures speak in a framework of beliefs and practices, outside of which they would be silent. This framework provides the key to meaning, filling in the gaps that the Scriptures have. Roman Catholic philosophers and theologians, such as Thomas Aquinas (1224/6–1274) and Francis Suárez (1548–1617), emphasize tradition in the proper understanding of the Scriptures. Outside these circles, however, tradition is also used, even if often disparaged.

Consider the important matter of Christ's appearance. How tall was he, and what kind of face did he have? The tradition in certain Christian circles is to take the image reputed to have been imprinted on Veronica's veil or on the Shroud of Turin as accurate representations of his appearance. The first—which is reported to have been kept in Rome until the fifteenth century, and of which there are pictorial renditions—is taken by many pious believers to have been the cloth with which Veronica cleaned Christ's face during his walk to Golgotha. The second— currently in existence—is considered to be by some the shroud in which Christ's body was wrapped after he died. The face portrayed in both is rather long, with features that have been reproduced in most movies about Christ. Gibson's Christ fits this image.

Another traditional view that Gibson accepts is the portrayal of Barabbas. In the Christian tradition this man is a terrible murderer, whose exchange for Jesus dramatizes the latter's plight. In the film, Barabbas is presented as horrible and wild. Christian art traditions also inspired Gibson. For example, it is common for art to depict the crucifixion in certain ways: Jesus carries a complete cross; the nails are driven through the palms of the hands, not the wrists; and a foot rest is added to the cross.

But traditions can be mistaken, as is the case with the ones mentioned derived from art. Moreover, why pick one tradition rather than another, and how do we decide which one is right? Some have argued that Barabbas was not a murderer, but rather a freedom fighter. And some Protestant churches dispute many of the traditions generally accepted by Roman Catholics.

Clearly, none of the approaches commonly used for the interpretation of the Scriptures is unassailable when taken by itself. It is also clear that the various ways of interpreting the Scriptures are themselves dependent on something else. Whether one holds that personal intuition, a certain authority, the Scriptures themselves, scholarship, tradition, or a combination of these, should be the determining factor in Scriptural interpretation, the choice depends on something more basic: the understanding of one's faith, that is, theology.

Theology presupposes belief, but goes beyond it to articulate doctrines that are entailed by, and necessary for, its understanding. Theology not only provides doctrines but also a context in which to place the Scriptures and a method for interpreting them. This means that theology ultimately determines the way Scriptures are understood. Particular theologies establish the proper place for personal intuition, authority, scholarship, the text, and tradition in the interpretation of the Scriptures. Arguments about the correct interpretation of the Scriptures, then, make sense only within a theological context, that is, they should consider the theological framework within which interpretations are developed. Otherwise, there is little hope of settling disagreements about the Scriptural message.

Let me summarize what I have said in three points. First, each of the ways to interpret Scriptures we have considered is inadequate by itself; all of them depend on certain beliefs that are part of a certain understanding of a faith, that is, on a theology. Second, from this it follows that theology is essential for the determination of the correct way of interpreting the

Scriptures; only within a theological context can one judge whether an interpretation is legitimate, for theology provides both the rules of interpretation and the criteria of evaluation. Third, it is at the level of theology that most disagreements about interpretation take place, rather than at the level of the interpretation itself. This entails that it is at the theological level that these disagreements should be addressed. But what does this tell us about Gibson's film?

Gibson's Take on Scripture

I began by noting that *The Passion of the Christ* is very controversial and that there are serious disagreements about whether it is a good film. Judgments about the film's value usually concern issues of Scriptural interpretation. Did the film picture the Jews correctly? Did it present Christ accurately? Was Gibson right in casting the devil as a woman or androgynous being? Is the violence in the film warranted? And so on. These questions cannot be answered unless one first determines the criteria Gibson used in his interpretation, and it appears that he used a variety of criteria. There is evidence of personal intuition, authority, attention to the text, historical scholarship, and tradition. But this is not enough for us to judge whether the use of these approaches and their corresponding criteria are justified. We need to go one step further, to the theological principles that Gibson was emphasizing in order to find any justification for the interpretation given in the film.

The issue breaks down into two questions: Did Gibson have a theology? And what is that theology? The first question can be answered easily. The presentation of the verse of Isaiah 53 at the opening of the film makes clear that Gibson takes a theological standpoint: He views Jesus as the Messiah. This textual connection is eminently theological–the product of the attempt by Christians to understand Christ in light of Old Testament prophesies. Another attempt at visually tying the New Testament to the Old occurs when Jesus crushes a snake released by the devil in the Garden of Gethsemane. The reference is to Genesis 3:15, in which we are told that "the woman" (Jesus's mother) will "bruise the head" of the serpent (through Christ). But there are many other instances of a theological background to the film, such as the assumption that the four Gospels are reliable accounts of the passion and that they tell only one story.

The second question, concerned with the particular theology that inspires the film, is more complicated. It could be answered on the basis of external evidence, based on what Gibson has said he had in mind. However, this is too facile an answer, for he may have intended to do something that he failed to accomplish. The real task is to figure out the kind of theology the film actually reveals. And there are some obvious indications of this. One piece of evidence of the particular Catholic theology that inspires the film is the prominence of Mary and her special connection to Christ—think of the moment in the movie in which she enters a place and senses the presence of Jesus above her. Another is the mentioned absence of brothers of Jesus in the flashback to his childhood. And still another is the connection between the sacrifice of the cross and the Last Supper through a flashback, which reminds us of the mystery of the Eucharist.

But this is not enough to settle the issue: the task is beyond the bounds of my present aim. This has been to show how a philosophical analysis of the problems of interpretation raised by Gibson's film can be helpful in evaluating the film. And in fact, philosophy has proven helpful in clarifying one aspect of the controversy concerning *The Passion of the Christ*: it has helped us see that evaluative questions about the film, when this is presented as an interpretation of a segment of the Christian Scriptures, cannot be effectively settled without considering the theology that inspired it.

Of course, key questions still remain. Did Gibson correctly use the theology he intended to use? Because it is possible that he did not, in spite of his intentions. Is the theology he used the correct theology for the Christian faith? This would certainly explain why there is disagreement among members of different Christian denominations about the value of the movie. And is the Christian faith correct? If one believes it is not, then Gibson's film can have little religious value. But these are not the questions I set out to explore here, and their answers will have to wait for another occasion.

For us, the important moral of the story is that Gibson's film makes sense as an interpretation of Scriptures only within a certain theological point of view, and that much of the polemic it has prompted is the result of looking at it from other theological perspectives. The same can be said about most other controversial interpretations of the Scriptures. In this, the examination of *The Passion* has also served to illustrate and clarify a philosophical issue that goes beyond the understanding and merits of the film.

SOURCES

Jorge J.E. Gracia. 2001. *How Can We Know What God Means? The Interpretation of Revelation*. New York: Palgrave.

————. 2003. *Old Wine in New Skins: The Role of Tradition in Communication, Knowledge, and Group Identity*. Marquette University Sixty-Seventh Aquinas Lecture. Milwaukee: Marquette University Press.

Philip A. Cunningham. n.d. Gibson's *The Passion of the Christ:* A Challenge to Catholic Teaching. http://www.bc.edu/research/cjl/metaelements/texts/reviews/gibson_cunningham.htm

Kevin Vanhoozer, et al., eds. 2004. *Dictionary of Theological Interpretation of Scripture*. Grand Rapids: Eardman's. In press.

Nicholas Wolterstorff. 1995. *Divine Discourse: Philosophical Reflections on the Claim that God Speaks*. Cambridge: Cambridge University Press.

QUESTIONS FOR DISCUSSION

1. What factors are important in determining the value of *The Passion of the Christ?*

2. What were the challenges that Gibson faced in making a film of Christ's passion based on the Gospels' accounts?

3. How does theology determine the various ways of interpreting Scriptures?

4. What difficulties does any film interpretation of a text face? Are there special problems when the text is regarded as God's word?

5. Can disagreements on the interpretation of the Bible be resolved? If so, on what basis?

13

The Women Who Loved Jesus: Suffering and the Traditional Feminine Role

CYNTHIA FREELAND

The Passion of the Christ offers striking versions of Jesus's mother Mary and his follower Mary Magdalene (played by Maia Morgenstern and Monica Bellucci, respectively). Both actresses, with their remarkably beautiful faces, are called on to portray deep reserves of love, strength, anguish, and pity. In the movie, Jesus's (Jim Caviezel's) suffering is so extreme that it becomes implausible and unreal—and after all, the film does want to show that he is more than human. By comparison, the suffering of the two women who love him is terribly human. Their sorrow actively echoes current TV and newspaper images of grieving mothers and wives of soldiers killed in wars or political and religious struggles.

Huddled together and restricted to a *passive* role as observers, the two Marys in this film each endure a *passion* of their own. They function like the chorus of a classical Greek tragedy. As they observe key actions from a distance, their emotions cue the audience's response. The two women's sustained grief and endurance evoke great empathy. In this chapter I want to reflect upon Gibson's portrait of the two key women in Christ's life. My ultimate aim is to bring to the film a perspective on the general meaning of physical suffering, considering also the traditional women's roles of care, love, and support for those who suffer.

The Movie's Other Women

There are other female roles in the film. Satan is played by a woman, Rosalinda Celentano, perhaps hinting at associations among women, sin, and evil. Such connections (sometimes said to be grounded in the story of Adam and Eve in Genesis) are common in Christianity. But I don't think we need to construe the film this way. Satan is troubling here because of being sexually ambiguous, not female. He/she has a deep husky voice and a body mostly obscured by heavy robes, though we once glimpse a hideous shaved head. This ambiguity might indicate that gender roles should be kept clearly separate. On the other hand, it is theologically appropriate, since angels—even fallen angels—are necessarily asexual. Art history is replete with depictions of angels as androgynous or even feminine-looking humans.

Two other women with small but important roles in the movie are Claudia, Pilate's wife; and Veronica, who brings Jesus a cup of water and offers her headscarf to wipe his bloody face. Each woman stands out as an example of sympathy, insight, and courage. Claudia warns Pilate against killing this Jewish subject because "he is a holy man"; she obviously disapproves of her husband's actions, and brings linens to Mary to use in cleansing Jesus's blood from the paving stones. Similarly, Veronica bravely steps through a line of brutish Roman guards to assist Jesus after he falls while bearing his cross. She too manifests deep sympathy and compassion. But there is no Biblical evidence for either of these portrayals. Belief in Veronica and her veil grew up only in medieval times, when it became codified as one of the Stations of the Cross. Similarly, the Biblical evidence for Claudia's kindness is scant. Gibson thus uses poetic license to foster a fictitious, stereotyped association between women and moral virtues like generosity, empathy, and spiritual strength. The scene with Veronica isolates her explicitly from the soldiers' male rudeness, depicting her in slow motion and haloed with bright light. Her scenes employ both a different pace and a distinct sound track from the main action. Accompanying her, we hear peaceful recorder or flute music, while the regular-speed scenes highlight the harsh jeers of the crowd and guards.

In fact, all of the "good" women in Gibson's movie are young and attractive. (Mary herself scarcely looks old enough to be the mother of Jesus; Morgenstern is forty-two to Caviezel's thirty-six.) The non-speaking roles of women in the film are confined to toothless "old hags" shown *en masse* as part of the angry Jewish rabble clamoring for crucifixion. The film thus offers a message about how women are "supposed to" look and behave: as uplifting, lovely moral exemplars and supporters for men.

Virgin or Whore? Women's Double Bind

Evidence is that Jesus's own attitudes to women were not so conventional or stereotypical. He was highly unusual in his time for accepting women as followers. He must have scandalized Jewish mores by accepting financial support from women and even traveling around with them in a culture where proper women were expected to travel only with male relatives. Reputable Biblical scholars like Elaine Pagels of Princeton and Karen King of Harvard have argued that Jesus took Mary Magdalene seriously as a leader among his apostles. Scripture too provides some support for this view; it was Mary Magdalene who went to Jesus's tomb (Mark 16:1; Matthew 29:8–10) and, according to John at least (John 20), was first to encounter him there, risen. He commanded her to spread the good news of his resurrection to the other disciples, making her in effect the first to preach his resurrection. Gibson allows viewers only a quick peek at the risen Christ at the end of his film, and so the film leaves no such significant role for Mary Magdalene, who is instead linked to Jesus's mother as another faithful female supporter.

Art history is clearly a source for Gibson's choice of actresses here, a selection which reflects a traditional Catholic dualism between types the two women represent. Morgenstern's strict, sober beauty makes her the perfect devoted, selfless, virginal mother. In a key scene where she witnesses her son's scourging, Mary's face stays steady as we witness one great tear sliding down her cheek. She looks like a Northern Renaissance Madonna from the sixteenth century. Monica Bellucci, on the other hand, fits the traditional conception of the Magdalene as a repentant sinner—a former prostitute, now redeemed by her faith in Jesus. Bellucci is well known for roles associated with voluptuous sensuality and eroticism, such as the whorish Persephone in the *Matrix* sequels (2003), or Malèna, the object of an adolescent boy's lustful desire in *Malèna* (2002). Her casting by Gibson seems no accident.

But feminist thinkers have been very critical of the traditional contrast between Mary and Mary Magdalene as two polar opposite types of femininity, the Virgin and the Whore. Mary is seen as typifying the reassuring, non-sexual (good) mother, while Mary Magdalene is the tempting (bad) sex object (even if now reformed). Women may still become trapped in a double bind of remaining selfless, asexual, and pure, but rejected as old maids; or exploring the erotic, risking labels like "nymphomaniacs" and "sinners."

Mary the Mother and "Feminine" Ethics

Let's look more into this dichotomous characterization of the two women who loved Jesus. Of course, Mary, the pure mother, manifests many very admirable traits. Who wants to banish good qualities like love, kindness, empathy, and selflessness from our lives? Most ethical theories and religious traditions value such qualities. However, certain moral qualities may not be beneficial or fair to those who are expected to manifest them, if not everyone in the society is equally asked to develop them. Some writers, like psychologist Carol C. Gilligan, have championed ethical outlooks that they describe as "feminine." Gilligan challenged Lawrence Kohlberg's studies of moral development, which concluded that males tend to apply a more rule-bound, universal conception of ethics than females, who think more relationally and contextually. Kohlberg regarded the "male" viewpoint as superior since it exemplified the moral standards of Immanuel Kant (1724–1804) as stated in his famous categorical imperative. Gilligan asked whether we should really infer that female outlooks on solving moral dilemmas are inferior to males', given that there are significant alternatives to Kant's ethics. Some of these, like Aristotelianism and moral virtue theories, are also contextual and relational—more "female." Gilligan's conclusion was not to favor either approach, but to argue that both are valuable. They have complementary strengths, and people of each sex should be encouraged to develop along both sorts of moral dimensions.

The thought that there may be specifically female approaches to ethics has been further elaborated by philosophers Nel Noddings in her theory of "maternal thinking" and Sara Ruddick in her account of the "ethics of care." Their approaches, like Gilligan's, are controversial. On the one hand, these theories strive both to describe and validate traditionally female attitudes and behavior, emphasizing that they are not just a matter of instinct or emotions but very reflective and complex. Maternal behavior, for instance, requires constant attention to the needs of the developing child with respect for its growing autonomy and future adulthood. Children must be *taught* and not disciplined like puppies. Again, Ruddick's outlook treasures the sort of selflessness valued by many different religious and ethical traditions. Caring activities, even if they appear rudimentary, such as a nurse emptying a bedpan or a mother feeding a child, require and reflect thought, training, and experience. How can sick patients be both cared for and encouraged to take on challenges? What is a healthy diet for a child at various ages, and how can a parent get a reluctant child to eat the proper diet?

On the other hand, these approaches to ethics are not universally endorsed by feminists. Some maintain that to emphasize supposedly "female" approaches may serve both to validate and perpetuate our current system of gender roles. In this system, women are often exploited, as when they are underpaid in many traditional caring professions like teaching and nursing. They may fail to develop self-respect or to seek authority in a broader social and political context. Women who focus too much on caring for others may fail to take proper care of themselves, and even fail at their own aims. Critics also argue that to promote caring could sustain a problematic gender distinction between men who often "care about" and women who "care for." "Caring about" tends to be higher status, since it means that a person's concerns extend beyond home and family to broader arenas such as government, politics, institutions, and principles. Ruddick insists that an ethics of care ought to apply to people of both genders: surely both types of caring are valuable and desirable goals for everyone. Gilligan's view is similar; she does not endorse women's approaches to ethics over those of men, but feels both approaches should be valued.

What do the controversies in feminist ethics tell us about *The Passion* and its women? In this movie Mary is defined by her role as loving mother from the moment when we first see her waking up, frightened about her son. Gibson employs flashbacks in key scenes to link Mary's current role in comforting Jesus with her maternal caring for him as a child and young man. In an especially moving sequence, Jesus falls in agony from his wounds, and Mary, who has run through crowded streets desperately seeking to get near him, reaches him to offer comfort. This sequence is cross-cut with flashbacks of her running desperately to assist the child Jesus when she anticipates and watches him falling amid hard rocks. In both scenes she assures him, "I am here." This is what we all want (and in fortunate cases, remember) from our own mothers.

But Ruddick emphasizes that mothering is not simply natural and instinctual in human females. It is emotional but also requires reasoning and thought. A mother's love is "attentive," an intellectual capacity reflecting knowledge and respect for the individual one loves. The mother must explore and insist on her own values while remaining open to the development of her child into an adult who may adopt alternative values and beliefs. Mary has obviously needed to reflect on how to bring up her son, what to teach him, and how to guide him as he enters into his adult role in life, a very specific role as the Messiah. But the film shows none of this.

Instead, Mary is one-dimensional, just as shown in tradition and in many paintings. She is simply and naturally a mother: stereotypically selfless, patient, beautiful, and loving. Some scenes use a shot/reverse shot structure and highlight her psychic communion with her son as they exchange lengthy deep gazes. These scenes suggest that mother and son share an intense psychic communion. When Jesus is raised on the cross, Mary Magdalene can't bear the sight and covers her head, but Mary gazes steadily into her son's one good eye (the other is swollen shut from blows). Indeed, in some interactions the mother and son appear almost like lovers. In the flashback scene that shows her preparing dinner while her handsome, strong young son works on his carpentry, Jesus's human father, Joseph, is notably absent. Mary tells her son to wash his hands before eating. When he responds by playfully splashing water on her, she giggles like a teenager. Viewers raised in a Protestant tradition may find this and other scenes unsettling (as I did), since they reflect a fascination with Mary's perpetual youth, beauty, and intimacy with her son that is more typical of Catholic Christianity.

Is Christian Ethics "Feminine"?

A deeper question suggested by considering the ethics of care is whether Christian ethics is itself "feminine." Christianity's moral outlook sounds much like the ethics of care approach. Christians are told to care for the meek, sick, and poor, even to love their neighbors as themselves. Jesus himself showed concern for people who were maimed or sick, healing the blind and freeing possessed people from devils. He paid no attention to their social class and even preached the virtue of Samaritans. He helped feed the hungry and provided wine for a wedding feast. His followers were admonished not to employ violence but to "turn the other cheek." In the movie, Jesus chastises Peter for cutting the ear off a guard's slave at his arrest, denouncing those who live by the sword.

Jesus was a revolutionary teacher within his cultural context, since he rejected traditional Jewish notions of justice as vengeance (an eye for an eye, a tooth for a tooth). In this regard, he resembles Socrates (469–399 B.C.), who similarly rejected traditional Greek codes of conduct four centuries before him. Christianity thus advocates many typically "female" behaviors of caring, love, passivity, and compassion. It's hard to judge, however, whether any particular view of Christian ethics is advocated by *The Passion of the Christ*, since the scope of the film is deliberately narrow. We see little of Jesus's active ministry. So we do not learn here of his revolutionary moral message or of how to put it into action.

Mary Magdalene: Scripture, Fiction, and History

I want now to turn to the character of Mary Magdalene. As I mentioned earlier, Bellucci fits this role well because of being a famous contemporary sex symbol. Gibson accepts the legend about Magdalene's former life as a prostitute or fallen woman. This is shown by his inclusion of a flashback where she is rescued from death by stoning. Cringing, she is saved when the handsome and upright Jesus draws a line in the sand against her accusers, then literally raises her up from the dirt.

Actually this scene has no Biblical support. Mary Magdalene is described only as a woman from whom Jesus had driven seven demons (Luke 8:1–3). But over centuries the western Catholic Church merged several distinct Marys and a nameless fallen woman so that Mary Magdalene acquired this persona. In fact, the current Catholic Church (the one Gibson's sect does not accept) acknowledged that the blending of Marys was not historically or scripturally correct in 1989, when it officially separated Mary Magdalene from the others. And the Eastern Orthodox Church never accepted any such association at all.

Another piece of lore about Mary of Magdala is that she escaped in a boat after Jesus's crucifixion and traveled to France with Lazarus. There she preached the gospel on her own before retiring to a cave where she lived out her life as a hermit, clad only by her luxuriant hair. In paintings by Renaissance artists like Titian and Botticelli, she is shown nude, her voluptuous sinner's body barely concealed by beautiful hair. As such, she very much resembles their paintings of Venus, the Roman goddess of love! True to this history, Gibson's movie sometimes shows Bellucci (but never Morgenstern) with her head uncovered, as gleaming long tresses flow around her exquisite face.

Judaism was historically a patriarchal religion, and in Jesus's time women did not have much independence; they were certainly not rabbis. But the historical conditions of women within early Christianity were more open and flexible. Many women who became followers of Jesus accompanied him in travels along with male believers. After his death, some of them continued to work with men in spreading the new religion, and some even went off on missions of their own. It was not until several centuries had passed and the new religion was seeking to consolidate its power and doctrine that an "official" line was arrived at denying women key roles (such as serving as priests). As a conservative or traditionalist Catholic, Gibson would no doubt agree with such a position. Whatever one's opinion it is important to realize that the tradition itself has a history and was modified over time.

And there is another tradition about Mary Magdalene that is more radical, which has recently been popularized by the bestseller *The Da Vinci Code*. Dan Brown's book makes sweeping and provocative claims about Mary Magdalene. Through his characters in it he asserts, for example, that the Magdalene's burial site is actually the Holy Grail sought for centuries. This fact was suppressed or hidden by its reinterpretation as the chalice of the Last Supper. *The Da Vinci Code* also advances the more controversial claim that Mary Magdalene was Jesus's wife and mother of his children. The book's title refers to Leonardo Da Vinci's alleged membership in a secret society that knew the truth about all of this. Leonardo supposedly symbolized Mary Magdalene's importance in his famous "Last Supper" painting. He placed a significantly feminine-looking person at Jesus's right hand—and no chalice.

This is not the place to debate the accuracy (let alone literary merits) of *The Da Vinci Code*. To set Dan Brown up against Mel Gibson as offering the only two interpretations of Mary Magdalene in early Christianity would be silly. Gibson's claims to some special historical accuracy and realism in his film can be challenged by better sources than Brown. Despite boasting of near-literal adherence to the Gospels, Gibson inevitably presents his own interpretations (as does Brown). There are significant alternative accounts of Mary in the Gospels, especially in John, which Gibson relies on least of all. Numerous scholarly studies, some feminist and some not, show that the Bible was an evolving text with a variety of authors, sources, and a complex and rich history. For several centuries members of various early Christian communities knew of and accepted alternative Gospels, such as those of Philip, Truth, Thomas, and even Mary. The fact that these did not become a part of the canonical New Testament requires understanding the complex cultural conditions and politics of early Christianity. Viewers of Mel Gibson's film who wish to use rational methods of studying religious questions should pursue the scholarly sources for themselves, starting with Elaine Pagels's very readable book *The Gnostic Gospels*.

Passion and Blood: The Savior Who Nurtures

What might be a feminist position on Jesus's passion? To witness the movie is itself to suffer, since it is a very painful film to watch. The scourging scene or the one where nails are pounded into a man's hands and feet seem so realistic, viewers may flinch from the screen. The sound track does not permit escape by closing one's eyes, since we still hear the amplified horrific sounds of whips tearing flesh, agonized screams, and squirting blood. In the Jewish Scriptures, physical suffering was the lot of all humans, specifically women in childbirth, as punishment for Eve's "sin." Gibson, like many film viewers, accepts a particular view of Christ's suffering as voluntarily undertaken, but also required by God, so that Jesus can purify humans of this sinful status. But this view of Christ's passion is not the only possible one in a Christian context. As Pagels explains, Gnostics during early Christianity favored an alternative view according to which Christ was a spiritual and not physical being who actually laughed as he hovered over the cross. The Gnostics and other early Christians did not interpret this as martyrdom, and were critical of Christians who chose martyrdom. Such people were even portrayed as choosing a self-serving route because they thought it would guarantee their salvation.

For the early Church Fathers who denounced Gnosticism as a heresy, Jesus's physical suffering had special meaning. This is also true of believers now: his blood is sacred, and it is symbolically drunk in the holy rite of communion. Gibson underscores this point with numerous cross-cuts between Jesus's final agony on the cross and scenes of the Last Supper.

Images of blood evoke associations between women and the flowing blood of menstruation and childbirth. In this film, women are comfortable with blood. That is, though they weep when it is shed, they soberly work to clean it up (even great pools of it!). During the final moments of Christ's time on the cross, Mary approaches and kisses his pierced feet. Her chin and mouth get smeared with blood, which she ignores. She holds and caresses her son's besmirched body in a rather graphic rendering of Michelangelo's famous *Pietà*. In Biblical times, it was women who tended bodies of the dead, cleaning and preparing them for burial. By undertaking traditional roles of giving birth, nursing young children, caring for the sick and cleansing the dead, women show an ability and willingness to address life as it is lived, not idealized life. They cope practically and lovingly with the messy details of embodied human existence.

The Christian doctrine of the Eucharist also associates Jesus's blood with nourishment for the soul. Symbolically, this amounts to a kind of feminization of his body. His wounds are often shown in medieval art, as in contemporary Mexican *retablo* paintings, spurting out blood that is precious enough to be gathered by angels into golden cups. Sometimes believers are even shown sitting below the cross, drinking the blood that flows from his pierced body, like infants nursed at their mother's breast. This strong imagistic association between Jesus and the maternal body was reinforced in medieval art by frequent inclusion of a pelican above images of the crucifixion. Pelican mothers were held to strike their own breasts so as to offer blood for their young to drink to survive.

Macabre as these images might seem to us now in the U.S.A., they were and are not uncommon in other times and settings. Mystics like St. Teresa of Avila in sixteenth-century Spain spoke lovingly about Christ's wounds and even dreamed of being absorbed into and sheltered by them. In a remarkable and provocative essay about female mystical language, "La Mystérique," the contemporary French feminist Luce Irigaray suggests seeing Christ's body, opened with wounds and flowing with blood, as very much like a female, maternal body. She explores the language and imagery of female mystics who saw these wounds as womb-like "nests" where they could find love and safety. Perhaps Irigaray's picture of Jesus's suffering body as "feminized" would strike Mel Gibson as outrageous, even blasphemous. Caviezel, the Jesus of this film, is strong and virile. His is not the slender, delicate body seen in many crucifixion paintings, but a modern lithe one, with corded muscles in his thighs and arms. Other commentators have noted that Gibson's earlier roles as heroes who endured tremendous physical torture foreshadowed his depiction of the suffering body of Christ in this film. Caviezel's performance in the physical challenge of this role is admirable, but the character's endurance of such extraordinary physical torture seems unbelievable. Even the most sadistic Roman guards express awe at this Jewish prisoner's apparent appetite for more punishment, as he rises again and yet again from his suffering under their whips to "take more, like a man."

Is Mel Radical Enough?

My point here has been first to show that while *The Passion of Christ* seems to admire the key women in Jesus's life, it also idealizes them in a way that reflects traditional gender stereotypes. They are not shown as having any significant interior life or moral development, or as able to think and choose for themselves. They seem so essentially kind, caring, and empathic that it appears to flow from their very nature. But faith, whether in God's choice of your destiny or in a new Messiah, is surely more complex than this.

The historical Jesus appears to have been more willing to challenge the accepted "truths" of his culture about appropriate male and female behavior than Mel Gibson is in this new movie. Another movie with the same subject matter, Pier Paolo Pasolini's *The Gospel According to St. Matthew* (1966), succeeds far better at portraying Jesus as a revolutionary moral leader and teacher. Through its exclusive focus on Christ's passion Gibson's movie fails to explore the potentially radical moral and social implications of Christianity, a religion that denounces wealth and power, rejects violence, promotes caring and love, embraces ethnic difference and radical equality, and accepts women into discipleship on an equal basis with men.

SOURCES

Dan Brown. 2003. *The Da Vinci Code*. New York: Doubleday.

Caroline Walker Bynum. 1984. *Jesus as Mother: Studies in the Spirituality of the High Middle Ages*. Los Angeles: Publications of the Center for Medieval and Renaissance Studies, UCLA.

Carol C. Gilligan. 1982. *In a Different Voice*. Cambridge: Harvard University Press.

Susan Haskins. 1994. *Mary Magdalene: Myth and Metaphor*. New York: Harcourt.

Luce Irigaray. 1985. *Speculum of the Other Woman*. Translated by Gillian C. Gill. Ithaca: Cornell University Press.

Karen L. King. 2003. *The Gospel of Mary of Magdala: Jesus and the First Woman Apostle*. Santa Rosa: Polebridge Press.

Nel Noddings. 1984. *Caring: A Feminine Approach to Ethics*. Berkeley: University of California Press.

Carl E. Olson and Sandra Miesel. 2004. *The Da Vinci Hoax. Exposing the Errors in The Da Vinci Code*. San Francisco: Ignatius Press.

Elaine Pagels. 1979. *The Gnostic Gospels*. New York: Vintage.

Sara Ruddick. 1999. Maternal Thinking. In Marilyn Pearsall, ed., *Women and Values: Readings in Recent Feminist Philosophy*. Third edition (Belmont: Wadsworth, 1999), pp. 110–131. Originally published in *Feminist Studies* 6, 2 (1980), pp. 432–467.

QUESTIONS FOR DISCUSSION

1. How did you react to the suffering of the two key women in the movie, as opposed to Jesus's suffering? How would you compare them?

2. Do you think that a "virgin-whore" double bind still exists for women?

3. Do traditionally female activities like mothering and caring for others involve thought? What sort of thinking is involved? How does it compare to the more abstract sort of thinking of scientists, engineers, or lawyers?

4. Most Christians believe that women like Mary Magdalene did play a key role in Christianity. What role was it, and what differentiates it in your mind from the role played by Jesus's male disciples?

5. Is it offensive, intriguing, natural, or surprising to you to consider Christianity a "female" ethical outlook, and Jesus's body (especially during the Passion) as being "feminized" by his suffering?

IV

Why Was Christ Killed?

14

The Craftiness of Christ: Wisdom of the Hidden God

DALLAS WILLARD

The Passion of the Christ is a work of art. This means that it uti-
lizes a *medium* to convey a *vision* of some serious aspect of the
human condition. The medium in the case of a film has several
levels: the roll of celluloid that can be produced, maintained or
destroyed like any other physical object; the visual and auditory
images that appear to the viewer; and the events represented by
means of those images. It is a mistake, often repeated, to take the
events presented as what the film is about. That might be true of
a strict documentary, if there is such a thing. But even a "home
video" is not just about the events recorded, but about the life,
the "happy family," and so on, which is seen *through* the events.

The events depicted in *The Passion* are those of the agonies,
torture, and death of Jesus Christ. Those events are depicted in
a certain way by the one who created the film, Mel Gibson, in
an effort to project *his* vision of the human condition. This is just
the sort of thing an artist does. The events selected, and how
they are presented, determine which vision of the human condition is, or can be, shared by the artist and the viewer. Although
the interchange between the artist and the viewer is very intricate, subject to many influences and liable to misfire, in the ideal
case the viewer would "pick up" the vision which the artist had
in creating, and which he has successfully embodied in the
work of art. Then the viewer would, in a manner, experience
the experience of the artist, and thereby have a new and more
profound grasp of what the artist "sees."

The Vision of Human Redemption

In the case of *The Passion*, the vision is one of human redemption according to one traditional Christian understanding. This involves two parts: the condition of human lostness and evil, and the act or process by which deliverance from that condition is made possible. The first part in turn has two elements: the appalling evil actually present in human life, and the effort of Satan to keep humanity from escaping its disastrous condition. The second part, the act or process of redemption, goes precisely contrary to anything that might be imagined from the human point of view, with its regard for power and its acceptance of the evil that is always "required" to make human power work. It is an act that allows corrupt humanity, ruled by Satan through its most exalted institutions, to have its way to the utmost extent, to do its "damnedest," without moving a finger to resist it.

The felt absence of God from the scene of the crucifixion in the movie—"Why hast Thou forsaken me"—is the ultimate point of "non-resistance." And the prayer for the forgiveness of the immediate perpetrators of such an evil and injustice—because they "know not what they do"—indicates the complete hopelessness of those in the grip of evil. Together, by contrast, the acts and words of Christ affirm the presence of another world—the world of truth and not power, of the kingdom of God—from which redemption and deliverance from overwhelming evil into goodness is possible.

Too Much Violence and Brutality?

Critics of *The Passion* have complained about the extent of the violence inflicted upon Christ, as presented in the film. The unrelenting bruising and beating and suffering shown has been rejected as unnecessary, and as undesirable for the viewer. I suspect that these critics come close to missing the entire point of the film, which is the nature of human redemption. Nowadays human redemption is not thought to amount to much, and what little there is to it can be dealt with by education and counseling, and perhaps a law here and there, or some improvement in living conditions. Gibson certainly is much closer to the core of traditional Christian teaching in his vision of the human heart and its world as a reservoir of unlimited capacity to hurt and to harm.

Those currently regarded as "in the know" about human life, with their remedies, have to turn a blind eye to the actual course of human events. Up to today, multitudes of human beings are tortured, slaughtered, and starved on a daily basis by those who have the power to do so, and lying, cheating, stealing, and sanctimonious hardness of heart are routine in societies which, nevertheless, take themselves to be "better" than others. Through the medium of the events of Christ's Passion, portrayed as an unceasing stream of wonton violence upon Jesus, tearing his body to shreds, the film communicates a vision of human evil that is off the scale of human capacity to deal with it.

Indeed, as the word 'evil' has tried to edge its way back into public discourse in recent years, the academic mind in particular finds itself threatened, precisely because the word suggests something that is beyond any human remedy. It is an affront to human pride to think that there is something about our condition that we could not fix—given the desire to fix it, and enough time to tinker with it. *The Passion*, by contrast, presents a humanity that takes delight in hurting people, that does not even want to "fix it," and a humanity that chooses to implement its will through permitting or perpetrating deeds of the most heinous quality. The unremitting violence depicted in the film is highly effective in forcefully presenting a vision of this aspect of the human condition.

The Demonic Dimension

Satan is essential to this vision. Perhaps this is what the contemporary academic mindset senses. His presence accounts for the seemingly unlimited extent of human wrongdoing. He has humanity in his grasp through the ideas and arrangements he has developed throughout history, and he wants to keep them there. His tools are gratification of desire, impressive appearance, and physical force. Recall how he tempts Jesus to use these in the three temptations of Jesus in Chapter 4 of the Gospel according to Matthew. Satan's focus in the film is upon Jesus, the one who, alone, can break his grip on the human world, devoted as it is to power and deceit, and can deliver human beings from the mire of sin and evil in which they flounder.

Satan knows Jesus to be the only truly radical person to enter human history; for Jesus, if undiverted, will refuse to use evil to defeat evil, and will set afoot a new order that does not employ the devices by which evil persons try to secure themselves and get their way. Satan's project was to stop Jesus from getting to his redemptive act of crucifixion. From the beginning of Jesus's earthly life, he had tried to destroy him or to deflect him. Now, in the final hours before the cross, Satan tries to break Jesus down by pressuring him with the hopelessness, in human terms ("No one man can carry this burden, I tell you. No one. Ever."), of what Jesus is attempting. After the crucifixion and death scenes, Satan's final appearance in the film shows his total exasperation and despair at having failed to keep Christ from doing the one thing that would open the doors to deliverance of human beings from the grasp of evil by demonstrating the power of good over evil.

Gibson's film is an amazing recovery of an understanding of Satan's role in human life, and in the "Passion," that has been almost totally lost from view in recent centuries. The bland or banal presence of evil among human beings is forcibly expressed in the face, words, and actions of the person who plays Satan. It is particularly effective in the striking figure of this person carrying a grotesque and contented human being in its arms through the crowd around the scene of the seemingly endless beating of Jesus. The look of self-satisfaction on the face of the dwarf in Satan's arms expresses the fact that Satan has humanity under his direction, and is using them, in their deluded condition, to torture Jesus. His aim is to see Jesus die in the beating—only the intervention of Pilate's man avoids this in the film—or to provoke Jesus into asserting his miraculous powers against those who are harming him.

In either case, the progression toward the cross, and the effectual insertion of the radical act of redemption into world history, would be prevented, and Satan would continue his rule. The wretched outcome of that rule for humans is seen in the film from its *effects* on human character, on human government (sacred and secular), in the plucking out of the eye of the unrepentant thief, and in the horrific progression of Judas toward his own tree and his suicide. But Jesus and God the Father have a strategy to break down the rule of Satan.

Who Was Really in Charge?

At one point in the film, on the *Via Dolorosa*, the way of sorrows, Jesus actually *embraces* his cross, saying, "I am your servant, Father." Simon of Cyrene, who has been forced to help him, is astonished that he would do this. But embracing the cross is the central moment in the wisdom of Christ concerning human redemption, and it finds its place in many forms of early and later Christian practice. It symbolizes a radical strategy in bringing humans back to God from their bondage to Satan and the "world." Embracing the cross *with* Jesus is to be our salvation. It is to release ourselves into the realm of God, into God's care, and to stop trying to work the human system of power and desire to get what *we* want.

This understanding of the human need freely to release ourselves into the realm of God, and to abandon our efforts to rule ourselves, makes clear the wisdom of Christ in embracing the cross. That need could only be redemptively met in a way that makes its satisfaction available to human beings world-wide, and without regard to their particular circumstances. Only by Jesus Christ publicly suffering and dying in circumstances of the worst kind—imposed by a range of different kinds of people, especially Romans and Jews—and then living on beyond all that in the power and goodness of God, could he open the possibility of a good and righteous life to everyone in the world.

Thus one might suspect that the very phrase, 'the Passion,' is misleading as to the nature of the events involved in Jesus's crucifixion. 'The Passion' is often understood to simply mean "the suffering" of Christ. It conveys the idea of *passivity*, of something being done to someone who is totally at the mercy of surrounding people or events. Jesus is thus often presented in the Garden of Gethsemane as cowering in the face of upcoming death, as begging God to allow him to live, and as unable to do anything about what was being done to him, a helpless rag tossed about by the dogs of hell. He was, in short, a pathetic victim.

But in the light of who, on the Christian reading, he really was and is, we would err badly if we were to describe his torture and death simply as "the Passion." Suffer he certainly did. But it is Jesus himself who was in charge of events and people involved in the story. He "played" them—not exactly like a piano, for the people involved still had their choices to make—

to achieve his end of blowing open a carefully prepared but tiny cultural enclave of redemption and stepping upon the stage of world history, where he has remained up to the present. As he said at a crucial turning point in his career: "I, when I am lifted up from the earth [in crucifixion], will draw all people to myself" (John 12:32). We need to see clearly the profound wisdom of his chosen path toward his goal.

Could There Have Been Other Ways?

As we look through the Gospels we see that Jesus very purposively turned away from "opportunities" to be a political or military leader or a king, or to leave Palestine and be a teacher in the larger world of the Roman empire (see the passage just cited). With his incredible power and attractiveness, there were many ways he could have avoided the cross had he wished to do so. He could have founded the ultimate welfare state, producing wine and food by a mere word. But, as he clearly told his followers at the time: "I lay down my life in order to take it up again. No one takes it from me, but I lay it down of my own accord. I have power to lay it down, and I have power to take it up again" (John 10:17–18). This was what "the Father" wanted him to do, and the Father loves and honors him for doing it (Philippians 2:5–11).

Exercises in imagining another path for Jesus besides a bloody crucifixion are not entirely lacking. We have *The Last Temptation of Christ*, the book and the movie, and now *The Da Vinci Code*, the book and movie soon to be. Now try to imagine yourself loving, worshipping, giving up your life for such a person as the Jesus of those books. Imagine a great civilization formed around *him*. Imagine, if you can, the saints and martyrs that have formed the core of Christian believers throughout the ages living and dying as they did for *that* "Jesus." Imagine the multitudes *now* dying for Christ in many places throughout our world doing that. For that matter, try to imagine the authors, Nikos Kazantzakis or Dan Brown, laying down their lives in devotion or in death for the Jesus they present in their writings. But of course multitudes of remarkable and unremarkable human beings have given and will give everything to and for the Christ of Mel Gibson's *The Passion*. One has to think that Jesus really *knew* what he was doing.

The Kingdom of God

No one can understand the events of "the Passion" unless they see them in the light of *the kingdom of God*, "the kingdom of the heavens," and thereby in the light of what God intends to bring out of human life and human history. Most any New Testament scholar will tell you that Jesus's life and message was all about "the kingdom." What they usually miss, however, is *exactly* what Jesus did and said about the kingdom. Simply, by his acts and words he invited anyone at all, no matter who or what they were, to live in the kingdom of God *now*, by trusting—relying on, putting their confidence in—him. The events of his "passion" and afterward, as traditionally understood, demonstrated to his followers and other observers that what Jesus said about the kingdom and its availability is true. To live *through and beyond* torture and the cross in resurrection life shows the presence of a world of God among men.

In the simplest possible terms, the kingdom of God is *God in action*. It is the range of God's effective will, where what God wants done is done. Jesus is a reformulation and embodiment of the message about God and his kingdom that runs through the history of the Jewish people recorded in the Bible. Jesus said: "Seek above all to live within the kingdom rule of God, and to have the kind of goodness he has, and all else you need will be provided with it" (Matthew 6:33 paraphrase). The Psalmist said simply and concretely, "The Lord is my Shepherd, I shall not want" (Psalm 23). In one of the historical books of the Old Testament a prophet is quoted as saying: "The eyes of the Lord move to and fro throughout the earth that He may strongly support those whose heart is completely His" (2 Chronicles 16:9). This is what Jesus knew as he went through his sufferings and death. In that knowledge he simultaneously wrote across the pages of human history the depth of human meanness and brutality and the unlimited reach of God's love and power.

It was knowledge of the presence and unfailing availability of God to those who trust him that led Jesus to say all the beautiful things (largely *already* recorded in the Psalms) which we wistfully acknowledge, but hardly believe to be true: all of those things about birds and flowers being in the care of God, of course, and about how we need never be anxious or afraid, no matter what comes, even crucifixion. The basic idea is that this world—with all its evil, pushed to the limit in what Jesus went through going toward and on the cross—is a perfectly good and safe place for anyone to be, no matter the circumstances, if they have only placed their lives in the hands of Jesus and his Father. We never have to do what we know to be wrong, and we never need be afraid. And Jesus practiced what he preached, even as he was tortured and killed. And so have multitudes of his followers.

The Hidden God

But the kingdom of God is not overwhelmingly *obvious*, to say the least. It's something one must seek, and therefore something we must want. Isaiah, the prophet, exclaims that "Truly, you are a God who hides himself" (45:15). He was the one who gave us the concept of *deus absconditus*, the hidden God, now deeply interwoven into Christian tradition. And why would God hide himself? Because God loves us, he wants to be known to us. That is the way of love. But because we, in our rebellion against him, are hardened in our insistence on having our own "kingdom," he must hide from us to allow us to hide from him and to pretend we, individually and corporately, are in charge of our life. He is such a great and magnificent being that, if he did not hide from us, we could not hide from him. He allows us the pretense of being our own god because that is what we want, what we choose. Pushed to the limit, this choice results in the terrible evils of which we have proven capable.

Only the hiddenness of God, then, allows people to define themselves. The existentialist philosopher Jean-Paul Sartre (1905–1980) had a point, though not the one he thought. He said that since there is no God, man has no nature. Man must therefore make of himself whatever he is to be. This view is logically incoherent, strictly speaking. Something with no nature cannot do *anything*. (Yes! Yes! I know. Something more can be said for Sartre here.) The Renaissance humanist Pico Della Mirandola (1463–1494) perhaps came closer to the truth. His view was that in man God had produced a creature that had the responsibility of becoming what he is to become by the choices he makes. God allows, indeed *requires*, that we choose to act on the basis of our desires, and that we freely decide what we will live for. What we choose in selecting among our desires for fulfillment determines what kinds of persons we become. What we decide to seek in life is the key to our character, and further determines what our character will be. God, like persons in general, wants to be wanted, and tries not to be manifestly present where he is not wanted. He is unwilling to impose himself on anyone if and as long as that can be avoided.

Would "More Evidence" Really Help?

Many individuals have protested that they *would* believe in God if they had more evidence. It needs to be pointed out, however, that just believing that God exists is not the only issue. What kind of God are we talking about? And is it indeed true that they *would* then believe? How much more evidence would it take? And would they then be glad there is a God? Would they then believe because they wanted God, wanted it to be his world, wanted not to be God—the ultimate point of reference in their lives—themselves? Would they be prepared to *love* God? More than evidence is required to bring a person to that point. And is it completely clear that the "more evidence" called for is not already available to those who are willing to seek it? Does the evidence have to be presented in a way that the unbeliever cannot avoid it, cannot not be aware of it?

It would be a small victory for God, if he exists, to wring belief out of a human being, but is that an outcome worth pursuing for him? In the *The Screwtape Letters*, C.S. Lewis has the senior devil, Screwtape, say to his protégé, Wormwood:

> You must have wondered why the Enemy does not make more use of his power to be sensibly present to human souls in any degree He chooses and at any moment. But you now see that the Irresistible and the Indisputable are the two weapons which the very nature of His scheme forbids Him to use. Merely to override a human will (as His felt presence in any but the faintest and most mitigated degree would certainly do) would be for Him useless. He cannot ravish. He can only woo. For His ignoble idea is to eat the cake and have it; the creatures are to be one with Him, but yet themselves. (Lewis 1962, pp. 46–48)

So we might say that God *lets* himself be known, for example, in the story and person of Jesus. He is available to those who really *want* him. "When you search for me," the old prophet said, "you will find me; if you seek me with all your heart" (Jeremiah 29:13). But he will not force himself upon you, not jump down your throat. And if you in your heart really want to be God yourself, you probably will not find him. You will find yourself.

Jesus's Low-Profile Approach

The craftiness of Christ in taking the cross is of a piece with the hiddenness of God. The means he employed to secure the end he had in view left God hidden to all. His end was to bring out of human history a world-wide, non-ethnic community of human beings who have the character of God, expressed in Jesus himself and in *agape* love: a character spelled out in a many-sided way by the contents of the New Testament and the lives of the best of Christ-followers throughout the ages. Jesus accomplishes this objective by showing us how to return good for evil in a power beyond ourselves. That has to be something we freely want, however, and something we choose to develop the character for. The wisdom of the cross makes this possible.

Remarkably, even after his resurrection Jesus continued his low-profiled ways. The human mode would have been to pay a post-resurrection visit to Pilate, perhaps, and to say something like, "Now could we have that discussion about power and truth once again?" Or perhaps to swing by the High Priest's house, or causally to drop in on the Sanhedrin in session. But no. That of course would have only been to give in to the temptations earlier posed to him by Satan. It would have been the "wisdom" of man, not the wisdom of God. Instead, "God raised him [Jesus] up on the third day and allowed him to appear, not to all the people but to us who were chosen by God as witnesses, and who ate and drank with him after he rose from the dead" (Acts 10:42). And then, of all things, he simply sent his bedraggled little friends out to the whole world to enlist students to him, promising his unseen presence with them. With nothing, to begin with, but his example, words and personal presence, they, to a striking extent, overcame a world of brutality routinely equal to that displayed in *The Passion*; often dying in the process, but also convincing multitudes of the vision and the ethical idealization incarnate in Jesus and his cross. All of this is simply a fact, as it is a fact that for the last two centuries or so historical force has been against this vision and idealization.

The Solution to an Unsolved Philosophical Problem

However, the philosophical problem of how to develop human beings into a character that will keep human life from being "poor, brutish, nasty and short," to use the words of Thomas Hobbes (1588–1679), has not been solved. It was not solved in antiquity. The route of education and law, which Plato (427–347 B.C.) and Aristotle (384–322 B.C.) tried to lay down, proved to be ineffectual for human nature as it is. The Greeks finally had to invite the Romans in to stop their fratricides. The route of careful soul-management, which Stoic and Epicurean philosophers later retreated into, more or less conceded the world to evil, and concentrated on telling individuals how to make life in a hellish world bearable. It was into this scene of intellectual despair that the community of Christ came, after his death, with its message of hope for the terrible "City of Man." This religious message was based on the presence of the "City of God" on earth now, taking all comers, and projecting them into a present and an everlasting future bright with hope. It was one of the cross combined with *agape* love: love first from God, seen in the cross, and then love filling human beings in all the dimensions of ordinary life. The message was an invitation to a love that "never fails" (1 Corinthians 13:8) and from which nothing can ever separate us (Romans 8:35–39).

The philosophical problem of how to develop moral character in human beings, so that they actually lead a moral life, has not been solved today. Indeed, though that problem was arguably the most important matter for moral thought in antiquity, it is now a problem that those known as the leading contemporary moral philosophers will hardly touch or try to relate to their theories. The main difficulty in solving it has always been that individuals and groups must start from a history of evil, and the way to overcome that history has, arguably, never been found outside of the pattern set by Christ and his people. Forgiveness has to be a massive reality in the heart of human affairs. This is available in Christ's way of crucifixion. If there are other promising ways, of course, they should be fairly and thoroughly considered, and the generosity of Christ is such that, if we can find a better way than his, he would certainly be the first to tell us to take it.

SOURCES

Jonathan Glover. 1999. *Humanity: A Moral History of the Twentieth Century*. London: Cape.
N.R. Hanson. 1972. *What I Do Not Believe and Other Essays*. Edited by Stephen Toulmin and Harry Woolf. Dordrecht: Reidel.
C.S. Lewis. 1962. *The Screwtape Letters*. New York: Macmillan.
Giovanni Pico della Mirandola. 1956. *Oration on the Dignity of Man*. Translated by A. Robert Caponigri. Chicago: University of Chicago Press.
Jean-Paul Sartre. 1947. *Existentialism*. New York: Philosophical Library.
Dallas Willard. 1998. *The Divine Conspiracy*. San Francisco: Harper.

QUESTIONS FOR DISCUSSION

1. Do you think that the religious answer provided by Christ solves the philosophical problem of how to develop moral character in humans?

2. What do you think of the idea that Jesus was actually "in charge" of the events associated with his "passion"?

3. Now suppose that *you* are in the position of Jesus, and you have his objectives. What would you do differently?

4. Let's suppose that Jesus responded to the taunts to come down from the cross by doing just that. How would the story go from that point up to the present?

5. Must God hide? How obvious would you like him to be?

15

The Death of Socrates and the Death of Christ

GARETH B. MATTHEWS

For a devout Christian the story of the death of Christ must be, in important respects, utterly unique and without parallel. Yet even the most devout Christian can still reflect on the similarities and differences between that story, as recounted in the Gospel narratives, and accounts of the deaths of other great figures in history. For a philosopher one obvious choice for comparison and contrast might be Plato's account of the death of Socrates in his dialogue, *Phaedo*.

On the surface at least, the stories of how these two figures died could hardly be more different. Mel Gibson's retelling of the Gospel stories in *The Passion of the Christ* makes the death of Jesus on the cross torturously painful. The relentless scourging and extended abuse Jesus suffers beforehand appear in the film as nothing less than a prolonged horror. By contrast, the end of the life of Socrates, as Plato portrays it in the *Phaedo*, is serene, rational, and remarkably civilized. According to Plato, Socrates spent the last day of his life in prison conducting a lively seminar on the immortality of the soul. Having, as he thought, defended his position successfully against the best counter-arguments the disciples gathered around him could come up with, Socrates then went into an adjoining room of the prison to have a bath. When he returned, he said goodbye to his wife and children. When they had left, the executioner entered and said this to him:

> I shall not reproach you as I do the others, Socrates. They are angry with me and curse me when, obeying the orders of my superiors, I tell them to drink the poison. During the time you have been here I have come to know you in other ways as the noblest, the gentlest and the best man who has ever come here. So now too I know that you will not make trouble for me; you know who is responsible and you will direct your anger at them. You know what message I bring. Fare you well, and try to endure what you must as easily as possible. (*Phaedo* 116cd)

A little later, when the man who was to administer the poison appeared with a cup of hemlock juice, Socrates said to him, "Well, my good man, you are an expert in this, what must one do?"

The poison bearer replied, "Just drink it and walk around until your legs feel heavy, and then lie down and it will act of itself" (*Phaedo* 117ab).

Socrates complied with the instructions. As he lay on his pallet, waiting for the poison to take effect, he turned to his disciple, Crito, and said: "We owe a cock to Asclepius; make this offering to him and do not forget" (*Phaedo* 118a). A scholarly footnote to the text explains that a cock was sacrificed to Asclepius by sick people hoping for a cure and that Socrates meant by his final remark that death is a cure for the ills of life. Soon after Socrates made that remark, his eyes glazed over and he died.

One can hardly imagine an account of the last hours of a human life that stands in greater contrast to Gibson's *The Passion of the Christ*. According to Plato, Socrates died calmly and quietly, after having conducted a lengthy and philosophically complex discussion of life, death, and immortality. According to Gibson, Christ died in a gruesome, even barbaric way, after suffering almost unbearable physical abuse and sadistic brutality. So far then, the comparison is all contrast.

Yet there are also important similarities between the deaths of Socrates and Christ, even as these deaths are portrayed by Plato and Gibson. By reflecting on the similarities, as well as the differences, we can come to understand Socrates and Jesus better. We might also hope to understand death better, including especially our own death.

Both Socrates and Jesus were condemned to death by a court. In the case of Socrates, the jury was a very large assembly of Athenian citizens, perhaps as many as 500 (or maybe 501, to prevent there being a tie vote!). Socrates's accusers brought their charges against him. And Socrates was given ample time and opportunity to defend himself against the charges. To judge from Plato's transcription of the trial in his *Apology* ('apology' in this context means 'defense') Socrates took the opportunity to explain his philosophical mission in life and to lecture the jury on their mistaken attitudes toward death.

Jesus was condemned by the Jewish Supreme Court, the Sanhedrin, and later put to death, somewhat reluctantly, to judge from Gibson's film, by the Roman governor of the province, Pontius Pilate. Instead of 501 members, the Sanhedrin had seventy-one, or, if it was the "Little Sanhedrin," only twenty-three. All the members of that court were themselves priests.

Both Socrates and Jesus were apparently tried for, and convicted of, religious offenses. Socrates, at his trial, seems to have faced two sets of charges. According to the second set, he was "guilty of corrupting the young and of not believing in the gods in whom the city believes, but in other new divinities" (*Apology* 24b). Jesus was charged with the "blasphemy" of declaring himself to be Christ, the Son of God (Matthew 26:63–65)

Behind the charge of impiety against Socrates and the charge of blasphemy against Jesus there were no doubt political, as well as purely theological motives. To Pilate Jesus must have seemed to be a potential insurrectionist. To the Council of Priests Jesus was most probably a heretic who promoted his heresy. So behind the religious charges against Jesus there were, in all likelihood, concerns among the Romans for the stability of the empire and, among the priests, for the authority of the priestly establishment in Judea.

With Socrates the political enmities seem to have been even more complicated. According to Plato, Socrates had made leading figures of Athens look foolish by showing through extended questioning that they could not explain in any philosophically satisfactory way what justice requires or what virtue is. He also seems to have infuriated leading figures of Athens by his acts of conscientious objection. For example, he had apparently refused what he considered to be illegal orders to help arrest someone the authorities wanted to hold in custody. Instead of obeying the order, he had simply gone home (*Apology* 32cd). Finally, some of Socrates's followers had been thought to have

acted dishonorably, and Socrates seems to have been held
responsible for their dishonorable behavior.

Are the death of Socrates and the death of Christ also similar
in being a model for us to emulate when we have to face our
own death? Certainly Plato has as one of his aims in the *Phaedo*
to help us learn how to die. Early on in the dialogue Socrates
says that "the one aim of those who practice philosophy in the
proper manner is to practice for dying and death" (64a). No
doubt Plato has Socrates say this because, in Plato's own view,
death is a liberation of the soul from the encumbrances of mortal life, including the lower pleasures of food and sex. On this
view we should welcome death, though not hasten it by suicide
(61e–62c). We should welcome death, since it will free us to
enjoy the pure pleasures of the mind, including, especially, philosophy.

The attitude toward death that Plato ascribes to Socrates in
the *Apology* is somewhat different from his attitude in the
Phaedo. To be sure, Socrates in the *Apology* is equally serene
about the prospect of his own death. But there he takes a more
agnostic position on our prospects for an afterlife. At no point
in the trial, according to Plato, does Socrates offer any proofs for
the immortality of the soul. Still, in his first speech to the jury
Socrates castigates his fellow Athenians for fearing death:

> To fear death, gentlemen, is nothing other than to think oneself
> wise when one is not, to think one knows what one does not
> know. No one knows whether death may not be the greatest of all
> blessings for a man, yet men fear it as if they knew that it is the
> greatest of evils. (29a)

Later on in the trial, in his final speech before the court, Socrates
offers a more extended line of argument. He begins with the
annunciation of these possibilities:

> . . . either the dead are nothing and have no perception of any-
> thing, or it is, as we are told, a change and a relocating for the soul
> from here to another place. (40c)

Concerning the first possibility he says this:

> . . . all eternity would seem to be no more than a single night. (40e)

Concerning the second he has this to say:

> I could spend my time testing and examining people there, as I do here, as to who among them is wise, and who thinks he is, but is not. (41b)

Put another way, Socrates in the *Apology* supposes that either death will be pure nothingness for him, and so can in no way harm him, or else it will offer him a further chance to do philosophy, which is the activity he most cherishes in life.

These are the thoughts of a man who has had, by his own lights, a good life. If death brings further opportunity to do what he has found most satisfying in this life, then it is to be welcomed. If it brings his extinction, at least it cannot harm him. Thus Socrates ends his defense with these words to the jury:

> Now the hour to part has come. I go to die, you go to live. Which of us goes to the better lot is known to no one, except the god. (42a)

Thus although the picture we get of Socrates's attitude toward death in the *Apology* differs significantly from the one we get in the *Phaedo*, each work gives us a philosopher's picture of how to die.

What now about the accounts we have of the death of Christ, and especially the re-enactment given us in *The Passion of the Christ?* Do they help us think about how to take up an appropriate attitude toward death?

Christians sometimes take the life of Christ to be a model for their own lives. Yet, for a Christian, there are obvious ways in which the death of Christ has to be different, much different, from our own deaths. These two items of Christian belief clearly stand in the way of any effort to draw conclusions about how we ought to die from the way Christ died:

(1) Christ was God in human form.

(2) Christ died for the sins of the whole world.

According to orthodox Christian belief, we are each of us made in the image of God. Yet none of us can literally be God in human form, as Jesus Christ was. So death for us cannot be what it was for Christ. In particular, we cannot have quite the same knowledge of God, or of an afterlife, that Christ had. We may, in the words of the Nicene Creed, "look for the resurrection of the dead and the life of the world to come." But we cannot have the same assurance of the world to come that Christ had. And so our death will have to be somewhat different from the death of Christ, no matter how fervently we believe in the world to come.

Second, we cannot possibly die for the sins of the whole world. We may die, when we do, and in the way in which we do, as a result of the sins of certain other people. But atonement for the sins of others, let alone for the sins of the whole world, is not something within the range of our life possibilities. And so the significance of our death cannot be anything like the significance Christian doctrine assigns to the death of Christ. Is there then nothing at all in *The Passion of the Christ* that could help us think about and meet our own deaths?

There are two sayings of Christ, both included in the Gibson film, that have been traditionally thought to help each of us face our own death. First, there is this saying of Christ in the Garden of Gethsemane:

> My Father, if it be possible, let this cup pass from me; nevertheless, not as I will, but as thou wilt. (Matthew 26:39)

This saying may be particularly helpful to people who face a prolonged and painful death. It may be comforting and inspiring to such a person to think that even the Son of God, facing the horrors of scourging and crucifixion, wishes he did not have to go through with it all. It may also be helpful to think that there may be some Divine purpose, or some act of Divine will, behind what seems otherwise to be only needless suffering. Gibson's film does not give any special prominence to this saying of Jesus; but faithful Christians, seeing the film, may need only a bare reminder of these words to have them in mind through the grueling scenes to follow.

The other words of Christ that have traditionally been thought to help us face our own death are the words he is said to have spoken from the cross, echoing Psalm 22:1:

My God, My God, why hast thou forsaken me? (Matthew 27:46)

This saying of Jesus may come to the Christian believer as something of a shock. How could Jesus Christ, the Son of God, even entertain the thought that God had forsaken him? The New Testament scholar, Oscar Cullmann has offered the following interpretation of this striking cry of despair:

> Because [death] is God's enemy, it separates us from God, who is life and the creator of all life. Jesus, who is so closely tied to God, tied as no other man has ever been, for precisely this reason must experience death much more terribly than any other man. To be in the hands of the great enemy of God means to be forsaken by God. In a way quite different from others, Jesus must suffer this abandonment, this separation from God, the only condition really to be feared. Therefore he cries to God: "Why has thou forsaken me?" He is now actually in the hands of God's great enemy. (Cullmann 1965, p. 17)

On Cullmann's interpretation this second saying of Christ can also be important to us as we face death. We, too, can expect to be abandoned to death, even if we have an abiding faith in God and a fervent hope for the world to come. No argument for the immortality of the soul can be counted on to give us protection against that sense of forsakenness and abandonment we can expect to have as we die. No reports from patients with "near-death" experiences that tell of a life "on the other side" can be guaranteed to save us from the threat of abandonment. Even the most steadfast faith in what we take to be God's promise of a life to come cannot be guaranteed to shield us against the feeling of forsakenness that Christ also experienced on the cross.

As I have said, both of these last sayings of Christ are included in the Gibson movie, although they are not given any special prominence. Anyone already familiar with the Gospel accounts of the passion of Christ will know to expect them, but they are not underlined or highlighted in the movie. So they are evidently not part of the movie's central message.

By contrast the suffering of Jesus in *The Passion of the Christ* is elongated and magnified, seemingly to the point of excess. Consider how much of the film is devoted to amplifying and drawing out what is stated so succinctly in these verses of St. Matthew's Gospel:

> And when they had mocked him, they stripped him of the robe, and put his own clothes on him, and led him away to crucify him. As they were marching out, they came upon a man of Cyrene, Simon by name; this man they compelled to carry his cross. And when they came to a place called Golgotha (which means the place of a skull), they offered him wine to drink, mingled with gall: but when he tasted it, he would not drink it. And when they had crucified him, they divided his garments among them by casting lots. (Matthew 27:31–35)

So why did Mel Gibson draw out the sadism of the soldiers and the agonizing suffering of Christ to the point that many viewers need to turn their eyes away from the screen? He must have wanted to show Christ as bearing the unbearable and suffering the insufferable. And that, in turn, means that Gibson was not focusing on the suffering and death of Christ as a model for how you and I might face our own suffering and death. Rather, he wanted to present Christ as doing something that we cannot possibly do for ourselves.

Of course, there is a way in which Plato also presents Socrates as doing something that, in all likelihood, none of us will be able to do ourselves. The philosophical argumentation Plato has Socrates present in the *Phaedo* includes a presentation of Plato's Theory of Forms, in some ways the most audacious and enduring metaphysical doctrine in the history of Western philosophy. It strains credibility to the breaking point to think that anyone, even Plato himself, could patiently set forth his most ambitious metaphysical theory on the very day of his own expected execution.

Still, developing a philosophical theory, even one as audacious as Plato's, is a human accomplishment. It is the accomplishment of an extraordinarily brilliant human being; but it is still the work of a human mind. Atoning for the sins of the whole world is not a purely human task, not even the task of a Mahatma Gandhi, or a Mother Teresa, or a Martin Luther King. I conjecture that Mel Gibson had Jesus Christ in his film suffer so inordinately to make the point that what he was doing on that first Good Friday was nothing less than atoning for the sins of absolutely everybody, even the most evil and cruel persons our sad and broken world has ever known.

One obvious point in emphasizing the inordinate suffering of Christ is certainly to inspire religious devotion. Among many Christians, Gibson's film seems, in fact, to have succeeded in inspiring devotion. But inspiring devotion to Christ may also have the effect of distancing Christ from us and so making His example less relevant to the way we think about our own death.

There is another way in which *The Passion of the Christ* makes the life and death of Christ more of an icon, and less of an example for us to reflect on in considering our own mortality and the end of our own lives. Consider this passage from the New Testament scholar and theologian, Rudolf Bultmann:

> I do not actually know what death and life are, for that could be truly known only when life is at its end—the end, when death is there, also belongs to it. Yet we have a peculiar preknowledge that death is not a mere natural event, not simply the cessation of life, but that it is the test of our life; that it is something unnatural, enigmatic, against which we struggle and in the shadow of which our whole life stands. (Bultmann 1966, p. 157)

Except in rare cases, for example, when patients have "near-death experiences," we cannot literally practice dying. Yet we can realize that our death may be, as Bultmann puts it, "the test of our life." Plato presents Socrates as clearly passing this test. In his trial, according to the *Apology*, he chides his fellow Athenians for thinking they know what justice and virtue are, when they don't. But, in a similar way, he also chides them for thinking they know that death is bad, when they don't. And in the *Phaedo* he carries on a complex and intricate philosophical discussion right up to the time of his execution.

Mel Gibson tries to use brief flashbacks to unify the life and ministry of Jesus with his agonizing death. But he so emphasizes the final suffering of Christ that the flashback to, for example, the Sermon on the Mount, becomes ironical rather than unifying. Even the resurrection of Christ, which is at the heart of Christian theology, becomes little more than a cameo appearance in the film. And so we are left with very little sense of how the gruesome agony of Christ's last day can be a test of the authenticity of the life that has gone before.

Plato tried to portray Socrates in a way that might help us deal with our own mortality, perhaps, as in the *Phaedo*, by coming to appreciate his arguments for immortality, but more likely, as in the *Apology*, by appreciating his reasons for being agnostic about death. Most importantly, he tried to show us in the *Phaedo* how one's life might have sufficient integrity that what is important to one at the hour of death is no different from what had been important throughout one's life.

A filmmaker could, no doubt, use materials from the Gospel stories of the passion and death of Christ to help us face our own death. Mel Gibson has not done that. No doubt it was not his intention to do that. What he has done instead is to give us a brutal account of the suffering and death of Christ that might inspire our devotion to someone who has done something for us that we could not possibly do for ourselves. But even if *The Passion of the Christ* is a splendid attempt to do that, we should not suppose that there are no other important ways to read the Passion story, ways that make Jesus less remote from you and me, and more relevant to what we may face at the hour of our own death.

SOURCES

Rudolf Bultmann. 1966. *Faith and Understanding*. London: SCM Press.

Thomas C. Brickhouse and Nicholas D. Smith. 1989. *Socrates on Trial*. Princeton: Princeton University Press.

Oscar Cullmann, et al. 1965. *Immortality and Resurrection*. Edited by K. Stendahl. New York: Macmillan.

Plato. 1981. *Five Dialogues: Euthyphro, Apology, Crito, Meno, Phaedo*. Translated by G.M.A. Grube. Indianapolis: Hackett.

C.C.W. Taylor. 1998. *Socrates: A Very Short Introduction*. Oxford: Oxford University Press.

QUESTIONS FOR DISCUSSION

1. What was your reaction to the abuse to which Christ is subjected in Gibson's film?

2. To judge simply from Gibson's film, what would you say was the point of the suffering and death of Christ?

3. Can you compare the suffering and death of Christ to the suffering or death of anyone else you know or have heard about?

4. What was the chief message you got from seeing Gibson's film?

5. Are there ways in which Mel Gibson's film helps you think about death? If so, what are they?

16

Dances of Death: Self-Sacrifice and Atonement

BRUCE R. REICHENBACH

Figures move, weaving, watching, reaching to each other in structured patterns. At times they connect at a distance, eyes meeting with an intense gaze of horror, uncertainty, distrust, or conquest. At other times in close proximity they dance in slow motion with the reach of a supporting hand, an intimate look, or a sensitive caressing touch. In *The Passion of the Christ* director Mel Gibson creates elaborate and carefully choreographed dances between the main characters. Each extended dance might be seen as a *pas de deux*, a dance between two persons with steps that form figures or patterns.

The figures and patterns formed between Jesus and his partners provide insight not only into the character of the dancers but, more relevant for our purpose, into their struggle to come to grips with the suffering and looming death of the Christ. By depicting individual encounters of people with Jesus, the dances provide a medium for Gibson to tell his own version of Jesus's passion story and present his understanding of its significance. In particular, he visually has something to say about Christ's atonement, that is, how Christ in his suffering and death reconciled humans to God.

Death and the Meaning of Life

The dances portrayed in the film form patterns that address the question of the meaning of death. The significance of death is an old philosophical problem, going back at least to Socrates, who questioned what significance his life might hold in the face of his impending death. If he took the offer of his friends, donned a disguise, and escaped from the prison where he awaited execution, would his life and calling to awaken the citizens of Athens to questions of knowledge and virtue (character) have any meaning? Citizens of the cities to which he would flee would see him as merchandizing his principles merely to live on a few more years in old age.

Recent philosophers also address the question of how we should face our own death. Martin Heidegger (1889–1976), for example, contends that persons become truly authentic when they come face to face with their own potential for death. We find ourselves thrown into a world not of our own making. We did not choose to be born, where to be born, or to whom to be born, yet here we are in the world. And we are in the world essentially in relation to others. Our connections with others help define who we are and how we understand ourselves. Heidegger notes that often we act unthinkingly, accepting what others say about who we are or what we will become without seeking to determine what we might desire as our own authentic existence. We choose conformity to society and culture that yields mediocrity. In not claiming our uniqueness we become alienated from real possibilities that might shape what we could become. Part of that destiny is that we will die. For Heidegger, death provides not only a temporal limit to our earthly existence, but more importantly it provides a boundary against which we conceive our identity and what we are about in life. A quick scan of the obituary page shows how people's lives are routinely summarized. Often, more attention is paid to naming past or surviving kin than to the accomplishments and character of the deceased. In a brief paragraph, others define the significance of our lives, continuing a pattern that occurs during life itself.

Often we deny our mortality; death happens to others, not to us. For Heidegger, affirming that *my* death belongs uniquely to me and is inevitable frees us to give meaning to our existence here and now. Instead of death simply happening to us, we should address it purposively by living in light of its certainty. Not that we should morbidly seek or constantly dwell on death. Rather, acceptance of the limits to our life opens us up to living in the present in a way that incorporates our past and present into a future of our own making. We need to create a meaningful, authentic existence by affirming our finiteness as an essential feature of living and to define our life's goals in light of that finiteness. We should not await but anticipate the future, and in its anticipation create it. Since the future has priority, we have a basis for hope regardless of our past and present states.

Self-Sacrifice and the Meaning of Life

The Jesus of *The Passion of the Christ*, in a style reminiscent of Heidegger, grasps his death authentically from the outset. Although he struggles with death, Jesus does not seek to evade, obscure, or conceal it. Neither does he merely await death, but rather approaches it with what Heidegger calls anticipatory resolve. True, Jesus has anxiety over his death. Yet he understands his death as that which gives meaning to all his other possibilities, to everything he has done (note the flashbacks to his Sermon on the Mount and the Last Supper). From the outset, both Satan and Jesus understand the cosmic significance of the choices Jesus makes. At the same time, Jesus departs from the Heideggerian motif in seeking to actualize his death, not as an act of suicide but as an act of self-sacrifice. Whereas our death provides the limit to our existence, Jesus's death is central to his project, the goal that gives his life its ultimate meaning. His project defines who he is and the mission he assumed. In that mission Jesus dies not for himself but for the Other, for Simon and the thief on the cross, for tormented Judas, and even for us.

Since Jesus's death is meant not for himself, it is relational, displaying what Heidegger terms "solicitude," that is, a deep concern for the Other. For example, Jesus does not bear a cross for Simon, but rather in bearing the cross together Jesus allows Simon to come to a realization of himself. Simon is freed to understand himself and to be himself authentically because he participates with Jesus in the dance of his death.

So the question of *The Passion of the Christ* is not how we can find meaning in our own death, but how the death of another can give us meaning. As Jesus crawls onto the cross, Gibson flashes back to the Last Supper that preceded the Passion. Looking at his disciples, Jesus says, "There is no greater love than this, that a man lay down his life for his friends." *The Passion* unfolds that saying. From the opening struggle in the Garden with the embodied Satan to the final "It is finished," the audience witnesses a man determined to carry his mission to its end, not for himself but for others.

Self-sacrifice exemplifies the highest moral ideal. It is generally not thought to be obligatory, although some Jewish literature prescribes one accept death rather than commit adultery, incest, or murder. The Talmud, for example, tells the story of Raba who, ordered by the governor to kill another, refused, offering himself instead. Self-sacrifice is supererogatory in that it is especially morally praiseworthy.

Whether a particular act is self-sacrifice (martyrdom) or suicide can be a matter of dispute, and sometimes fundamentally a matter of perspective. A different judgment might be rendered by the one who dies than by the ones affected by the death. Assessment of the deeds of the 9/11 hijackers illustrates the point; how they viewed their actions differs immensely from those trapped in the burning towers. In their study, *A Noble Death: Suicide and Martyrdom among Christians and Jews in Antiquity*, Arthur Droge and James Tabor note five characteristics of martyrs: they reflect situations of opposition and persecution, their choice to die is viewed as necessary or noble, they are often eager to die, a presumed vicarious benefit results from their suffering and death, and their death is vindicated beyond their death. *The Passion of the Christ* evinces all of these characteristics in portraying Jesus as a martyr, not as determinedly suicidal.

So what might be the significance of someone's sacrifice for another? Here let us return to the motif of the dance to see how Gibson portrays the significance of Jesus's self-sacrifice.

The Dance with Satan

The film opens with an anxious Jesus in the Garden. "I don't want them to see me like this," he moans as he approaches his sleeping disciples. He agonizes over his impending death, seeking to avoid it while struggling with what appears to be the inevitable should he accept his role—"Save me from the temptations they set for me." Into the midst of this personal struggle Gibson introduces a choreographed *pas de deux* with Satan, a dance whose steps here form a pattern of a conquest struggle. Satan appears as a hooded, androgynous, attractive yet sinister figure who verbally counters the moves of Jesus, even to the point of taking on the role of Jesus's counter-ego. "Do you really believe that one man can bear the burden of sin?" Jesus replies, "Shelter me, oh Lord." Satan takes up the refrain, "No one man can carry the burden. It is far too heavy." Jesus replies, "Father, you can do all things. If possible, let this chalice pass from me. Yet not my will but yours be done." The dance continues as Satan tempts Jesus to question the one who demanded the role of agony foretold of the suffering servant in Isaiah 53, the scripture that opens the film. The camera moves between the two, the one prostrate in agony over his anticipated role, the other a tempter offering what appears to be release from the fated suffering. "Who is your father? Who are you?" Who will conquer whom in this deadly dance?

In Jesus's weakest moment, Gibson visually recalls the Garden of Eden story in Genesis, where the crafty serpent successfully tempted the first parents with a series of provocative questions and half-truths. The battle resumes in the Garden of Gethsemane, where a serpent emerges from between the legs of Satan, poised to strike the weakened Jesus lying prostrate from his agony. In the first movement of this dance sequence, Jesus gathers his strength (as Gibson has him do repeatedly in the film) and, raising himself up from his despair, crushes the head of the serpent with his foot. The violent destruction of the serpent fulfills Genesis 3:15, which prophesies that the man's offspring would crush its head. Jesus's strong will produces the first victory.

Satan reappears in his conquest dance during the endless flogging of Jesus. Passing through the on-looking religious elite, Satan circles the agonizing Jesus, perhaps again recalling Genesis 3:15 as Satan bruises Jesus's heel by means of the sadistic acts of the Roman henchmen who whip both upper and lower body. Staring at the suffering Christ and carrying a deformed, adult-faced child (the illusion of innocence) dressed in black, he wears the look of "you could have escaped all this if." The second movement of conquest belongs to Satan.

The dance continues on the path to the cross (the *Via Dolorosa*, the way of suffering), as both Satan and Mary parallel Jesus on the agonizing last journey. The one tempts, the other strengthens since no one can bear the cross singly.

In the crucifixion scene Gibson brings ultimacy to the *pas de deux* between Jesus and Satan, creating a pattern by moving the camera's vantage-point from the horizontal to the vertical. Gibson uses a pair of reverse photographic scenes. In the first, the crucifixion is photographed from above. A descending drop of water symbolizes the agony of the crying Father as he from high above surveys the crucifixion. The camera descends from the heights overlooking the three crosses to the human witnesses struggling to process the death. In a subsequent scene, the camera commences with an up-close focus on Satan, who tears off his wig and lets out a primal scream as the camera ascends to view him from above. The scene shows Satan in a caked, cracked desert, trapped within his own circle of hell. The dance is completed: by sheer courage and determination Christ has conquered his tempter.

For Gibson, the significance of Jesus's sacrificial death for the conquest dance between Christ and Satan is that it signals the defeat of the demonic. Historically, this theme is embodied in the *Christus victor* view of the atonement, versions of which were advocated by Church Fathers such as Irenaeus (who died in A.D. 202), Origen (185–254), Gregory of Nyssa (died after 385), and Augustine (354–430). The doctrine of atonement, central to Christian theology, describes what is required to end the estrangement between humans and their creator brought on by the fall. According to the *Christus victor* view, a great cosmic drama rages between the forces of good and those of evil. Satan, because of human sin, conquered or gained possession of humanity and controls it, bringing both evil and death. Sin pays off in death, Paul teaches. Christ's death and subsequent resurrection destroy the power of the demonic. With Christ's suffering and crucifixion the hold of sin and death has begun to weaken. As noted in Jesus's response to Pilate, atonement is not accomplished by the power of divine conquest; no great angelic or human battles are envisioned. Rather, our reconciliation with God comes through Christ's humanity and his obedience to the will of God. Death is not the final word. Its conquest fulfills what the film signified at its outset with the crushing of the serpent's head and finalizes by the resurrection of Jesus, who strolls naked, scarred but healed, from the tomb.

Gibson, in his visualization of Satan, suggests a realist view of good and evil. Evil is not merely the privation of the good, as

Augustine taught, but itself a force, powerful, cunning, tempting, alluring, even killing (Gibson has Satan present at the final torment of Judas). Since evil has reality, its conquest must itself be real.

The puzzle of the *Christus victor* view of atonement has always been precisely how this conquest occurs. Since God does not use force, some Church Fathers such as Origen and Gregory of Nyssa suggested that God deceived Satan in Christ's sacrifice. This was viewed as appropriate, since Satan had taken possession of humans by a series of half-truths. Yet this fails to accord both with moral standards (the end—the redemption of humans—does not justify the means) and the character of God. So Gibson, like his patristic predecessors, does not tell us how this conquest occurs, only *that* the dramatic death of Christ accomplishes this feat. But perhaps, as the Church Father Gregory Nazianzenus (born about 330) observed, one cannot push metaphor into definiteness.

The Dance with Simon

The second *pas de deux* occurs in the striking encounter between Jesus and Simon of Cyrene. As Gibson portrays the scene, Simon is passing through Jerusalem with his daughter when he is conscripted by the drunken Roman soldiers to carry the cross of the beaten, staggering, failing Jesus. (Although Gibson does not flashback to the Sermon on the Mount at this point, one hears its message—if someone conscripts you to go one mile, go two instead.) Simon wants nothing to do with Jesus. "What do you want from me? I can't do that. It is none of my business." He then proclaims to the surrounding crowd his complete disassociation with this convicted criminal. "I am an innocent man forced to carry the cross of a condemned man." As Simon hoists the cross, he looks with a mixture of curiosity and suspicion at his newly acquired partner.

Gibson departs from the text of Luke, which has Simon following Jesus, to show Simon partnering to carry the cross with the convicted criminal. The dance is a paired dance, with each partner bearing his own weight. The dance steps lack rhythm and harmony as the two struggle unequally on the journey. As the procession continues, Simon becomes more protective of his fellow bearer. When Jesus falls and the crowd begins to pummel him, Simon steps in to protect the fallen. He even refuses to go on: "If you don't stop, I won't carry the cross one step further." Eventually, when Jesus falls again Simon not only lends his hand to lower and then lift his partner, but even carries his partner along with the cross. In the dance Simon bears the weakened Jesus up the hill. "We're nearly there. Almost done." Ironically, Simon carries to the hill both the instrument of death and the man who is to die and in his death carry the sins of the world. The irony is compounded when Gibson makes the Satan of the Garden a truth teller in the same way that the serpent in Eden proposed half-truths. Gibson's Satan proposed to Jesus that no one man could bear the burden of the cross, which is precisely how Gibson portrays the bearing of the cross. Simon becomes the bearer both of the cross and of the crucified, rather than the other way around. The dance ends after an eye-to-eye encounter between the exhausted cross bearers. The horror of the crucifixion both attracts and repels Simon, who is forced to flee the crucifixion, not of his own will, but by the same Roman soldiers who conducted the death march.

The atonement here takes on a meaning different from the first dance. The atonement is no longer *Christus victor* but a subjective view championed in the twelfth century by Peter Abelard. According to this position, Christ's death reveals God's love for us. Christ's dying out of love inspires us to show love to others; his suffering and death show how we can be transformed to live authentic lives for others. If Jesus, as fully human, could voluntarily die for others, so can we.

From the moment Simon takes up Jesus's cross, Jesus's only communication with Simon is nonverbal. Not words, but Jesus's resilience to the beatings, his hanging in there under the burdens of the journey, gradually overcomes the hardness of Simon's suspicions. The Simon who reluctantly leaves the crucifixion site is a different Simon from the one who protested his conscription. He is beginning to be transformed by the sheer resilience of Jesus. The dying of Christ is a motivating example.

Gibson misses, however, that a moral transformation theory of atonement requires more than a resilient death, more than the example of one irrepressible convict. A transformation atonement theory requires that it be love, not fortitude, that transforms. Simon is not changed by the loving Jesus; Simon's gaze into Jesus's eyes shows a Jesus who will not quit, not a Jesus who has compassion. Simon already has departed down the hill before we hear Jesus forgiving his torturers and caring for Mary. Gibson's story of redemption omits the love manifested in the sacrificial death.

The Dance with Mary

Simon's dance comes to a tortured end when he disappears beneath the brow of the hill just when Gibson has the trio of Mary the mother of Jesus, Mary Magdalene, and John approach the crucifixion site over the same brow. With their appearance Gibson continues their dance begun at the beginning of the film, when John stumbles into a home to inform the Mary, the mother of Jesus, and Mary Magdalene of the arrest of their son and friend. Gibson envisions their connection with the passion in a light different from that of Satan and Simon. For this trio the atonement involves sharing in the agony of the suffering and the shedding of the blood.

The dance with each of the two Marys and John runs through the film. We will focus on Jesus's *pas de deux* with his mother. From the time of Jesus's arrest, she partners with Jesus, assuming several roles. Gibson's portrayal of Mary's presence at the Sanhedrin trial inaugurates the significance of the Jesus's death for Mary. She is to suffer alongside of Jesus. When Mary senses Jesus's presence beneath the Sanhedrin, she presses her ear to the floor in sympathetic communication with her suffering son, while Jesus, shackled in the cell below, looks up, in turn sensing her presence. Mary's presence lends him strength.

Thus fortified, Jesus is brought to the flogging pillar: "My heart is ready, Father." Mary witnesses the flogging, suffering with each stroke. Though beaten down, Jesus again senses his partner suffering with him. He sees her and with every ounce of strength pulls himself upright, to the amazement and anger of the exhausted floggers. Mary gives Jesus the strength, the will to continue. When Jesus cries out, Mary with incomprehension turns, crying, "My son, when, where, how will you choose to be delivered of this?"

Mary soaks up the blood of her beaten son with Claudia's gift of burial linens. Gibson has in view the sacredness of the life-bestowing blood that oozed from the flogging given her son. In Catholic theology, nothing is more precious than the Blood of

Christ (I Peter 1:18). This emphasis on the suffering and the blood, connected to the Stages of the Cross, begins somewhere around the fourteenth century and represents a departure from the *Christus victor* motif of regal conquest advocated by the Fathers. According to Dominican theology and following the Council of Trent, Christ's blood is deemed not an accidental feature but an essential part of his humanity. Except for that which became part of the relics (witness Veronica's possession of the bloodied towel), the blood would be returned to Christ in the resurrection. The blood is essential to the humanity of Jesus, and Mary does her best to reclaim what was lost.

The *pas de deux* between Jesus and Mary becomes more pronounced on the *Via Dolorosa*. The figure is not a circle dance (as with Satan at the Roman beating), nor a partnered dance (as with Simon), but a parallel dance where their movements mirror each other—although this time with an intruder, Satan. The agony of the one is mirrored in the agony of the other, until their parallel lines briefly meet and Mary touches the head of her son. Mary announces her presence: "I am here," to which Jesus responds, "See, mother, I make all things new." This is Heidegger's "moment of vision," "the resolute rapture with which the Self is carried away to whatever possibilities and circumstances are encountered in the Situation as objects of concern, but a rapture which is *held* in resoluteness. [It is] a phenomenon which *in principle* cannot be clarified in terms of the '*now*'" (Heidegger 1996, pp. 387–88). Renewed by Mary's presence, Jesus rises and again takes up the cross. Again irony prevails, for Satan's earlier statement in the Garden rings true; the cross is too heavy for only one to bear. But instead of preventing Jesus from bearing the cross, as Satan would have it, Mary assists in the process in the only way possible for her, inspiring him with her own strength. Simon is not the only one who assists in cross bearing.

Once on the hill, Mary again plays a role in the dance of death. Seeing his mother, Jesus gathers the strength to stand as the soldiers strip off his clothes. Mary and the others suffer through the agony of the actual crucifixion, and in the end Mary approaches the cross, touches and kisses Jesus's feet, getting bloody in the process. The blood again becomes symbolic as Mary takes on herself the blood of her dying son. His life extends to her; she participates in the bloody event. The denouement is a re-enactment of the *pietà* portrayed in many religious works of art, where Mary, still unable to understand, cradles her dead son as her agony reaches its height.

Christ's atonement in the case of Mary does not connect with traditional themes, for from the Roman Catholic perspective from which Gibson made the film, Mary was sinless and hence not in need of atonement. So a penal substitution theory or moral transformation theory of the atonement would be out of place for her. Her dance with her son must take on a different character and significance. For Mary the significance of the event is not only that she participates in the agony of her son, but also that she provides the assistance of her strength throughout the process. If Jesus's main characteristic is fortitude, it is surely assisted by the indomitable spirit of Mary. No atonement emerges here; rather, the dance of death is the breaking of the heart of the mother who participates in the agony from the outset.

Gibson's Mary thus appears in the role of a co-redemptrix. As Jesus's cross is raised, Mary rises from the ground: "Let me die with you," she utters. Gibson thus reaffirms Pope Benedict XV's pronouncement that Mary not only suffered with Christ, but with him she redeemed the human race: "When her Son suffered and died, she so to say suffered and died with Him, renouncing for the salvation of men and the appeasement of the justice of God her maternal rights over her Son—and immolating her Son, as much as in her lay, so that we are entitled to say that she, with Christ, has redeemed the human race." At the foot of the cross Mary, united in her maternal agonies with those of her son, participates in a subordinate role in the mystery of Christ's passion.

Strangely, then, the self-sacrifice of Jesus has been transmuted into the sacrifice of Mary in giving up the one she loves. Although Mary cannot quite understand the events (she wonders when Jesus will end them), she engages in self-sacrifice, even to the point of being willing to die with him. Gibson views Mary as part of the salvation process when she sacrifices to torture and death the son she voluntarily bore. Here the doctrine of Christ's atonement takes a strange turn.

Self-Sacrifice and Healing

Gibson opens the film with a passage from Isaiah, where by his stripes the Suffering Servant assumes the infirmities and sins of the afflicted and effects a cure for the human predicament. Although Gibson uses the Isaiah passage to lay the groundwork for the violence and blood that characterizes the film, he makes little attempt to create a *pas de deux* of healing. Jesus's healing ministry is completely ignored.

The healing atonement model recalls that traditional societies connect sickness with moral lapse, the influence of other persons and things, or supernatural causes. One practice of traditional healers involves the alleged extraction from the body of the cause of the illness. Healers suck out the illness either directly or through removing from the body what appear to be foreign objects or fluids. The illness is then transferred to the healers, who for a time take the illness upon themselves until they can dispose of it. The process is risky for the healer, full of anxiety, since assuming another's illness can bring about the healer's own death. But even where death does not result, by assuming the illness the healers sacrifice their good for the other. Applied to the atonement, in Christ's suffering and death God addresses not merely the symptoms but also the root causes of the human predicament, initiating and implementing the atonement healing. Christ takes on the illness of sin in his own beating and death, which are curative in that they address our fundamental human predicament of sin by removing it from us, and they are restorative in returning persons to personal wholeness and to a relation with God. The difference from the traditional view of healing is that Christ's atonement provides more than temporary reprieve; his self-sacrifice is curative and finally restorative. Resurrection finally overcomes death.

Compensatory Atonement

In Gibson's rich series of dances what is missing is almost as interesting as what is present. It is somewhat puzzling that in a Catholic film about the sacrifice and death of Jesus, Gibson ignores the traditional Catholic view of atonement, developed by Anselm in the eleventh century. Anselm held that Christ restores us to God by voluntarily substituting for the reparations we owe but cannot pay God.

In a recent philosophical treatment of this view, Richard Swinburne argues that a person who has done something wrong is under obligation to atone for the action. Atonement involves four features: repentance, apology, reparations, and penance. As Anselm noted, humans cannot supply the reparations, since no matter what humans repay, the payment already belongs to God as his normal due. Some greater compensation for sin is required, which is supplied by God himself. However, since God cannot make reparations to himself, it must be supplied by someone who is both divine and human. Hence, the voluntary incarnation and death of Christ are necessary to provide genuine satisfaction for the sins committed. The atonement has significance in that it satisfies what we owe to God, giving us freedom and life.

In Gibson's emphasis on violence, blood, and fortitude, the substitution theme is lost. The film contains nothing of sin, repentance, apology, reparations, or penance. Gibson's dances, variously hellish, gory and violent, and ennobling, point to great truths about the meaning of the suffering and death of one person for another. But no dance captures the substitutionary, compensatory motif.

Yet real life provides noteworthy examples of substitutionary, supererogatory self-sacrifice. Probably one of the most well-known cases of a life-bestowing act occurred in 1941 in the Auschwitz concentration camp. According to the camp rule, if one person escaped, ten others would be executed. After one attempted escape (the escapee later was found dead in a latrine) the commandant demanded that ten men be selected to starve to death. Father Maximilian Kolbe, a Polish priest, stepped forward and requested to die in the place of one of the chosen. Surprisingly, the commandant granted his request, and Kolbe starved while ministering to the other condemned men. Kolbe's sacrificial act challenged the demonic powers that sought to dehumanize all who were compelled to enter those hellish gates.

Our Dance

It's one thing to try to find meaning in anticipating one's own death. Mitch Albom writes in *Tuesdays with Morrie*, "We don't get into the habit of standing back and looking at our lives and saying, Is this all? Is this all I want? Is something missing?" (1997, p. 65). But even more profound is the discovery of meaning in the sacrificial suffering and death of another for us. Gibson consciously assumes this task. By its *pas de deux* structure *The*

Passion draws the viewers into the atonement drama, reminding us that Christ's passion is neither abstract nor general, but cosmic and individually transforming. What remains is our response to the invitation to dance.

SOURCES

Mitch Albom. 1997. *Tuesdays with Morrie: An Old Man, a Young Man, and Life's Greatest Lesson.* New York: Doubleday.

Anselm. 1998. *Cur Deus Homo.* In *Anselm of Canterbury: The Major Works,* edited by Brian Davies (Oxford: Oxford University Press).

Gustav Aulén. 1931. *Christus Victor.* New York: Macmillan.

Margaret Cormack. 2001. *Sacrificing the Self: Perspectives on Martyrdom and Religion.* Oxford: Oxford University Press.

Martin Heidegger. 1996. *Being and Time.* Albany: State University of New York Press.

Richard Swinburne. 1989. *Responsibility and Atonement.* Oxford: Clarendon.

QUESTIONS FOR DISCUSSION

1. In what ways might one find meaning in one's own death?

2. What is the difference between finding meaning in one's own death and the meaning that another's death might have for someone? How is this illustrated in the film?

3. What theories of atonement are suggested by the film? How do they differ?

4. What characteristics distinguish martyrdom from suicide? How might this distinction be applied to the Jesus portrayed in the film?

5. What significance, if any, might Jesus's suffering and death have for us in the twenty-first century? Why did Gibson make the film? How might this significance connect to why Gibson made the film?

17

The Crisis of the Cross: God as Scandalous

PAUL K. MOSER

The Passion of the Christ suggests that the God and Father of Jesus Christ is scandalous. How could an all-loving God allow His innocent Son and Prophet to undergo barbaric torture and death by Roman crucifixion? Surely, accordingly to many philosophers and other people, this could not be part of an all-loving God's plan. The torture and the death of Jesus by Roman soldiers are, we hear, incompatible with God's loving intentions. Likewise, according to many people, *The Passion* portrays "needless violence" and "misrepresents" the person and mission of Jesus—recall the seemingly endless scourging of Jesus and its bloody aftermath. These objections come from philosophers and others of widely divergent perspectives, including many Christians, Jews, Muslims, agnostics, and atheists. Are such objections answerable? If so, how?

This chapter uses the movie to address two philosophical questions. First, could an all-loving God have purposes served by the scandalous death of Jesus? Second, how could one come to know the reality of such a God? These questions require that we begin with two other questions: Who is this "Jesus Christ," and what is his avowed purpose in undergoing crucifixion? We will understand the crucifixion of Jesus only if we understand *the one* who was crucified. Perhaps we will understand *ourselves* only if we understand Jesus and *our* role in his crucifixion.

"Who Do You Say I Am?"

Jesus asked his disciples: "Who do you say I am?" (Mark 8:29). The disciples were puzzled by this question, as are many people today, even Christians. Jesus responds by talking about his impending death and subsequent resurrection, thus suggesting that we must understand him in terms of those events. He could have pointed to his teachings, his healings, or his influence on his followers, but he did not. Why not? We need some background. It is fitting, we shall see, that *The Passion* begins with the prophecy from Isaiah 53 that God's servant would be "crushed because of our iniquities."

Jesus claims that he is the unique Son and *sole* revealer of God as Father (Matthew 11:25-26; Luke 10:21-22). Such a claim would seem delusional on the lips of any other human. In making this claim, Jesus portrays his Father as *hiding* His plans from "the wise and the intelligent." This fits with the Biblical idea that God is elusive, and it should caution us against easily presuming that we adequately understand God's purposes. A recurring Biblical theme is that God's ways are not our ways and God destroys the wisdom of the wise (Isaiah 29:14, 55:8–9; 1 Corinthians 1:19; Hebrews 3:10). *The Passion* vividly portrays God's Son as being mocked, beaten up, clad in rags, and even tortured and murdered. How could this be? How could it be part of God's loving purposes? Is God's love hidden somehow in the cross of Jesus?

The earthly life of Jesus exhibited authority and power unique among humans. According to the New Testament, Jesus has unsurpassed authority and power in human history. The movie portrays his disarming authority in a flashback where Jesus rescues the woman caught in adultery. Jesus remarks that acceptance (or rejection) of him amounts to acceptance (or rejection) of God (Matthew 10:40; 1 John 2:23). In addition, Jesus claims authority to forgive sins apart from God's Temple (Mark 2:1–12) and to oversee the final judgment as God's king (Luke 22:29–30). Likewise, Jesus symbolically presents himself as the everlasting king of Israel, after Zechariah 9:9, in his humble entry into Jerusalem on a colt (Mark 11:1–10). *The Passion* captures this with the scene of a crowd celebrating Jesus's entry into Jerusalem. The celebration is actually ironic, since Jesus was going not to a throne but to his scandalous death.

Jesus suggests that he is King David's Lord (Mark 12:35–37), and that he is greater than even King Solomon (Luke 11:31). Indeed, in reply to a question from John the Baptist (Luke 7:18–23), he alludes to Isaiah 61:1–2 and 35:5–6 to suggest that he is God's Messiah. Similarly, as the movie dramatically portrays, Jesus claims to be the messianic Son of God in response to the chief priests (Mark 14:61–64). This claim elicits the charge that Jesus is guilty of blasphemy, of exalting himself in a way that demotes God. Even if Jesus is King David's Lord, he does not promote worldly power as the way to triumph. The movie thus begins with Jesus's healing of an enemy injured by Peter's use of a sword to "protect" Jesus (Mark 14:47; John 18:10). In the movie this person appears to be puzzled and deeply moved by the mercy of Jesus. Should we be similarly moved?

In his own earthly life and ministry, according to Jesus, the *kingdom of God* had arrived: "if it is by the finger of God that I cast out the demons, then the kingdom of God has come to you" (Luke 11:20). This is a central theme of the Good News he preached and exemplified. In the parable of the vineyard (Mark 12:1-12), Jesus suggests that he is God's beloved Son who is heir to the things of God but who will be rejected by humans. Jesus predicted on at least three occasions that he would be put to death by humans but then resurrected (Mark 8:31, 9:31, 10:33–34).

Despite his predicted death, Jesus saw himself as the one sent by God to fulfill the hopes of Israel for an everlasting kingdom under God. No other human could make such an authoritative claim with any real plausibility. Jesus thus transcends the limits of human authority in a way that merits our attention. In the movie, Jesus leaves Pilate shaken by his remark that his kingdom "is not of this world" (John 18:36). Jesus is no mere moral reformer, spiritual guru, or philosophical sage. He leaves us with three options. He is either (i) patently insane (Mark 3:21), (ii) Satanic (Mark 3:22), or (iii) God's unique Son (Mark 15:39). Clearly, he was not insane. If he were, we should all become similarly insane and thereby improve the world. His not being Satanic should go without saying, after one attends to his compassionate life and teaching. The movie rightly portrays Satan and Jesus as in ongoing conflict with each other. We see this conflict in Gethsemane, at the scourging of Jesus, and while Jesus carries his cross. The third of our three options thus recommends itself. We are thus back to our opening question: How could God allow His innocent Son to be brutalized in the way portrayed by the movie?

The Scandal of the Cross

What exactly is "the scandal of the cross" (Galatians 5:11)? It stems from the *One* who was crucified. *Jesus* himself is the scandal, the scandal of his Father's reconciling love for His enemies, including us. Jesus stands absolutely alone, among leaders of the world's religions, as the self-proclaimed *atoning sacrifice from God for human sin.* As *The Passion* shows in a flashback, Jesus announces this unique role at the Last Supper. The rest of the New Testament consistently echoes this Good News: "This is my blood of the covenant, which is poured out for many" (Mark 14:22–25; Matthew 26:26–29; Luke 22:15–20). Jesus claims that his death will inaugurate the (new) covenant of God for people. He thus suggests that his death on the cross has saving (or, redemptive) significance for others. Some ancient Jewish literature acknowledges that human suffering can atone for sin (4 Maccabees 6:27–30, 9:23–25). The novelty is that Jesus, the Galilean outcast, regards his death as the means of God's new *covenant of redemption.* The covenant is God's loving promise and plan to save humans from their destructive ways via reconciliation with God as a gift unearned by humans. Could the cross of Jesus be the anchor of such a covenant?

Matthew's Gospel represents Jesus as saying that he will die "for the remission of sins" (Matthew 26:28). The atoning (= reconciling) sacrifice of Jesus as God's covenant offering for humans sets Jesus apart, decisively, from Abraham, Moses, Elijah, Confucius, Krishna (counted by some as a god), Gautama the Buddha, Muhammad, the Dalai Lama, and every other religious leader. None of these religious leaders offered himself as God's atoning sacrifice for humans.

People outside the Jesus movement have typically shared the apostle Peter's doubt that the gruesome death of Jesus is integral to God's plan of reconciliation for humans (Mark 8:31–32). Many have doubted that the crucifixion of the Son of God would be compatible with God's character of merciful love. Given that *The Passion* focuses unabashedly on the passion and the crucifixion, many Christians object to it on the ground that

the resurrection of Jesus should be given more attention than
the cross. The apostle Paul faced similar uneasiness among
Christians in Corinth. His response was forthright: "I resolved to
know nothing while I was with you except Jesus Christ *and him
crucified*" (1 Corinthians 2:2). Why? The obedient death of Jesus
is no less important than his resurrection. We shall see why.

The crucifixion seems to brand Jesus as a dismal failure. *The
Passion* shows him being held at the mercy of his enemies,
offering no resistence, and suffering excruciating abuse. Even
so, the cross is the place of God's turnaround *victory*. Out of the
crushing defeat of Jesus, God brings proof of His love and forgiveness toward us, His enemies. The cross is God's *grand
reversal* of the darkest human tragedy. As Paul says: "the message of the cross is foolishness to those who are perishing, but
to us who are being saved it is the power of God. Jews demand
miraculous signs and Greeks look for wisdom, but we preach
Christ crucified: a stumbling block to Jews and foolishness to
Gentiles, but to those whom God has called, both Jews and
Greeks, Christ the power of God and the wisdom of God. For
the foolishness of God is wiser than man's wisdom, and the
weakness of God is stronger than man's strength" (1 Corinthians
1:18, 22–25). The power of God's self-giving love is demonstrated in the crucified Jesus, the One whom God approvingly
raised from his death. This invincible power of divine merciful
love overcomes even death, thereby surpassing any human
power. Jesus's resurrection is God's indelible signature of
approval on His crucified, obedient Son. His resurrection gets
significance from the cross, where Jesus gave full obedience to
his Father to redeem us.

God sent His Son, Jesus, for a definite purpose: to prove
God's merciful love for all people, even His enemies (Romans
5:6–8). *The Passion*, accordingly, portrays the crucified Jesus as
asking for forgiveness for those who have crucified him (Luke
23:34). He came to identify with us in our troubles, while he represented his Father in faithful, self-giving love. He thus represents *both* God *and* humans, seeking to reconcile humans to his
Father via his gift of merciful love. His obedient death shows
how far he and his Father will go—even to gruesome death—to
bring us to God. Jesus gives us all he has in love to demonstrate
that God loves us without limit and offers us the gift of unearned
friendship with Himself (John 3:16–17, 15:13–14).

God uses the cross of Jesus as the place where our selfish rebellion against God is mercifully judged and forgiven. This does *not* mean that God punished Jesus. The New Testament does not teach this, contrary to some theologians. God sent Jesus into our nexus of rebellion to undergo suffering and death that God would deem adequate for dealing justly, under divine grace, with our rebellion against God. Jesus thus pays the price on our behalf, and removes the need for fear, condemnation, shame, guilt, and punishment among us (Romans 8:1). Jesus thereby reconciles us to his Father, as he becomes our Lord and Redeemer.

The cross of Jesus is the focal point of divine-human reconciliation. It is the very heart of the Jesus movement and its Good News of God's amazing gift of gracious love (1 Corinthians 2:2). The self-giving, crucified Jesus is the power and the mirror-image of the all-loving God. Jesus himself, as the human image of God, serves as distinctive *evidence* of God's reality and unsurpassable love. He fulfills his Father's loving plan to reconcile us to Himself. We need to look for the right kind of evidence of God, while we set aside our misleading preconceptions of such evidence. *The Passion*'s shocking portrayal of torture should not obscure God's use of the torture for good, even our good. The movie is right in putting the cross first and dwelling on its inhumanity and humiliation. The sacrifice of the cross, in all its gruesome horror, is essential to a correct understanding of Jesus's significance. The scourging that precedes it, to which the movie gives abundant attention, prepares the way for the defining moment and sacrifice of Jesus.

The ultimate motive for the cross is the Father's *holy, righteous love* for us humans (Romans 3:21–26). Paul remarks: "God proves His own love for us in that while we were still sinners, Christ died for us. . . . Since we have now been *justified by his blood*, how much more shall we be saved by him from *the wrath* [of God]! . . . [W]hen we were enemies [of God], we were *reconciled* to Him through *the death* of his Son. . . ." (Romans 5:8–10). The living God of love is also a God of *righteous wrath* (Romans 1:18), and *because* He loves us and all other sinners, He has wrath toward sin. He seeks to *reconcile* us to (relationship with) Himself in a way that exceeds mere forgiveness and satisfies His holy standard of genuine, *righteous* love. Through the loving self-sacrifice of Jesus, *God* meets this standard *for us*, when we could not and would not. He thereby welcomes us to Himself as our righteous loving Father. As Paul says, "God was in Christ reconciling the world to Himself," not counting our sins against us (2 Corinthians 5:19). This is the heart of the Good News of Jesus Christ. This is God's scandalous holy love. It should shock us and shake us to our core. We typically hold a different, less demanding standard of love, and we thereby domesticate God. *We* thus pretend to be God. God meets our selfish pretension with scandalous love that is righteous and merciful. In emphasizing this, the movie shocks us. The image of a suffering self-giving God is nothing but scandalous. Coercive power giving way to self-giving love makes no sense to us in the ordinary terms we use to deal with the world.

The heart of the cross *for Jesus* is his perfectly loving *obedience to his Father on our behalf*, and not just his physical suffering. We see this exemplified by Jesus in Gethsemane. The movie rightly begins the passion there, where Jesus resolves to obey his Father, and then crushes the snake's (Satan's) head (Genesis 3:15). Later, it shows Jesus resolutely, even eagerly, embracing the cross. Paul vividly identifies the crucial role of Jesus's obedience. He refers to: "Christ Jesus, who, being in the form of God, did not consider equality with God something to be grasped, but he emptied himself, taking the form of a servant, being made in human likeness. Being found in appearance as a man, he humbled himself and became *obedient to death*, even death on a cross" (Philippians 2:6–8; Romans 5:19). Jesus can be and is our "Passover lamb" (1 Corinthians. 5:7), our "sacrifice of atonement" (Romans 3:25), because he is perfectly obedient, fully righteous, in the eyes of his holy Father. He became "a curse for us" to save us from the law's curse (Galatians 3:13). His perfectly obedient life toward God is an acceptable sacrifice to God for us. Gethsemane and the Last Supper, as depicted by the movie, manifest these lessons. Gethsemane shows Jesus passionately resolving to put his Father's will first, and the Last Supper shows Jesus portraying, with the bread and the wine as his body and his blood, the ultimate self-sacrifice pleasing to his Father.

Given God's righteousness and our sin, we desperately need a perfect atoning sacrifice, and *only* the *perfectly obedient* Jesus can and does provide it in his sacrificial love for us, at the command of his Father. God's power of sacrificial love is made perfect in Jesus's weakness on the cross (2 Corinthians 12:9). Without Jesus, we have no reconciler to bring us to the holy living God. Jesus alone voluntarily pays the price of our selfish rebellion against God by obediently meeting God's standard of righteous, sacrificial love. For this reason, Jesus alone is Lord and Savior who takes away the sin of the world (John 1:29; 1 John 2:2).

The Myth of a Nice God

God is not "nice," contrary to popular expectations. Nor is God out to win a popularity contest. God's purposes are much more profound than popularity contests, and they are not constrained by human purposes, expectations, or standards. God's own character is the ultimate constraint for God's purposes and plans.

Any being worthy of the pre-eminent title "God" must be worthy of worship. This means that God must be morally perfect. A being merits the full commitment of worship only if that being is morally perfect. It follows further that God must be all-loving, even perfectly loving. A being is morally perfect only if that being is perfectly loving. God, then, must care about us perfectly, in a way that seeks to bring about whatever is truly good for us. What is truly *good* for us, however, is not always the same as what we *want*. Hence, God is not required to be "nice" by ordinary standards. God is not a "people-pleaser" in the way that many humans seek to be. The all-loving God is too loving to be a people-pleaser. God cares too much about us to settle for satisfying our wants, and for this we should be grateful.

The myth of the "nice" God looms large in ordinary and philosophical thinking. It leads to misguided conceptions of God and misleading standards for evidence of God's reality. As a result, the God of scandalous love is domesticated, trivialized, and even rejected. We domesticate God when we approach or even portray God on our terms, by our standards, without "the scandal of the cross." Natural theology, advanced by philosophers with various "arguments for God's existence," typically domesticates God in this way. It leaves us at most with the abstract and innocuous "god of the philosophers," and not the living and suffering God of Abraham, Isaac, Jacob, and Jesus. The "nice" god of the philosophers does not need the cross of

Jesus, for this god is not set on redeeming humans from their rebellious ways. The nice god would say "I'm OK, you're OK, and we have no need for the cross." This, of course, is *not* the self-giving suffering God who sends Jesus to a scandalous death on the cross for human sinners. The movie does not promote the nice god of the philosophers. Its God, in keeping with Jesus, goes against our "nice," shallow, and selfish approaches to love. *The Passion* captures God's character of self-giving love by showing Jesus as the obedient Son who gives all he has for the sake of his Father's plan to restore us to Himself. Jesus, in agreement with his Father, provides us with what we truly need, not just what we may want.

Gethsemane and Forgiveness

Humans must *receive* the undeserved gift of (1) God's sacrifice for us in Jesus and thereby (2) God's Holy Spirit sent by Jesus (Galatians 3:1–2). We receive this gift by *faith*, or *trust*, in God, which includes *obedience* to the Good News of Jesus (Romans 10:16–17; 2 Thessalonians 1:8; Hebrews 5:9; Matthew 7:21). In saving faith, we are "crucified with Jesus" in our obedient love toward His Father. The theme of *our cross-bearing with Jesus* pervades the New Testament (Mark 8:34–35; Matthew 10:37–39; Luke 14:25–27; Galatians 2:20–21, 5:24–25; Romans 6:5–11). *The Passion* shows the cross-bearing of Jesus to be deliberate and slow, and thus suggests that our own cross-bearing will not be coincidental or rushed.

We *receive* the gift of life in the saving cross of Jesus *only as we live out the cross of self-sacrificial love toward God on behalf of others*. Faith in God includes dying with Jesus as we respond to his Father's love with obedient love as exemplified by Jesus in Gethsemane: Not what I will, Father, but what *You* will! (Mark 14:36; Matthew 26:39; Luke 22:42). This attitude is the heart of obeying God. The shocking love of his cross is exactly what we need, as an atoning gift *and* as a way of life. *The Passion* suggests this lesson in its opening scene, where Jesus in Gethsemane resolutely sets his life on a path that will prove God's self-giving love for us.

A dominant Biblical theme is that people are alienated from God owing to their rebellion against God. The Last Supper message in the movie assumes this. The rebellion stems from our selfish disobedience to God's love commands: the commands that we love God with all we are and have and that we love others as we love ourselves (Mark 12:28–31). We habitually live our lives as if we have no need of either these commands or the all-loving God who issued them for our own good. Hence, we all share to some degree in the rebellious attitude that led to the scandalous crucifixion of Jesus. Mel Gibson thus fittingly gave *himself* a role of holding one of the nails in the movie's crucifixion scene. We reject our God-given status as creatures, and we presume to know better than God regarding what is good for us. In willfully exalting ourselves, we demote God from His status as Lord of our lives. We pretend to be God. Like the Roman soldiers, we seek to be the true God's executioner. Jesus's crucifixion shows this.

In opposing God, we undermine our own lives. We choose to cling to sources of supposed security that hinder our loving and trusting God. These include wealth, health, education, and fame. We lapse into idolatry. We move toward bondage and death, and away from freedom and life. When faced with God's standard of unselfish love in the crucified Jesus, we experience fear, guilt, shame, and hiding. Judas Iscariot, who betrayed Jesus, represents this vividly in the movie. He finally senses his alienation from the merciful Jesus, and becomes overwhelmed with guilt and shame, even to the point of suicide. Our own alienation from God deepens and widens. We become weary and devoid of joy and peace. Death looms large. We have no escape. We are lost indeed, despite the diversions and distractions we use to avoid the God who calls us from death into His life. Will we follow Judas Iscariot into suicide?

In the midst of our self-made mess, the living God comes to us. Amazingly, God comes not with condemnation but rather with forgiveness, with merciful love. He comes not to meet our twisted expectations but instead to give us what we truly need. He meets with resistance and rejection from us, but He does not give up. Instead, He goes for broke: He sends His beloved Son. He stoops low, humbly, to meet us in self-giving compassionate love, in Jesus. God is, in Jesus, proclaiming forgiveness to His enemies (including us), and extending an offer of reconciliation, of friendship on God's life-giving terms of unselfish love. The movie ascribes to Jesus, on his way to be crucified, a line from the book of Revelation spoken to his mother: "Behold I make all things new!" (Revelation 21:5). In particular, Jesus renews relationships with his Father.

God's call to us is a Good News call of compassionate forgiveness. When God pronounces forgiveness upon us, we are being *judged* by God's love as having fallen short of His love commands. We are judged as needing forgiveness and as being worthy of judgment, owing to our rebellion against God's love commands. We expect judgment as condemnation, but instead we receive judgment as merciful forgiveness in Jesus. This is the core of the Good News, the Gospel, of Jesus Christ. Part of this core is that we receive, as a free gift, the very Spirit of Jesus and of His Father. *The Passion* vividly illustrates God's forgiveness in a flashback to Jesus who frees a woman caught in adultery from punishment by stoning.

In Jesus, God has taken care of any supposed or self-imposed ground for human alienation or hiding owing to human rebellion. In Jesus, God offers compassionate forgiveness to all people, however alienated and rebellious they are. God counts the death of Jesus as any needed payment for justly forgiving our rebellion. God's offered reconciliation of us to Himself is a free, unearned gift. It undermines any of our distorted conceptions of a "just" reconciliation. God's gracious gift of Jesus sets the standard for justice in reconciliation. This is a central theme of Paul's letter to the Romans (Romans 3:21–26), and it is foreshadowed in the parable of the workers in the vineyard (Matthew 20:1–16). Divine reconciliation comes in a kind of unselfish, suffering love foreign to us and our inferior, "nice" and selfish ways. It shatters our distorted ideas, including our philosophical preconceptions, about God and about our value before God.

In receiving Jesus as our Lord, we receive God's gracious offer of forgiveness and reconciliation. We thereby receive the gift we need to live in unselfish freedom and love. Receiving Jesus as Lord consists in loving, trusting, and obeying him in the spirit of Gethsemane: His will must be authoritative over our wills, just as in the Garden Jesus gave his Father's will priority over his own. We must forgive others as God has forgiven us (Matthew 6:15); otherwise, we are not truly receiving God's universal offer of forgiveness. This is a tall order, because our forgiving others, including our enemies, requires that we love them (Matthew 5:43–45), but we lack the power to love our enemies on our own. Such rare forgiveness and love must be empowered by our trusting God to be faithful to us. Otherwise, our selfish fears will hinder us. *The Passion* powerfully represents Jesus as resisting the temptation to be selfish in Gethsemane, where he obeys his Father's call to offer his life on our behalf.

The proper reception of God's forgiving love requires that I subject my faulty, selfish will to God's perfect, loving will. This is an ongoing struggle, and not just an intellectual commitment. It requires that I seek help from God, and it cuts to the core of my intentions and desires, the attitudes that motivate me. It is thus a power struggle between God and me, and in the end I will not defeat God. I am thus well advised to fold now, without delay.

Our second opening question concerned how we can know the God of self-giving love. We can now appreciate the answer. The extent to which we know God as our loving Father depends on the extent to which we are gratefully willing to acknowledge God's non-coercive authority for us and, as a result, to participate in God's life of redemptive love (1 John 2:3–6). It thus becomes obvious why we humans (not just atheists and agnostics) have difficulty in knowing God as our loving Father. The difficulty comes from our resisting God's authority for us, just as Satan does in the movie when he tries to dissuade Jesus from his atoning purpose. The heart of this resistance is our resisting God's desired *agape transformation* of us: that is, our change in the direction of God's morally perfect all-loving character. We contradict Gethsemane in saying or in acting as if we are saying: "Not what You will, God, but what *I* will." We thus supplant God's will, and thereby steal the place of God. We do this whenever we yield to selfishness. We are then at odds with the only One who can give us lasting joy and peace. "The one who does not love does not know God, because God is love" (1 John 4:8).

Our knowing God as loving Father, requires our welcoming and embracing a child-parent, or filial, relationship to God. It includes filial trust in God as one's rescuer from all that is bad, including moral failure and death. Its heart of obedience emerges in Gethsemane, in Jesus's obedient prayer to his Father: "Not what I will, but what You will." Such filial knowledge rarely, if ever, emerges in philosophy of religion or even in

Christian approaches to knowledge of God. The result is wide-spread misunderstanding of suitable knowledge of the living God. We need to understand knowledge of God in terms of the Gethsemane of Jesus rather than the Athens of philosophers.

The Real Jesus as Scandalous

The scandal is that despite God's self-giving love for us, we rebel in ways that call for the suffering of God's innocent Son. This is the crisis of the cross. The crucified Jesus is a scandal to us and to religion as we know it, but the crucified Jesus is the only real Jesus. So, the real Jesus is, as always, the odd man out. He stands outside and knocks, with his cross and wounds of love, awaiting a receptive entry. *The Passion* conveys this Good News message clearly. It vividly portrays God and His Son as taking the merciful initiative in coming to us with self-giving, suffering love on our behalf. Jesus suffers long and lays down his life for us, and his Father raises him up again, with love's approval.

Will we welcome the real, scandalous Jesus? We move now from a movie to reality. As we stop pretending to be God, the true God will emerge as real in our lives. Will we let God be God? Will we let Jesus be Jesus? Will we come to see who we really are, through the eyes of the crucified Jesus, the savior of the world?*

SOURCES

Wesley Carr. 1992. *Tested by the Cross*. London: Harper.

Michael J. Gorman. 2001. *Cruciformity: Paul's Narrative Spirituality of the Cross*. Grand Rapids: Eerdmans.

Luke T. Johnson. 1999. *Living Jesus: Learning the Heart of the Gospel*. San Francisco: Harper.

Leon Morris. 1981. *Testaments of Love: A Study of Love in the Bible*. Grand Rapids: Eerdmans.

Paul Moser. 2002. Cognitive Idolatry and Divine Hiding. In Daniel Howard-Snyder and Paul Moser, eds., *Divine Hiddenness: New Essays* (Cambridge: Cambridge University Press), pp. 120–148.

Helmut Thielicke. 1959. *The Waiting Father: Sermons on the Parables of Jesus*. New York: Harper.

* Many thanks to Linda Mainey for very helpful comments.

QUESTIONS FOR DISCUSSION

1. Would an all-loving God allow God's innocent Son to suffer and to die by crucifixion? If so, why?

2. If God is perfectly loving, could God be a "people-pleaser" who aims mainly to satisfy our wants? Would an all-loving God seek to satisfy our true *needs* rather than our wants?

3. If God wants humans to be transformed into God's all-loving character, what place would obedience have in our coming to know God? Would God seek to change our *wills* (and our desires and intentions) and not just our beliefs?

4. Who is in a position to say how God must relate to us, in giving us evidence and knowledge of God? God or humans? Do we naively presume to be able to say how God must reveal Himself to us?

5. What is idolatry? Do we commit a kind of idolatry when we demand that God meet our standards for how God should be revealed to us?

V

Who Is Morally Responsible?

18

Christ's Choice: Could It Have Been Different?

JONATHAN J. SANFORD

> No one takes my life from me, but I lay it down of my own accord. I have power to lay it down and power to take it up again. This command is from my Father.
>
> —Christ, in Gibson's *The Passion of the Christ*

One set of questions Gibson's *The Passion of the Christ* brings to the fore center around why the way of Christ was the way of the cross. Why did it have to be like that? The movie vividly presents the pain, physical and emotional, that Christ suffered. Think of the scourging scene where Christ's flesh is flying from his body, or of the anguish in his eyes as he looks at his chief apostle, Peter, after being denied three times. We ask ourselves why Christ, or anyone for that matter, would willingly go through with it. Did Christ have to? Central to Christ as he is depicted in the film is that he *chose* to suffer. We see the full moon, the olive trees in the garden, and Christ, alone, imploring his Father: "Hear me, Father. Rise up, defend me. Save me from the traps they set for me."

Satan knows of Christ's anguish, and arrives on the scene to suck hope from Christ by ridiculing his goal of saving humanity through suffering as foolishness. We see the curl of triumph about to wrap itself around Satan's mouth as Christ is on the verge of cracking. He asks his Father to take his chalice—his allotted portion of suffering—from him, but nonetheless *chooses* to submit his will to his Father's: "But let your will be done, not mine." Satan makes one last attempt to strike at Christ, this time seeking to sting the very core of his being: "Who is your father? Who are you?" But Christ knows the answers to those questions, and his choice is already made as he rises and smashes the head of the serpent which represents temptation, emboldened for his passion. Why this choice? Was this the choice of a madmen? Did he really have a choice? In what sense might it be necessary that Christ suffer and die? Could Christ's choice have been different?

Was It Necessary?

Perhaps you have given no thought to your use of the term 'necessity' and its cognates. But if you have, you probably noticed that you use the term to mean different things. For instance, let's say you suddenly realize that if you don't return home immediately to turn off the burner on your stove, your house will catch on fire and burn to the ground. You'd like to spend time with your friend, but you hardly need to reflect on the decision to hurry home. There is the force of necessity in this example, but you are also exercising choice. We might call this *necessity of the end*. If the end is to be accomplished, it is necessary that you do one thing and not another.

There are other kinds of necessity where you don't have any choice in the matter. The way gravity causes you to fall on things you'd rather not serves as a ready example of this sort of necessity. We might call this *necessity of compulsion*.

Another sort of necessity where you don't have choice is on the order of nature, or the way things are. For instance, because you are human you don't fly on your own accord like a bird. It is not in your nature. But there were no birds in my local theater when I watched *The Passion of the Christ*, and if there were some in yours then we can be sure they missed the central points of the film. It is not in the nature of birds to understand films. The point is that beings are what they are, and this puts certain limits on them that are intrinsically tied to their capabilities. We might call this last instance of necessity *necessity of nature*. Although you don't have a choice about this necessity, it is not in every case incompatible with choice. This is so because some beings are, by their very nature, choice-makers. Human beings are one example: We have a nature that necessarily involves the exercise of free choice.

In determining whether Christ's choice could have been different, we need to examine it from the vantage point of these three different kinds of necessity: Was Christ's choice necessary to accomplish an end? Was Christ's choice compelled by some external force? And, was it in Christ's nature that he *had* to die on the cross?

Redeeming Humanity

Consider again the words of Satan to Christ in the Garden of Gethsemane: "Do you really believe that one man can bear the full burden? . . . No one can carry this burden, I tell you. It is far too heavy. Saving their souls is too costly. No one. Ever. No. Never". Satan knew what Christ was up to. This androgynous being chides Christ that it is not possible for one man to bear the sins of all, that his earthly mission is without hope. Why try? Why suffer for nothing? Why indeed, unless Christ had some reason to hope that his passion would be effective, unless he *knew* that it was possible to bear the sins of humanity on his back on his way up Golgotha. And he *does* know, or at least thinks he knows. Consider the scene where Mary watches her son fall beneath his cross. Christ's flesh is in tatters and he's covered in filth, laying on the ground unable to get up–seemingly as low as a man can get. Mary runs to him: "I'm here." You'd expect a man in that situation to weep, to complain, to lie there in piteous agony. Christ should be broken by now. But he's not. He encourages his mother with words—amazing words which are so incongruous to the plight he's in—that explain the whole meaning of his passion: "See, mother, I make all things new."

Why on earth would Christ be in a position where he would have to suffer for everyone else in order to save them? Why in heaven would God the Father allow, or even require, such punishment? What sort of logic is behind this? To answer this we have to consider justice and mercy, and consider them from God's point of view.

The traditional account of justice conceives it as "to give each his or her due." The Judeo-Christian Scriptures have it that our first ancestors, Adam and Eve, failed in this. Instead of giving to God his due they robbed him, and they stained their offspring with the same sin in the process. But did they really do harm to God himself? How could that be possible if God is all-powerful and complete in his own being? Well, it is not possible regarding God himself. Rather, they harmed their relationship to God, the harmony that existed between God and his human creatures.

Why did God make this law, knowing full well that Adam and Eve would violate it? Doesn't this seem to make God a fickle tyrant playing games with his subjects, teasing Adam and Eve like some dog trainers who dangle meat in front of a dog only to spank it when it goes for it? Hardly. The law regarding the tree stands for all of God's laws: They are for *our* own good. They are meant to ensure healthy relationships among humans and between humans and God. Right living, the happy life, necessarily requires regulation, for we can't flourish except in doing what's right. But still, couldn't God just waive the consequences of the offense? Why does he permit the natural consequences of contravening his laws? Wouldn't simply ignoring our offence be more merciful?

Well, frankly, no. First of all, it would make a liar of God, like the bad parent who threatens his or her child with interminable groundings or other varieties of "big trouble when you get home!" only to never follow through. Second, it makes a mockery of sin by making it of no consequence. We've all felt the weight of wrongdoing, and the desire to "make things right again" with whomever we've offended. But making things right again with God is no easy matter, because the force of the consequences of Adam and Eve's free choice is that they harmed themselves in such manner that they *couldn't* live in a proper relationship with God.

And so here we come back to why Christ *had* to suffer. He stands in, as the perfect sacrifice, for all sinful humanity. His passion is both a rectifying of all past and future wrongs, and an enabling of all future rights. He not only repairs the disharmony between human beings and God, but he repairs humanity's wounded nature, making it even better than before we messed up. God needs nothing, but justice is what it is because God is what he is. Justice is always relational, between two or more parties, and it is the relation between human beings and God that is in need of restoration.

Rather than pointing to a bloodthirsty or fickle God, humanity's need for redemption points to God's mercy in several ways. First, it reveals how we are blessed, or some would say cursed,

with the burden of free choice. We can choose to harm ourselves and others with our choices, but we can also do great
good, and enjoy experiences entirely unknowable to a being
not so endowed. Second, it shows that God performs the great
honor of taking us seriously. All of us, like Adam and Eve, want
something that cannot be ours. We want to be God, but we
can't. When we act in such a manner that we try to take what
doesn't belong to us, God allows us to fail. Finally, God himself
gives us the means to be restored to the right relationship with
him. He gives the Christ, his very self in the person of his Son,
to bear the brunt of the consequences of our own actions. This
is a free act. God was not forced to do this. He could have let
us suffer forever the effects of our poor choices. Redeeming
humanity does not involve the necessity of compulsion. But it
does involve the necessity of the end. *If* justice is to be repaired,
then *something* has to be done by God to repair it. Could God
have found another means besides the passion of his son? No
doubt he in his power and wisdom could. But there are better
and worse ways to accomplish goals, and it is more reasonable
to assume that God chose the best way, one that would heal not
only the offense to justice, but humanity itself.

Who Is This Christ?

The Christ we discover in *The Passion* is no ordinary man, he is
the God-man. At least, he certainly appears in every respect to
be a man, for he looks like a man, eats like a man, speaks like
a man, loves his mom like a man, and bleeds like a man. But
this man, with bloodied face and his good eye trained on
Caiaphas, also claims to be God—He Who Is: "I AM, and you
will see the Son of Man seated at the right hand of power and
coming on the clouds of heaven." Christ could, we might suppose, be a liar. But this would be out of sync with the rest of his
actions, all of which exhibit moral excellence.

But perhaps, we might suppose, Christ was mad. But again,
this too would be out of character for the man who so wisely,
so sanely, turned back the would-be-executioners of the woman
caught in adultery, which Gibson identifies with Mary
Magdelene when she recalls first meeting Christ as she sops his
blood from the paving stones around the pillar. The same calm-
ness is on display just after Judas betrays the Son of Man with a

kiss: guards and Christ's followers are swirling in a confused frenzy while Christ alone remains calm, admonishing Peter, "Put it down. Those who live by the sword die by the sword," and commanding a Temple guard to also lay down his weapon. He tends to the severed ear of the guard, Malchus, who is subsequently so astounded–and perhaps experiencing the first moment of conversion–that he remains behind, spellbound. Christ, unlike so many other characters in the film, is presented as calm and in his right mind throughout.

Finally, if Christ were either a liar or a madman, then he could have freely laid down his life—as he says he does in the quote at the beginning of this chapter—but he could not take it up again, as he does in the very last sequence of the film. God cannot die, but a man can. A man can't raise himself from the dead, but a God-man can.

So, who is this Christ? *The Passion of the Christ* makes it plain that he is the Son of the living God, who calls God his *"Abba"*, his daddy; a man, who suffers and dies; and God, who encourages his friends around the table at the Last Supper to have faith in him: "You know that I am the Way, the Truth, and the Life." He is one person, who in his humanity suffers terribly, and who in his divinity is capable of elevating the rest of humanity to perfect communion with himself, because he has joined humanity to himself in himself. As a man who has been completely unified with God in his own person, Christ exercises both his human and divine wills to execute single choices that accomplish singular ends, and in this case to accomplish the end of redeeming humanity through offering himself as sacrifice.

Christ's Struggle

But wait a minute, if Christ is such a perfect unity of man and God, why does he struggle so much in the Garden of Gethsemane? In that first scene he is doubled over in agony, and beads of sweat and blood pour down his face and drip from his beard. Doesn't this indicate that at least some element in Christ is working against the purpose of offering himself as sacrifice? Sure, as a man Christ is inclined to those things that are good for human beings, and against those things that are bad for human beings. In the Garden Christ is anticipating what the movie unfolds, that he is to be betrayed, falsely accused, convicted, abandoned, spat on, hit, dragged about, scourged, mocked, and crucified. These are all certainly natural evils for a human being. It would be truly perverse of Christ to be inclined to any of these things. He doesn't want these things, his human nature is repulsed by them, and yet his human nature in its higher faculties is capable of recognizing that these things are necessary to accomplish the end which he wants more than he doesn't want the means to that end: The end of redeeming humanity. And so he struggles, he *must* struggle, to quiet his natural repugnance to torture and death in order to conquer death. What we see in Christ's struggle to conform the whole of his self to the will of the Father in the Gethsemane scene, and then later in the scourging scene when Satan appears with a demon child to mock the strength that Christ draws from his mother, is not a lack of perfect union between his humanity and divinity, but rather the difficulty of maintaining this unity. There is drama in the execution of Christ's choice. It doesn't come easily, but it does come, and necessarily so.

What is the alternative to Christ's choice? There are, I suppose a myriad of other possible actions we could imagine. All of them would involve, however, the essential aspect of *not* doing what he knew to be right. Nonetheless, in refusing to drink the cup poured him, he might have done many things that are good in some respect. It is good to preserve one's life, for instance. But Christ tells his disciples in one of the Last Supper flashbacks of the movie that "there is no greater love for a man than to lay down his life for his friends," and he knows that this is the time to put aside the good of preserving his own life in order to die for others. It is good to stop people from doing evil things. He knew not just that one of his disciples would betray him, but who and when and how. He could have stopped Judas from betraying him, though he might have only stopped Judas from trying to betray him through force. If he wasn't imprisoned, he could have prevented Peter's denials of him, at least *those* three. Maybe if Christ chose to speak eloquently at his trial before Caiaphas and like a good politician avoided answering the question of whether he was the Messiah, or if he had not met Herod with perfect silence and instead performed some minor miracle as requested, or if before Pilate he would have convinced him that it was far worse to allow this innocent man to be crucified than it would be to satiate the crowds calling for

his death, he could have then prevented them from condemning him, and so saved them the offense of having done just that.

But it was the better choice for Christ to allow these people,
and so many others, to contribute to his passion. For Christ, just
like his Father, has a way of taking us seriously—which means
respecting our freedom to choose good or evil. Judas was permitted to betray Christ, but he could have fully repented his
deed instead of killing himself, and been the better for it. Peter
did repent of his denials, and certainly became better for it.
Who knows what might have happened later in the hearts of
Caiaphas, Herod, or Pilate? For just as they were free to condemn Christ, they were free to repent of their deeds.

The deepest problem with any other choice than the one
made by Christ is that none of them would have been in accord
with the will of the Father, none of them would have been in
accord with Christ's own divine will. None of them, no matter
what good might have come from them, could ever be wholly
good because Christ would have failed in obedience, and at the
same time failed to effect the immeasurable and total good of
conquering death and redeeming humanity.

Still, in this chapter we are not so much asking whether
Christ's choice *should* have been different, as whether it *could*
have been different. Much of what I've argued already has been
to show that, far from being the choice of a madman or liar,
there is a deep reason why Christ had to suffer, die, and rise
again. This helps us answer whether Christ's choice could have
been different, by suggesting that it should have been just what
it was. The two questions are intimately related. And yet, there
is still the lingering possibility that Christ's choice could have
been different, even if in being different it would not have been
the best. He is tempted in the Garden by Satan, just as he was
in the desert. He struggles interiorly at different stages of his
passion, as in those moments in the scourging scene before he
rises to receive the second and even more severe round of
scourging. So often in Gibson's film Christ looks to his mother
for support and inspiration, mirroring with his actions the words
she utters when Christ is first brought before the Sanhedrin and
by which she has lived since first learning of her special role in
God's plan: "So it has begun, Lord. So be it." Why don't all of
these examples, and more besides, suggest that Christ's choice
to go through with his passion, and each of his successive

choices to keep going through with it, hangs delicately upon Christ's perpetual choice to sacrifice himself?

I want to suggest that they do: Christ's choice really is precarious, as precarious as every genuine choice, but also it *could not have been different*. Perhaps this answer sounds contradictory. After all, how can one claim that something necessarily happens the way it happened, and that what happens is through the execution of a genuinely free choice? Seeing how these two claims are not in opposition to each other requires that we reflect further on the person of Christ, a person who is a unity of two natures.

Christ is the perfect God-man. This implies that not only does the unity of God and man achieve perfect personal unity in the one Christ, but that this person, the Christ, is perfect in his humanity as well as in his divinity. Christ is wholly without the stain of sin, original or otherwise. He has the perfection of every human virtue, one of which is practical wisdom–or what philosophers used to call "prudence." Practical wisdom is a perfection of the human intellect which is concerned with directing actions toward what has been determined to be the morally best course of action. This best course of action is accomplished with the help of additional virtues, such as courage and temperance, that have as important aspects of their function keeping all of our various desires and appetites in proper order. Those moral virtues are tested when Christ struggles to maintain the course of action he already knows in his wisdom to be the best. But it is crucial to see that Christ, considered in his humanity, is already of such a character that for him to do something that is not in accord with what he knows to be the best action would be so wholly out of character as to be nearly unimaginable. His character was so noble and good that it had become, as Aristotle (384–322 B.C.) would call it, a second nature: His human nature was not just that of any human nature, but that of an individual human nature that is fully flourishing. There were no apparent flaws in this character whatsoever, and so no apparent underlying currents of disordered appetites that might prompt an act of disobedience.

Nevertheless, 'nearly unimaginable' does not yet take on the force of 'impossible'. If only a perfect man, it indeed would only be nearly unimaginable for him to overtly disobey what he knew to be the will of God. But perhaps if we throw into our considerations here the fact that Christ would have foreseen exactly the toll to be leveled against him in his passion—every curse hurled at him, every lash of the scourge, every thorn shoved into his head—it is much less unimaginable that he would have made a choice out of character. But even if an alternative choice for Christ were nearly unimaginable, we are still a long way from it being impossible. It is always possible for a human being to fail, but is it ever possible for God? We have to say "no," if in fact God is truly all-powerful and so always effective in bringing to fruition his goals. When we consider Christ's situation as he reflected on his soon to occur passion, we need to keep in mind that he is more than a man, he is a man-God. And it is, I suggest, Christ's divinity that keeps Christ's humanity on course, so to speak, in its perfection. If only a man, Christ may well have made a different choice, but as a man in perfect union with God in his very person, Christ could not have but made the choice he did.

But someone might ask, what happens to the supposed freedom of Christ's choice? If he could not but choose to submit himself to the will of God the Father, how is it that he had any choice in the matter whatsoever? To answer this, we must first recognize that there is not that sort of necessity involved in his choice which is by its very nature wholly incompatible with freedom, namely the necessity of compulsion. There is nothing, so to speak, behind Christ forcing his choice in the way that one billiard ball forces another to move. There is no exterior fate acting upon Christ in the way that Greek dramatists imagined the workings of necessity. There is no overwhelming urge within Christ blindly compelling him to do what he did in the way that Friedrich Nietzsche (1844–1900), for instance, would describe his will to power, or the way that Arthur Schopenhauer (1788–1860) might describe his will to annihilation. Christ's choice was entirely contingent, it follows upon an act of his intellect and will. And yet, his intellect and will being *his*, informed as they were with the plan of the Father and emboldened as they were with the grace of union with God himself, this contingent act could not but be what it was. Christ, in his humanity, enjoyed that very subjection to the Truth in his very person which is the goal of human life. He enjoyed perfect freedom in each of his actions, and necessarily brought to fruition the plan of God—and does so in perpetuity.

Through Christ's divine nature he necessarily accomplished the will of his Father, a will he shared as his very own. Christ as God shared everything with the Father, knew the Father's plan for salvation, and had the common purpose of effecting it. It is in the necessity of the nature of Christ, insofar as he is the Divine One, that he made the choice he made. But Christ in his humanity is a different matter. Humans have rebelled, and continue to rebel, against God's will. But in Christ, there is not *just* a human nature *and then* a divine nature; here is a human nature that is perfectly wed to the divine nature in the same person. In Christ, humanity is elevated and made not just as good as it can be, but as good as it can be *insofar* as it is joined to the living God—and that's pretty good, indeed! So, although in human nature considered in itself we don't find the sort of necessity of nature to accomplish what we know to be right, we do find that sort of necessity in a human nature conjoined to the divine nature in the second person of the Trinity.

The Two Necessities in Christ's Choice

Recall that we talked about three different sorts of necessity. Two of them apply to Christ's situation, whereas one does not. The necessity of the end plays a large role in his choice insofar as God really does, in his great mercy and love, want not just to restore the former harmony that humans enjoyed with him, but to make this union incomparably greater. But justice, being what it is, requires that a sufficient atonement be made to repair the relation: There is an order to all that has been made, which reflects the order of the Creator, and that order cannot simply be laid aside out of convenience because without it there is nothing but chaos. Christ's passion does not sate a bloodthirsty God, it rather restores a right order between God and humanity. More than that, it opens the door to complete union with God; a union modeled on the union of God and man in Christ himself. If this is to be accomplished, Christ must suffer, die, and live again—just as we see him go through this sequence of events in Gibson's film. Christ knows this at the moment of making and continuing to make his choice to sacrifice himself for our sake: he does it for us. He wants us to continue to be in union with his Father, even as he is himself a union of a human nature and the divine nature, and so he chooses the means to the end; he accepts the necessity of the end.

There is also the necessity of Christ's nature which is found in Christ's choice. Christ, in both his human and divine natures, already desires the redemption of humanity. Through his divinity he elevates his humanity to perfection. In his own person there is as intimate a relationship between his human and divine wills as possible. The weaknesses of humankind, which he did indeed feel, made it a struggle to keep his humanity in unanimity with his divinity; but this is a struggle that necessarily would lead to success. Christ's choice was, and is, free, perfectly so, but it could not, cannot, but be what it was and is.

There is nothing interior or exterior that forces him to do what he did. He makes his choice freely. But, making a free choice does not mean following a whim, or chasing a passion, or acting randomly. It means deliberating about what is the best thing to do, and then doing it. Freedom is by no means incompatible with reason. We are free to follow the dictates of our intellect, or not to, but we are more free when we follow the dictate of our intellect. This is so because if we do not, we are instead in some manner compelled by something like a lower desire. It is also true because more often than not our intellect is going to hit upon what really is the better course of action. In the case of Christ, rather than saying "more often than not" we say "always." His human intellect was in perfect union with the divine intellect, and so was informed with the knowledge of what really was the best course of action. To be informed is not to be forced.

The Passion of the Christ presents a Christ who not only struggles physically and mentally in enduring his passion, but a Christ who *permits* his passion to occur in the first place. He permits himself to be subjected to others, tortured, and crucified. He allows himself to be so bound because he is necessarily bound to himself. This self, as the movie also reveals, is not just a man, but a man who is God. He, in freely planning the redemption of humanity, freely submits himself to the means necessary to accomplish it. This was his choice from the beginning, knowing as he did as the second person of the Trinity that human beings would abuse their freedom and that he would have to repair the fault preventing their good which is full union with him—and this choice could not have been different at the time appointed for his passion.

SOURCES

Aristotle. 1980. *Nicomachean Ethics*. Translated by W.D. Ross, revised by J.L. Ackrill and J.O. Urmson. Oxford: Oxford University Press.

Plato. 1981. *Five Dialogues: Euthyphro, Apology, Crito, Meno, Phaedo*. Translated by G.M.A. Grube. Indianapolis: Hackett.

St. Anselm of Canterbury. 1988. *On Free Choice (De libero abitrio)* and *Why God became Man (Cur deus homo?)*. In *St. Anselm of Canterbury: The Major Works*, translated and edited by Brian Davies and G.R. Evans (Oxford: Oxford University Press).

Augustine. 1993. *On Free Choice of the Will*. Translated by Thomas Williams. Indianapolis: Hackett.

Thomas Aquinas. n.d. *Summa theologiae*, III, qq. 46–47. In *The Summa theologica of Saint Thomas Aquinas*, translated by the Fathers of the English Dominican Province. Available at http://www.newadvent.org/summa/.

QUESTIONS FOR DISCUSSION

1. What is justice? Can it be just that one person suffer and die on behalf of all other humans?

2. What does it mean to say that you are, in your very nature, free?

3. How can one argue that Christ's *inability* to make a different choice is a sign of freedom and power rather than of weakness?

4. Can you think of any situations in which it would be right for you to choose to die for others?

5. What are the different senses of necessity explained in this paper? Can you think of others?

19

Forgiving Judas: Extenuating Circumstances in the Ultimate Betrayal

ANNA LÄNNSTRÖM

I have felt sorry for Judas ever since I heard the Easter story for the first time. Even though I was told repeatedly that pity was not the appropriate reaction to the worst traitor in history, the sentiment still lingered. It returned stronger than ever as I watched Gibson's *The Passion of the Christ*.

This film begins with Jesus praying in the garden. In the next scene, Judas goes to the High Priest and tells him where to find Jesus. The high priest throws him thirty silver coins for his services. The guards soon arrive in the garden, and Judas helps them to identify Jesus, betraying him with a kiss on the cheek. Soon after, Judas experiences deep remorse. In Gibson's version, Judas is present when Jesus is brought before the High Priest. Overcome with guilt, he rubs his lips against the rough stone pillar, trying to remove the kiss of betrayal still lingering upon them. He then returns to the high priest and tries to undo the deal—"I have sinned by betraying innocent blood"—and throws the money at the priest's feet. He is turned away.

The next time Judas appears in *The Passion*, he has begun descending into madness. His lips are bloodied, his eyes frenzied, and the young boys who find him declare that he is cursed. Judas runs, terrified by a vision of Satan's face and chased by boys who seem to turn into demons. Ultimately, as in the Gospel of Matthew, Gibson's Judas takes his own life.

Certainly, what Judas did was horrible. He betrayed a friend for money, and with a kiss—a gesture of love. If it were a simple matter of guilt or innocence, I would have no qualms about declaring Judas guilty. But our reaction to Judas is much more than a declaration of guilt. What is it about his betrayal that makes it such an outstandingly terrible crime in the popular imagination? Even Jesus seems to think that Judas's guilt is deeper than that of any other person. In *The Passion*, Jesus reassures Pontius Pilate, who seems unwilling to condemn him: "It is he who delivered me to you who has the greater sin." The words hang there, rich with the implication that Judas's guilt is greater than Pilate's. In the Gospel of Matthew, Jesus puts it even more strongly: "Woe to that man by whom the Son of Man is betrayed! It would have been good for that man if he had not been born" (Matthew 26:24). It sounds as though no one in history is guilty of a worse crime than Judas.

Many treatments of Judas suggest just this. Dante places him in the lowest circle of hell, along with Brutus and Cassius, the betrayers of Caesar. The nineteenth-century theologian Carl Daub views Judas as evil incarnate, Jesus's evil opposite. He argues that Judas embodies unparalleled evil and that he is utterly condemned. There is no possible excuse or repentance for him (see Klassen 1996, p. 5). To this day Judas's name is uttered with hush and dread. But is Judas really so much worse than all others?

In *The Passion* Judas is clearly more guilty than Pilate, presented by Gibson as a noble man forced to execute Jesus against his better judgment. But why is Judas's guilt greater than that of Caiaphas, the High Priest? Why is he more guilty than the Roman soldiers who derive great pleasure from whipping Jesus? Why is he worse than the blood-thirsty crowd Gibson puts in the courtyard? Is he guilty of the worst crime in history? Is his crime worse than the crimes of Hitler or Stalin, Caligula or Nero? Philosophy, specifically the branch of philosophy known as ethics, helps us think about these questions.

Did Judas Freely Choose to Betray God?

A crucial consideration in determining guilt is whether the person freely chose the bad action. In other words, was the bad action voluntary? If it was not, then the person can't be held morally responsible. Aristotle's analysis of voluntary and involuntary action is instructive. Aristotle (384–322 B.C.) points out that we excuse people, in whole or in part, if we believe that they were forced to do what they did. Thus, we partially excuse Peter for denying Christ in *The Passion* because of the threatening crowd surrounding him. We understand that his freedom to choose was limited.

Aristotle uses the example of throwing the cargo overboard in a storm in order to save a ship. The owner of the cargo would normally be furious if the captain jettisoned his property, but given the circumstances, he might consider the action excusable and even say it was the best thing to do. Or consider a situation in which a prisoner is ordered to kill another prisoner and told that unless he does so, both of them will be executed. The prisoner doesn't want to kill, but he knows that the other man will die regardless of what he does and that, if he refuses, he will die too. Under these circumstances, he might decide that killing is the best option available to him because the other man's life is lost anyway.

In these situations, the person is free to do otherwise. Peter could have said that Jesus was his rabbi even though that would have been a very dangerous admission; the ship's captain could have decided to risk the life of everybody on board instead of abandoning the cargo; and the prisoner could have refused to kill his mate, accepting that he too would die. As Aristotle notes, the circumstances of these actions provide excuses, but the actions are still a lot like voluntary actions. The circumstances don't eliminate moral responsibility; they just alleviate it.

By contrast, consider the kind of case in which the person didn't choose the action at all—for instance, if he was possessed or insane or if the action was accidental. In such situations, we wouldn't consider him guilty. In *The Passion*, when Jesus falls, carrying the cross, he almost makes Simon fall as well. But Jesus would never be held responsible for making Simon fall because he didn't intend for him to fall. It was an accident, caused by exhaustion.

Consider Judas's betrayal and final suicide in this context. In Gibson's version, Judas was tormented and chased after the betrayal. John goes one step further by saying that "Satan entered [Judas]" at the Last Supper (John 13:27; see also Luke 22:3). We might interpret this metaphorically to mean merely that Judas decided to betray Christ at that point. If so, Judas remains responsible. If we interpret it literally, however, the entry of

Satan lessens, and might even eliminate, Judas's responsibility for the actions that followed. If Judas acted while he was controlled by Satan, then Judas didn't choose to betray Jesus. Satan *made* him do it or, perhaps Satan even *used* Judas to do it.

Similarly, Gibson's portrayal suggests that Judas might have been driven insane by his guilt and by the boys chasing him. Insanity alleviates responsibility very much like accidents do, because a truly insane person doesn't choose his actions; he doesn't know what he is doing. Thus, if Judas was insane when he killed himself, he isn't morally responsible for his suicide. The basic issue here is freedom of choice. Did Judas choose to do what he did, and could he have done otherwise? If the answer is yes, he is responsible; if the answer is no, he isn't. If Judas was insane or possessed, he was not responsible for his actions; but if he was not, he bears responsibility.

Could Judas Have Done Otherwise?

Did Judas act freely? Was Judas free to do something other than what he did? Was it possible for him not to betray Jesus? These questions lead us to the thorny issue of divine foreknowledge. In the Last Supper scene in *The Passion*, Jesus tells his disciples that one of them will betray him and that another will deny him three times. They all react in horror, assuring him that they will do no such thing. Yet, when Christ starts his painful journey, carrying the cross to Golgotha, Peter has denied him three times and Judas has betrayed him.

If I make a prediction of what another person will do, it doesn't impinge upon her freedom because I am a fallible human being and I could be wrong. I might predict that Peter will deny Jesus tomorrow, but Peter might still do something completely different. Given Christian theology, however, divine predictions are different because God is all-knowing. This means that he cannot be wrong. If God knows that Judas will betray him tomorrow, Judas can't avoid doing it. But then, how can Judas be held accountable for his betrayal? How can he be responsible for what he did? He had no choice. To make the situation worse, the problem recurs for each and every one of us because God knows what we will do ahead of time. All of us seem to lose our freedom and, with it, the moral responsibility for our actions.

Philosophers and theologians have wrestled with this problem for millennia, trying to reconcile human freedom with divine foreknowledge, and they have come up with a variety of solutions. Boethius (around 480–524) tried to solve the problem by arguing that God is outside of time. Human beings exist in time. Only the present moment is truly there for us, and we can only act in it. We remember the past, experience the present, and imagine the future. God's existence is different, Boethius argues. His entire existence and the entire history of the world are fully present to him at once: "His knowledge transcends all movement of time and abides in the simplicity of its immediate present. It encompasses the infinite sweep of past and future, and regards all things in its simple comprehension as if they were now taking place" (Boethius 1962, Prose 6, p. 116).

How does Boethius's explanation enable us to hold Judas responsible for his betrayal? Because God can see Judas's entire life at once, it is all present to him: God's knowledge is not *fore*-knowledge, but eternal knowledge. He doesn't *foresee* Judas's betrayal; he simply *sees* it, just as the people who were there could see it—the only difference being that, while those present saw it for a brief moment, He can see it eternally. And because God merely watches Judas act, His knowledge doesn't impact Judas's freedom. We can still say that Judas acted freely and he is morally responsible.

This solution is ingenious but problematic. First, it isn't clear that it makes sense to say that God is outside of time. Second, saying that God is *outside of* time seems to make it impossible for Him to act in the world because all actions take place in time. This is not acceptable because one of the most important things about the Christian God is that He acts in the world. Third, saying that God is outside of time and hence doesn't have foreknowledge doesn't seem to solve the problem. If God eternally knows that Judas will betray Christ, then it was true a hundred years before the betrayal that God eternally knows that Judas will betray Christ. And if it was true a hundred years before the betrayal, then we are back to the original problem: Judas *had to* betray Jesus, or God would have been wrong.[1] So, we ask again, can his decision to do so be free?

---

[1] I'm paraphrasing Gregory Bassham's formulation of this objection in "The Prophecy-Driven Life: Fate and Freedom at Hogwarts," in David Baggert and Shawn Klein, eds., *Harry Potter and Philosophy* (Chicago: Open Court, 2004).

A better solution was first proposed by Jonathan Edwards (1703–1758) and then clarified by Henry Frankfurt (born 1929). Edwards suggests that we need to rethink our understanding of freedom. I've said that freedom requires the ability to do otherwise. This means that Judas betrayed Jesus freely only if he could have avoided betraying him. Edwards argues that this reasoning is mistaken. A free action simply is one in which we do what we want to do. To ask whether Judas was free to do otherwise is to ask the wrong question. Instead, we should ask whether he chose to betray Jesus. If he made that choice, he betrayed Jesus freely even if he couldn't have done otherwise.

Applying Edwards's and Frankfurt's insights, we can think about Judas's betrayal in the following way: God ordained that Jesus would die for our sins and he knew that Judas would be the instrument. So, He needed to make sure that Judas really did betray Jesus. This means that God couldn't permit Judas to do anything other than betraying Jesus. Were Judas to hesitate, we'd have to assume that God would interfere and force him to go through with the betrayal. If that had happened, Judas's action would have been involuntary and he would not have been morally responsible. But it didn't happen that way. Judas believed that he had a choice and he made it; he betrayed Jesus. Judas could not have acted otherwise because God would not have permitted it, but Judas did not know that. In fact he didn't try to act otherwise because he didn't want to, and this means that he acted freely.

What Was the Result of Judas's Betrayal?

If Judas freely betrayed Jesus and Jesus is God, then Judas betrayed God. But we still don't know the extent of Judas's guilt. We also need to know why he betrayed Him (his intention) and what happened as a direct result of his betrayal (the consequences or outcome). Consequentialists like John Stuart Mill (1806–1873) argue that our moral assessment of actions should focus upon the outcome. When we try to figure out what to do, we should choose the action that provides the greatest good for the greatest number. We often think in this way. We assign more or less responsibility, depending on outcome: less if the outcome is better, more if it is worse. Think about the legal distinction between attempted murder and murder: The intention is the same in both crimes, but attempted murder receives a lesser punishment because the outcome is different.

What happens if we focus on outcome in judging Judas? We might be tempted to say that Judas's betrayal produced an outcome which otherwise wouldn't have occurred, namely Jesus's death. But surely this is not true. The Jewish authorities could have found Jesus without Judas's help. Jesus was not in hiding and there is no reason to assume that he was planning to go into hiding. In fact, he was a famous preacher, and great crowds gathered as soon as he appeared. Judas might have helped the authorities to find Jesus sooner, but they would have found him soon enough without his help. So, Judas's initial betrayal in the Temple did little or nothing to produce a different outcome.

What about his second betrayal, the disturbing kiss in the garden that identified Jesus? Again, this didn't change the outcome at all in Gibson's version of events. In *The Passion*, by the time Judas kisses him, Jesus had already identified himself. We must conclude that Judas's actions did little to change what ultimately happened. Judas revealed the location of a man whose whereabouts were already known or could easily have been discovered; he identified a man who had already identified himself.

Indeed, one might even argue that Judas's betrayal had good consequences. His action led to Christ's death, and Christ's death redeemed us, saving countless human beings from eternal damnation. If any action in the history of the world has produced the greatest good for the greatest number, surely this one did!

Nevertheless, this assessment seems to miss something crucial. Even if we accept that Jesus would have been arrested and executed without Judas's help, and even if we accept that Jesus's death had good consequences, betraying Jesus was still morally wrong. Consequentialists recognize that an action can be bad even if it has a good or neutral outcome. They argue that an action is bad if others like it usually have bad consequences. Even though betrayal did little to change the outcome on this occasion and even if it helped produce a great good, in most cases it would have had harmful effects. Therefore, they conclude, betrayal, and especially the betrayal of a trusted friend, is a wrongful action.

Still, the focus upon outcome seems unsatisfactory. We generally believe that when we assess the moral worth of an action and the culpability of the agent who carries it out, intentions are central. For instance, we distinguish between manslaughter and murder, unintentional and intentional killing, and consider the killer more culpable if he acted intentionally. Indeed, deontologists such as Immanuel Kant (1724–1804) argue that considerations of intention are all-important in assessing the character of an agent and the moral worth of his actions—consequentialists think they are relevant only for the evaluation of character.

To evaluate Judas's guilt, then, we must take into account what he intended to do and whether or not the intended action is moral. Here, matters quickly become complicated. Outcomes are relatively easy to judge because they can be seen. By contrast, motives are hidden in the human heart, sometimes so well hidden that we don't even understand our own motives. We know that Judas chose to betray Jesus. But we don't know what his motive was, and we don't know if he was aware that he was betraying God and not just a man.

Why Did Judas Betray Jesus?

Tradition offers a couple of possible motives for Judas's action, and our evaluation of Judas must differ radically depending upon which of these we ascribe to him. In *The Passion*, the scene in the Temple when Judas receives the money suggests that he betrayed Jesus for money: his motive was greed. Two of the Gospels support Gibson's interpretation. In the Gospel of John, Judas protests the use of expensive ointment for Jesus's feet, saying that the oil could be sold and the money given to the poor. John stresses Judas's greed: "He said this not because he cared about the poor, but because he was a thief; he kept the common purse and used to steal what was put into it" (John 12:6). Matthew indicates that Judas betrayed Jesus immediately after the argument about the oil: "Then one of the twelve, called Judas Iscariot, went to the chief priests and said, 'What are you willing to give me if I deliver Him to you?'" (Matthew 26:14–15). If he couldn't get money by stealing the money from the poor, he would get it by betraying Jesus. This might be the worst possible motive Judas could have had. To betray anybody is bad enough, but a person who betrays a friend out of greed deserves utter contempt. This interpretation, I suspect, underlies the complete condemnation of Judas.

Another possible motive stems from the traditional identification of Judas as a Zealot. This means that he was among those who believed in the imminent return of a Messiah who would be a king and a leader in this world. The Messiah would lead the Jewish people in an uprising that would end Roman occupation. If Judas was a Zealot and a follower of Jesus, he probably believed that Jesus was going to be that leader.

If this were Judas's motive, he may not have intended for Jesus to die or even to be arrested. Judas might have been trying to force Jesus to reveal himself as the future king, provoking him into picking up the sword and attacking the oppressor. If this was Judas's hope, it was of course thwarted. Gibson shows how Jesus meekly went with the guards. He didn't fight them but instead told Peter to put down his sword. Instead of witnessing the king take power, Judas saw him humiliated and beaten. As Jesus says in the Gospels and in *The Passion*, his kingdom isn't of this world. Judas had misunderstood what sort of king Jesus intended to become and what results he'd deliver. Finally realizing that Jesus was no worldly king, Judas killed himself in despair, recognizing too late that he had betrayed "innocent blood" and perhaps understanding that he had betrayed God.

Regardless of what his motive was, Judas's actions after Jesus was arrested in *The Passion* suggest that he had not realized what would happen to Jesus. He seems genuinely shocked to see that Jesus is chained and abused. If he sold Jesus for money, perhaps he didn't fully understand what they would do to him. He might have expected them to let him go after a light lashing, some version of a slap on the wrist. Or perhaps he knew what would happen, but still was unprepared for actually seeing it done.

If he thought Jesus was the new King David, he must have been completely unprepared for watching what would happen next. He didn't intend Jesus to die or suffer; he intended to catalyze Jesus into starting a revolution. He misunderstood, and perhaps he should have known better. Still, if intentions are what counts, Judas's ignorance reduces his guilt; he is responsible only for what he intended to happen.

If Judas was truly unaware that the man he betrayed was also God, we shouldn't hold him responsible for betraying God, "only" for betraying a man. If he didn't understand that Jesus would be killed and tortured, we shouldn't regard him as fully responsible for that either. His ignorance excuses him, although not completely. Even if Judas didn't know what would happen, the fact remains that he handed over Jesus to the authorities. Furthermore, we might say that he should have known, that he should have suspected, or that he should have made more of an effort to predict it. Perhaps he ought to have looked to heaven instead of hoping for worldly power and an end to Roman occupation. Perhaps somebody who had spent time with Jesus should have understood that Jesus was not a worldly king at all, but something different and better. Indeed, perhaps his lack of understanding was a sign of his too worldly character, symbolized by his interest in money.

Was Judas a Treacherous Person, or Did He Just Mess Up This Once?

In reports of trials for gruesome crimes, one of the most damning statements that audiences and juries make about culprits is that they show no remorse. If intentions and outcomes were all that mattered, remorse would be irrelevant. Whatever a killer feels after a murder doesn't change his intention or the outcome in the least. Yet, we consider remorse relevant because it provides evidence about character. It tells us whether the culprit would have acted differently if he had to do it over again. By focusing upon character, Aristotle provides a third way of thinking about morality which philosophers call virtue ethics. Virtue ethics considers intentions and outcomes too, but it mainly uses them as evidence of character.

Virtue ethics often stresses the circumstances of an action. Consider Peter's betrayal of Christ. Gibson's version makes Peter's denial of Jesus seem more excusable than it otherwise might have been. Surrounded by an angry mob, Peter is asked whether he is one of Jesus's followers. Frightened, he denies knowing Jesus three times in a row. Peter's denial isn't good, but it is understandable, and it doesn't cast a deep shadow upon his character for two reasons. First, we think about the circumstances: Identifying himself as one of Christ's followers would have done nothing to help Christ and might have resulted in Peter's own death at the hands of the angry mob. Second, Gibson shows Peter drawing his sword, trying to defend Jesus in the garden, and full of remorse soon after the betrayal. Peter's betrayal appears to be a lapse rather than a deeper flaw. He isn't a bad guy; he's a good guy who, on one occasion and under great pressure, did a bad thing.

Can we say the same about Judas? Imagine if *The Passion* had shown Judas laughing and spending the money on wine and prostitutes as he watched Jesus being tortured. Then, without hesitation we would have judged him harshly. But this isn't what Gibson shows us. Like Gibson's Peter, his Judas experiences regret almost immediately. He tries to undo his action, begging the priests to release Jesus, and he doesn't keep the money. This remorse suggests that he would have acted differently if he had another chance, and it should make us judge him less harshly. He is not completely bad. On the other hand, we may still have strong doubts about his character. If Judas has always been greedy, it appears plausible that he betrayed Jesus for money, and then his greed wasn't merely a lapse. This is why the passage about saving the oil for the poor in John and Matthew is crucial. It paints Judas as consistently greedy, suggesting that he didn't simply give in to the temptation to have thirty silver coins in a moment of weakness; he was a greedy man who lived a life of weakness. And Judas is without the circumstantial excuse that Peter has. Judas didn't betray Jesus out of fear for his own life; he betrayed him while under no particular pressure.

Final Judgment

So how should we judge Judas, and how did God judge him? Surely, the answer must depend upon why he betrayed Christ, whether he understood what would happen to Jesus, and whether he was a treacherous person or only a man who succumbed to weakness at the wrong time. Gibson doesn't answer these questions for us, and neither do the Gospels. This means that we have no way of knowing how we should judge Judas or how God judges him. Still, I'd like to think that Jesus meant to include Judas in his compassionate plea from the cross: "Father, forgive them for they do not know what they do" (Luke 23:34).[2]

---

[2] I am grateful to Gregory Bassham for several useful suggestions, and to him, John Lanci, and Joel Marcus for bringing my attention to some pertinent secondary literature.

SOURCES

Aristotle. 1999. *Nicomachean Ethics*, Book 3. Translated by Terence Irwin. Second Edition. Indianapolis: Hackett.

Boethius. 1962. *The Consolations of Philosophy*, Prose 6. Translated by Richard Green. New York: Macmillan.

Jonathan Edwards. 1969. *Freedom of the Will*. Edited by A.S. Kaufman and W. K. Frankena. Indianapolis: Bobbs-Merrill.

Henry Frankfurt. 1971. Freedom of the Will and the Concept of a Person. *Journal of Philosophy* 68, pp. 5–20.

Immanuel Kant. 1993. *Grounding for the Metaphysics of Morals,* Sections 1 and 2. Translated by James W. Ellington. Indianapolis: Hackett.

William Klassen. 1996. *Judas: Betrayer or Friend of Jesus?* Minneapolis: Fortress.

Hyam Maccoby. 1992. *Judas Iscariot and the Myth of Jewish Evil.* New York: Free Press.

John Stuart Mill. 1993. Utilitarianism. In Mill, *On Liberty and Utilitarianism* (New York: Bantam).

QUESTIONS FOR DISCUSSION

1. What other possible motives could Judas have had for betraying Jesus, and how would they affect his guilt?

2. What is worse, betraying a friend or betraying God? Why?

3. When is ignorance a legitimate excuse, and when is it not?

4. Is Judas worse than Hitler?

5. If Judas had come to the cross, would Jesus have forgiven him?

20

Resist Not Evil! Jesus and Nonviolence

GREGORY BASSHAM and DAVID BAGGETT

The Passion of the Christ has been described as the best movie people don't want to see twice. It gives horror and slasher films a run for their money. Mel Gibson's relentlessly graphic depiction of the death of Christ presents us with gruesome violence that goes well beyond anything described in the Gospels. Jesus is beaten by Jewish guards prior to his trial before the Sanhedrin, he is dropped off a bridge, his arm is dislocated during the crucifixion, and he endures an unusually severe flogging and scourging at the hands of sadistic Roman soldiers. What is the purpose of all this violence? Clearly, it is to amplify emotional impact.

Not often noticed, but equally worthy of attention, however, is Jesus's non-violent response. At no point does he attempt to avoid or resist it. In the opening scene he reveals his anguish in a remarkable prayer: "Father, you can do all things. If it be possible, let this chalice pass from me. But let your will be done, not mine." We see a man who seems to know the horrors in store for him, in fulfillment of prophecies he takes as applying to himself. With all his might he wishes he could avoid these horrors, but he senses that such suffering is God's plan, and so he's willing to submit to it. Accepting of his fate, he endures the suffering, refusing to resist, obedient to his calling. Indeed, at times he seems almost to invite it, as when he painfully climbs to his feet after his hideous flogging by Roman guards. Refusing to hit back, refraining from complaint, he remarkably endures the pain and shame.

In these ways the film's extreme violence subverts itself by showing the ultimate emptiness of violence in the face of all-conquering love. Indeed, in some ways the film's depiction of Jesus's *practice* of non-violence goes beyond Christ's teachings, a fact that will prove important for us. Such a vision seems plainly to be Gibson's faith-based conviction as a Catholic filmmaker. One of the questions that we will consider is whether this belief in the futility of violence can be justified as a reasoned conclusion from evidence that does not presuppose any theological commitments.

Jesus's Teachings on Nonviolence

Jesus's practice of nonviolence during his Passion remarkably resembles his teaching of nonviolence during his ministry. Several scenes in the film focus specifically on Jesus's teachings on nonviolence. These include the flashback to the Sermon on the Mount, in which Jesus preaches forgiveness and love of enemies, which he then later models on the cross himself. Another flashback features Jesus washing his disciples' feet, while warning them to expect persecution as followers of him, which they must meet meekly and without fear—in contrast to Peter's vehement denial of knowing Christ when persecution for it seemed likely. Also pertinent is the scene in the Garden of Gethsemane, where Christ watches sadly as his disciples fight the Jewish guards and he instructs Peter to put down his sword, quoting the Jewish proverb that "all who live by the sword shall die by the sword." Jesus, far from joining in the fight, instead restores the ear of the guard that Peter had cut off, to the guard's utter astonishment. Peter's greater willingness to brandish a sword to defend Jesus than to be persecuted for Jesus was the exact opposite of the harder path to which Jesus had called him. Christendom's lamentable history of holy wars, inquisitions, and crusades is sad testimony that Peter has too often indeed been its guiding example.

Admonitions to "turn the other cheek" and "go the extra mile" derive from Jesus's instructions (Luke 6:27–28; Matthew 5:39–41), and examples could be multiplied. Included among such teachings are "hard sayings"—like "resist not evil"—that Jesus himself put into practice and also expected his disciples to follow, even unto death (Matthew 10:17–22; 10:38–39).

What did Jesus mean by these strongly pacifist-sounding sayings?

The earliest Christian communities seem to have taken Jesus's teachings on nonviolence and love of enemies quite seriously, refusing military service, declining resort to secular courts, praying for their persecutors, and submitting unresistingly and even joyously to the lash, sword, or cross (Bainton 1960, pp. 66–84). Taken literally, however, these sayings are so demanding that attempts have been made at least since the time of St. Augustine (A.D. 354–430) to limit their scope or blunt their force. Let's look briefly at five leading interpretations, several of which may contain insight into this matter.

The Two-Class Ethics Interpretation

The traditional Catholic approach to Jesus's hard sayings is to treat them as "counsels of perfection" addressed only to a select few who choose to pursue a higher calling of moral and spiritual perfection. On this view, Christ laid down two kinds of moral directives: "precepts" and "counsels." Precepts are commandments binding on everyone that cannot be disobeyed without mortal sin. Counsels, by contrast, are recommendations for those who wish to undertake, either for a lifetime or a period of time, a more perfect imitation of Christ's example (by, for instance, taking vows of voluntary poverty or chastity). Protestant Reformers strongly opposed the Catholic doctrine of super-meritorious actions, insisting that Christ called all his followers to be perfect, as their heavenly Father is perfect (Matthew 5:48).

Even if we grant that some of Christ's ethical directives are counsels, it's doubtful that his teachings on nonviolence fall into this category, since they occur in the midst of directives that are clearly commands (don't divorce, don't swear, and the like). Moreover, some of the ethical directives the Catholic tradition treats as commands, such as the commandment to love God with all one's heart and mind, are in fact *more* difficult to fulfill than many of the alleged counsels, such as turning the other cheek or going the extra mile. So the Catholic two-class ethic interpretation is problematic. In fact, as Catholic theologian Hans Küng notes, the counsel-precept distinction has largely dropped out of post-Vatican II Catholic moral theology (Küng 1976, p. 245).

The Interim Ethics Interpretation

Another way of understanding Jesus's radical ethical teachings that makes them largely irrelevant to most Christians today is to see them as short-term emergency legislation for the end-time. On this view, first popularized by the German theologian and medical missionary Albert Schweitzer, Jesus fully accepted the "futurist eschatology" endorsed by Jewish apocalyptic sects of his day. Believing that God would intervene immediately and dramatically in human history, Jesus taught a rigorous, perfectionist ethic that makes sense only if one assumes that practical concerns like burying one's dead father (Matthew 8:22) or giving away all one's money or clothes (Luke 6:30; Matthew 5:40) are unimportant given that God's apocalyptic kingdom was immediately at hand. Why worry about hanging on to your coat if there's never going to be another winter?

Although Jesus's ethical teachings may have been colored by his beliefs about the end of the world, it doesn't follow that those teachings were intended only as short-term crisis legislation or lack permanent validity. Jesus's commandments to avoid swearing, anger, divorce, lust in one's heart, showy displays of religiosity, and so forth were clearly intended as intensifications of the Old Law, but there is no reason to believe that Jesus saw these as being applicable only for a few short weeks, months, or years. The same should be said of Jesus's teachings on nonviolence, which are also presented as sharpenings of Old Testament demands.

The Lutheran Penitential Ethic Interpretation

Many Protestant theologians, following the great Reformation thinker Martin Luther (1483–1546), argue that the real purpose of Jesus's demanding ethical teachings was to bring us to our knees by showing us the impossibility of achieving righteousness through good works. In Luther's view, when Jesus commanded his disciples to "resist not evil" and "turn the other cheek," he didn't mean to exclude legitimate secular duties such as protecting one's family, punishing criminals, and taking up arms to resist foreign invasion or domestic insurrection. Jesus's ethical teachings nevertheless demand absolute, uncompromising obedience to God's holy will, a standard of perfection that no fallen human being can achieve. Such teachings, therefore, humble our pride and teach us that salvation comes through faith and grace, not through any righteousness of our own.

Certainly Jesus lays down a highly demanding ethic and rules out any sort of boasting before God (consider Luke 18:9–14). Recent New Testament scholarship, however, has argued that Jesus's teachings on nonviolence cannot be limited to purely individual, non-civic actions, as Luther claimed, but have social and political implications as well (Yoder 1994). Further, many of Jesus's ethical teachings, while demanding, are not impossible to fulfill (don't swear, don't pray ostentatiously, and so forth). And as John Howard Yoder points out, if Jesus's purpose was simply to teach the futility of achieving salvation through good works, it's hard to see why he offered such detailed ethical principles or felt it necessary to sharpen Old Testament rules that in many cases were already extremely demanding (Yoder 1994, p. 43).

The Absolute Pacifism Interpretation

Some have claimed that when Jesus said "resist not evil" he meant exactly what he said: all violence and resistance to evil is wrong, regardless of the reasons, circumstances, or costs. Such absolute pacifism has been defended by Leo Tolstoy, the great Russian novelist, as well as by some of the historic "peace churches" such as the Anabaptists and Mennonites. Tolstoy goes so far as to claim that Christ totally forbids armies, police, and criminal courts, since these all involve the use of force and violence (Tolstoy 1940, p. 323).

Absolute pacifism has implications that most people would understandably find very hard to accept because they grate against deep intuitions. An absolute pacifist, for example, would have to condemn any use of force, no matter how moderate and restrained, to protect a helpless child from assault, arrest a serial killer, or prevent a terrorist attack that could kill thousands. Refusing to use even minimal force to protect the innocent seems inconsistent with Christ's teachings to love one's neighbor as oneself (Mark 12:31) and to treat others as we would like them to treat us (Luke 6:31). Consequently, Christians should not conclude that Jesus commanded absolute pacifism unless this is the only plausible interpretation of his teachings.

Fortunately, other interpretations are possible. Jesus himself used force in driving the money-changers out of the Temple with a whip of cords (John 2:14–16). At least some of Jesus's disciples carried swords (Luke 22:49), although Christ would not permit their use to prevent his arrest. The Old Testament clearly sanctioned the use of force in a variety of contexts, and although Jesus heightened the demands of certain Old Testament teachings, he rarely if ever explicitly rejected them. Most of Jesus's pacifist sayings are focused on individual, self-regarding conduct ("if any one strikes *you* on the right cheek . . ."), not on conduct involving the welfare or protection of others. And St. Paul, after repeating Jesus's commandments never to avenge wrongs or repay evil for evil (Romans 12:17–19), urges Christians to obey the governing authorities, since these authorities are ordained by God to restrain the wicked and serve the common good (Romans 13:1–5). In light of these facts, it's unlikely Jesus believed in absolute pacifism.

The Implicit Qualifier Interpretation

None of the four leading interpretations of Jesus's teachings on nonviolence considered so far seems entirely satisfactory. How, then, should these teachings be interpreted? Perhaps part of the solution lies in two characteristic features of Jesus's teaching: his occasional resort to hyperbole and his opposition to the kind of letter-over-spirit approach to rules adopted in Jesus's day by many Pharisees.

The use of hyperbole (deliberate overstatement or exaggeration) was commonplace in Near-Eastern cultures of Jesus's time, and Jesus himself often used exaggerated language to drive home a point. "If any one comes to me and does not hate his own father and mother and wife and children and brothers and sisters, yes, and even his own life, he cannot be my disciple" (Luke 14:26). This is just one example of Jesus's sayings that, while clearly extravagant, would not have deceived his listeners. It may well be that there is a similar touch of hyperbole in his pacifist sayings, which Jesus certainly intended to be taken seriously, even radically, but probably not literally or without qualification.

Jesus's opposition to treating rules as rigid absolutes supports this reading. In his view, even divine commandments like

"Remember the Sabbath day, to keep it holy" (Exodus 20:8) must be interpreted flexibly and with an eye to core Biblical values. Contrary to the Pharisees' approach to religious rules, which too often stressed the letter of the law over its spirit, Jesus taught that the Sabbath commandment should not be interpreted as prohibiting hungry people from eating (Mark 2:23–28), or sick people from being healed (Luke 6:6–11), or children or animals from being rescued from a well (Luke 14:5). In a powerful scene in the film, Mary Magdalene is prevented from being stoned according to the prescribed punishment for her transgression. Rules aren't impersonal, he believed, but come from a personal lawgiver and are often phrased in broad, general language and should not be construed with wooden literalness or rigid legalism in disregard of higher values or the rule-maker's general purposes and intentions.

Jesus's teachings on nonviolence, likewise, lay down a general norm that must be applied intelligently in light of Jesus's other teachings. Roughly, Jesus seems to be saying this: "Be zealous agents of peace and reconciliation; respond to hatred with love and forgiveness; when abused, be prepared to suffer hardship, loss, or indignity rather than to respond with violence or vengeance; never use force without need and never in ways inconsistent with fundamental Gospel values." This paraphrase brings out clearly how Jesus's sayings on nonviolence were intended as implicitly qualified general norms rather than as absolutes without exception.

Why Did Jesus Believe in Nonviolence?

We have argued that Jesus taught an extremely demanding but not absolute or unqualified ethic of nonviolence and nonresistance. On any plausible interpretation, this ethic is a deeply challenging one, not "reasonable" by the world's standards. Jesus's explanations for his teachings on nonviolence bring out their radical nature.

First, he says, we should respond to violence and hatred with love and forgiveness because this is what God does, and we should imitate God and seek to fulfill his will in all things, even as he himself did what he saw his Father doing. "[L]ove your enemies, and do good, and lend, expecting nothing in return; and your reward will be great, and you will be Sons of the Most

High; *for he is kind to the ungrateful and the selfish*. Be merciful, even as your Father is merciful" (Luke 6:35–36; emphasis added). Recall the beginning scenes of *The Passion*, where Jesus interferes with the violent resistance put up by his disciples in the Garden of Gethsemane.

Second, Jesus undermines many of the usual justifications for violence by pointing out that, with the dawning of God's kingdom, many things that seem to be unmitigated evils are in fact blessings to those who love and serve the Lord. "Blessed are you when men revile you and persecute you and utter all kinds of evil against you falsely on my account. Rejoice and be glad, for your reward is great in heaven" (Matthew 5:11–12). The thought is well dramatized in the scene toward the end of the film in which the "good" thief is promised happiness the very day of the crucifixion. Blessed are the poor, the hungry, and those who weep, for God has great things in store for them (Luke 6:20–21). Are you concerned that if you don't respond to violence with violence, evildoers will escape punishment? God will give them the punishment they deserve (Matthew 25:31ff.). Are you worried that if you don't fight back, you may be robbed, beaten, or killed? "Do not fear those who kill the body but cannot kill the soul" (Matthew 10:28); "whoever loses his life for my sake will find it" (Matthew 16:25).

In short, what Jesus calls for is a radical reversal of worldly values and "common-sense" assumptions, a thoroughgoing conversion (*metanoia*) to a God-centered way of thinking and living. From a worldly point of view, it is an unqualified evil when a good person is robbed or mistreated, and aggressors deserve to be repaid in kind. But from a God-centered point of view, such concerns fade in importance. As Peter asks (sounding here a bit like Socrates and the ancient Stoics), "who is there to harm you if you are zealous for what is right?" (I Peter 3:13). Nothing that the violent can do to a person, or take from them, can cause them deep or lasting harm if God is on their side. From a personal standpoint, therefore, all that ultimately matters is faithfulness to God—His "kingdom and His righteousness" (Matthew 6:33).

The Ethics of Nonviolence

Jesus's willingness to endure the cross seems rooted in a profound moral faith that entrusting ourselves to God's hands and suppressing our violent impulses will be vindicated and can play an important part in ushering in God's kingdom. Is such trust in nonviolence promoting the cause of peace likely to be justified by unassisted reason alone? Suppose that we understand such trust as grounded in the conviction that we ought, morally, to be strongly committed to the cause of peace and nonviolence. This question can then be posed: Can standard secular moral theories undergird a strongly pacifist commitment to live nonviolently in the face of temptations to do otherwise?

Philosophers generally distinguish between two broad types of ethical theories: consequentialist and non-consequentialist. Consequentialists believe that one should always act for "the greater good," whereas non-consequentialists believe that some acts are wrong even if they do produce the best net outcomes for everyone affected by the action. Caiaphas, the Jewish High Priest in the film, reveals his commitment to consequentialism when he defends Jesus's execution by saying, "It is expedient that one man should die for the people, and that the whole nation should not perish" (John 11:50).

Utilitarianism is the most common version of consequentialism, and comes in a couple of varieties. Act utilitarianism mandates those individual actions that best promote overall utility (for example, the maximizing of pleasure and minimizing of pain for the greatest number). An act utilitarian would probably say, in extreme cases, it's morally permissible, indeed morally obligatory, to torture an innocent child if that's the only way to get a terrorist to reveal where he's hidden a nuclear bomb. Rule utilitarianism, in contrast, dictates that there are certain kinds of actions that should never be done, even if on occasion they promote utility in the short term, because in the long term they are likely to undermine it. So the rule utilitarian would probably insist that torturing an innocent child, for whatever ultimate purpose, is morally ruled out because it's the sort of behavior that, if practiced, will likely detract from long-term utility.

Can Jesus's ethic of nonviolence be defended on consequentialist grounds? It's easy to think of examples in which, say, jailing an innocent person or murdering a political opponent would promote the best consequences for everyone involved, yet Jesus's ethic would plainly condemn such acts. When it comes to act and rule consequentialism, only rule utilitarianism holds any hope of justifying a strongly pacifistic approach to life, and only if it were based on the highly questionable assumption that no rule permitting forcible resistance to evil could promote long-term utility. This however would entail an absolute pacifism that goes beyond Jesus's ethic and that we saw we have good reasons to reject. So whereas act utilitarianism seems to permit actions it morally shouldn't, rule utilitarianism at best justifies an absolute pacifism that seems to yield unpalatable results.

Models of the Passion

If we take the Passion of Christ as a faithful application of Jesus's teachings about nonviolence, and interpret his teaching of nonviolence as identifying a moral obligation to renounce violence in most cases and in his own death particularly, then Jesus would have been obligated to do what he did, based on a duty that ruled out any right of his to refuse to do it. And if Jesus in fact was laboring under such an externally imposed moral obligation that precluded any right of his to do otherwise, then he would have been blameworthy for refusing to follow through with his mission. In the movie, when mockingly challenged to come down from the cross by the defiant thief, for instance, Jesus would have been sinful to do so. Given the extraordinarily difficult obligation that was imposed on him, though, he still might be deemed praiseworthy for doing it. We can call this the "duty model" of the Passion.

A quite different account insists that Jesus was under no obligation at all, but was perfectly free morally to avoid the cross. Jesus's sacrifice was, on this view, an act of pure generosity and grace. Jesus is praiseworthy for having gone to the cross, for he didn't have to in any moral sense, so he wouldn't have been blameworthy for refusing to do so. We can call this the "freedom model" of the Passion.

Is there a principled way to split the difference and characterize Jesus's going to the cross both as obedience to God's perfect will and something that Jesus morally had to do, on the one hand, while also something altogether praiseworthy, gracious, and as more than just doing his duty, on the other? Perhaps there is, but we suspect that to find this synthesis we need to introduce aspects of ethics beyond just rights and duties. Surely the Passion isn't properly understood merely as Jesus's discharging a moral duty and thereby avoiding wrongdoing. Rights and duties are not all that ethics is about, and Jesus's Passion just doesn't seem reducible to such categories.

There's another way to capture a way Jesus may have "had to" go to the cross. As God the Son, Jesus shared in divinity that, on classical interpretations, is perfectly loving. Jesus, being who he was, couldn't be less than perfectly loving. His obedience was tested somehow in his human vulnerability and in the crucible of pain, but his divine perfection dictated he should do all he could to make the resources of God's grace available. The moral constraints on his behavior, on this view, are internal to his character, rather than externally imposed standards. So it's accurate to say Jesus morally had to do it, given his identity and nature, and it's also appropriate to accord Jesus maximal praise for his willing sacrifice. Knowing that his sacrifice would make God's grace so available, Jesus was morally constrained by his own perfection to express his love sacrificially. We can call this the "character model" of the Passion.

Where does pacifism fit in? It depends on which model of the Passion we adopt. The duty model would dictate that nonviolence is a moral obligation imposed by Jesus's teachings and faithfully discharged by Christ himself. Applied to a nonabsolutist understanding of pacifism, it would imply that we generally have no right to self-defense, even if we retain rights to defend others. On the freedom model, in contrast, pacifism would be a purely supererogatory act, one that we are praiseworthy for performing but not blameworthy for not performing. We would be under no obligation at all to follow Jesus's hard sayings on nonviolence, though the choice to follow such sayings would be praiseworthy. Opting out of pacifism would not be at all blameworthy. Rights to defend oneself and others would be consistent with this approach. This view conspicuously resembles the two-ethic analysis discussed earlier.

Our favored take on pacifism and nonviolence, however, follows the character model. As all followers of Jesus are called to perfection, all have been called to follow Jesus's example and to become the kind of people for whom violence is less and less an option. To say merely that nonviolence is a moral duty or that self-defense is not our moral right is to conduct the discourse on the wrong level. Perhaps we do retain a right of self-defense. But Jesus would call us, on occasion at least, not to exercise all the rights we may have, even as he didn't exercise all his own prerogatives, like his moral authority to assert his innocence or point out that what was happening was unjust. This is a useful reminder that rights, despite their importance, need not always dominate ethical discussions. The greater the sacrifice the more likely we may need to forego genuine rights, but Christ's Passion teaches us that nothing we might be called to sacrifice compares with what he sacrificed for us.

Either Jesus meant to teach that we don't have a general right of personal self-defense or that, even if we do, we're often called to lay it aside, following his example. Recall from the movie that Jesus said nobody took his life from him, but that he laid it down of his own accord to accomplish the work to which God had called him (see John 10:18). Those inclined to affirm such rights are hard-pressed to do so on consequentialist grounds. Non-consequentialists, though, can correct what they consider to be this deficiency among the utilitarians. Seeing whether Jesus's teachings on nonviolence can be defended on non-consequentialist grounds is more difficult, because non-consequentialist theories are so varied. Some non-consequentialists, like Immanuel Kant (1724–1804) and certain contemporary situation ethicists, claim that ethics can be reduced to a single fundamental ethical principle (for instance "Always act on principles that you would like to see everybody act upon" or "Always do the loving thing"). Others hold that there are several basic moral principles ("Tell the truth," "Do no harm," "Act justly," and so forth) and then offer ways of prioritizing the principles to reach concrete outcomes.

In general, however, it's hard to see how a non-consequentialist theory could do the job. All leading non-consequentialist theories accord primacy to a right of self-defense that conflicts with Jesus's radical ethic of nonresistance. And from the standpoint of natural reason, how can such a right be denied? There are times, as Jan Narveson notes, when "it's either him or us. And the pacifist seems to be insisting that it always ought to be *us*. But why? The *other* guy is the guilty party, for heaven's sake!" (Narveson 1986, p. 139). So the non-consequentialist is going to have a difficult time making sense of either denials of rights to self-defense or exhortations to lay such rights aside.

Historically, of course, most advocates of radical nonviolence have been motivated by religious conviction, including

Buddha, Mahatma Gandhi, Martin Luther King, Jr., and Dorothy Day. Secular accounts of ethics seem ill-equipped to imbue us with the sort of confidence in the ultimate workability of such an approach and the power of love to conquer evil. In the end, as Dietrich Bonhoeffer wrote, "the cross is the only justification for the precept of non-violence, for it alone can kindle a faith in the victory over evil which will enable men to obey that precept. Only such obedience is blessed with the promise that we shall be partakers of Christ's victory as well as his suffering."

SOURCES

Roland H. Bainton. 1960. *Christian Attitudes toward War and Peace.* Nashville: Abington Press.

Hans Küng. 1976. *On Being a Christian.* Translated by Edward Quinn. Garden City: Doubleday.

Martin Luther. 1956. *The Sermon on the Mount and The Magnificat.* In *Luther's Works*, Volume 21, edited by Jaroslav Pelikan, translated by Jaroslav Pelikan and A.T.W. Steinhaeuser (St. Louis: Concordia).

Jan Narveson. 1990. At Arms' Length: Violence and War. In Tom Regan, ed., *Matters of Life and Death: New Introductory Essays in Moral Philosophy.* New York: McGraw-Hill.

Leo Tolstoy. 1940. *A Confession, The Gospel in Brief, and What I Believe.* Translated by Aylmer Maude. London: Oxford University Press.

John Howard Yoder. 1994. *The Politics of Jesus.* Second edition. Grand Rapids: Eerdmans.

QUESTIONS FOR DISCUSSION

1. Should Jesus have allowed himself to be tortured and crucified?

2. What did Jesus mean when he said "Resist not evil"? (Matthew 5:48)

3. Did Jesus believe in absolute nonviolence? If not, what was his view of violence and retaliation?

4. Would Jesus say that all wars are wrong? If not, what kinds of wars would he say are justified?

5. What is pacifism? Are there good theological or religious grounds for pacifism? Can pacifism be defended on nonreligious grounds?

About the Authors

DAVID BAGGETT is an Assistant Professor of Philosophy at King's College, Pennsylvania. He is co-editor of *Harry Potter and Philosophy* (with Shawn E. Klein, 2004) in Open Court's Popular Culture and Philosophy series, and is currently working on a book entitled *Vanquishing Euthyphro* with Jerry Walls.

GREGORY BASSHAM is Director of the Center for Ethics and Public Life and Chair of the Philosophy Department at King's College, Pennsylvania. A frequent contributor to volumes in Open Court's Popular Culture and Philosophy series, he is the co-editor of *The Lord of the Rings and Philosophy* (2003), the author of *Original Intent and the Constitution: A Philosophical Study* (1992), and co-author of *Critical Thinking: A Student's Introduction* (second edition, 2005).

ERIC BRONSON heads the Philosophy and History Department at Berkeley College in New York City. He edited *Baseball and Philosophy* (2004) and co-edited *The Lord of the Rings and Philosophy* (2003), Volumes 6 and 5 in Open Court's Popular Culture and Philosophy series.

J. ANGELO CORLETT is Professor of Philosophy and Ethics at San Diego State University. He is the author of several books, including *Analyzing Social Knowledge* (1996), *Responsibility and Punishment* (2001), *Race, Racism, and Reparations* (2003), *Terrorism: A Philosophical Analysis* (2003), *Ethical Dimensions of Law* (2005), and *Interpreting Plato's Dialogues* (2005). He is editor of *Equality and Liberty: Analyzing Rawls and Nozick* (1990) and Editor-in-Chief of *The Journal of Ethics*.

CYNTHIA A. FREELAND is Professor and Chair of the Department of Philosophy, University of Houston. She was formerly the director of the Women's Studies Program at the University of Houston. Her publications include *But Is It Art?* (2001), "Penetrating Keanu," in William Irwin, ed., *The Matrix and Philosophy* (2002), *The Naked and the Undead: Evil and the Appeal of Horror* (1999), *Feminist Interpretations of Aristotle* (1998), "The Sublime in Cinema," in Carl Plantinga and Greg Smith, eds., *Passionate Views* (1999), and *Philosophy and Film* (1995), which she co-edited with Thomas E. Wartenberg.

JORGE J.E. GRACIA holds the Samuel P. Capen Chair in Philosophy and is State University of New York Distinguished Professor at the University at Buffalo. Among the thirty-five books he has published are *A Theory of Textuality* (1995), *Texts* (1996), *Haw Can We Know What God Means?* (2001), *Old Wine in New Skins* (2003), and (co-editor with Carolyn Korsmeyer and Rodolphe Gasché) *Literary Philosophers: Borges, Calvino, Eco* (2002).

WILLIAM IRWIN is Associate Professor of Philosophy at King's College, Pennsylvania. He is the author of *Intentionalist Interpretation* (1999) and several articles in aesthetics, and editor of *The Matrix and Philosophy* (2002), *The Simpsons and Philosophy* (2001), and *Seinfeld and Philosophy* (2000). He is editor of the Open Court Philosophy and Popular Culture series.

PAUL KURTZ is Professor of Philosophy Emeritus at State University at Buffalo. He is Editor-in-Chief of *Free Inquiry* magazine and Chairman of the Center for Inquiry. Among the forty-five books that he has written or edited are *Skepticism and Humanism: The New Paradigm* (2001), *Embracing the Power of Humanism* (2000), and *The Courage to Become* (1997).

ANNA LÄNNSTRÖM is Assistant Professor of philosophy at Stonehill College. Her recent and forthcoming publications include: "Am I My Brother's Keeper? An Aristotelian Take on Responsibility for Others," *Boston University Studies in Philosophy and Religion* 26 (2005), "The Matrix and Vedanta: Journeying from the Unreal to the Real," in William Irwin, ed., *More Matrix and Philosophy* (2005), and (as editor) *The Stranger's Religion: Fascination and Fear, Boston University Studies in Philosophy and Religion* 25 (2004) and in *Promise and Peril: The Paradox of Religion as Resource and Threat*, in *Boston University Studies in Philosophy and Religion* 24 (2003).

JAMES LAWLER is an Associate Professor of Philosophy at the State University at Buffalo. He is the author of *The Existentialist Marxism of Jean-Paul Sartre* (1976), and *IQ, Heritability, and Racism* (1978), and the editor of *Dialectics of the U.S. Constitution: Selected Writings of Mitchell Franklin* (2000). He is currently writing a history of early modern philosophy, *Matter and Spirit: the Battle of Metaphysics in Early Modern Philosophy before Kant*. He primarily teaches courses about and writes on Kant, Hegel, and Marx.

GARETH B. MATTHEWS is Professor of Philosophy at the University of Massachusetts at Amherst. He is the author of *Thought's Ego in Augustine and Descartes* (1992), *Socratic Perplexity and the Nature of Philosophy* (1999), and *Augustine* (forthcoming).

RALPH MCINERNY is Michael P. Grace Professor of Medieval Studies at the University of Notre Dame. He is author of two dozen books and many articles of philosophy, as well as numerous works of fiction, including novels and short stories, and has authored or edited many other books, some dealing with religious topics. Among his books are *Art and Prudence* (1988), *The Question of Christian Ethics* (1993), *The God of Philosophers* (1994), *Ethica Thomistica* (1997), and *What Went Wrong with Vatican II* (1998).

PAUL K. MOSER is Professor and Chair of Philosophy at Loyola University of Chicago. He is the author of *Philosophy after Objectivity* (1993), *Knowledge and Evidence* (1989), and "Jesus and Philosophy," in *Faith and Philosophy* (forthcoming). He is also co-editor of *Divine Hiddenness* (2002), and editor of *The Oxford Handbook of Epistemology* (2002) and *Jesus and Philosophy: New Essays* (forthcoming).

BRUCE R. REICHENBACH is Professor of Philosophy at Augsburg College. He has written over fifty articles and book chapters on diverse topics in philosophy of religion, ethics, theology, and religion. His most recent books are *Introduction to Critical Thinking* (2001), *On Behalf of God: A Christian Ethic for Biology* (1995), and *Reason and Religious Belief* (third edition, 2003), co-authored with Michael Peterson, William Hasker, and David Basinger.

JONATHAN J. SANFORD is Assistant Professor of Philosophy at Franciscan University of Steubenville. His publications include *Categories: Historical and Systematic Essays* (as co-editor and co-contributor, 2004), and "Scheler *versus* Scheler: The Case for a Better Ontology of the Person," *American Catholic Philosophical Quarterly* (forthcoming). He has contributed several articles to volumes in Open Court's Popular Culture and Philosophy series.

CHARLES TALIAFERRO is Professor of Philosophy at St. Olaf College. He is the author of *Consciousness and the Mind of God* (1994) and *Evidence and Faith* (2005) and *Contemporary Philosophy of Religion* (1998). He is co-author of three other volumes, including the *Blackwell Companion to Philosophy of Religion* (1997).

JERRY L. WALLS is Professor of Philosophy at Asbury Theological Seminary. Among his books are *Hell: The Logic of Damnation* (1992), *Heaven: The Logic of Eternal Joy* (2002), and most recently, with Joe Dongell, *Why I Am Not a Calvinist* (2004).

THOMAS E. WARTENBERG is Chair of the Philosophy Department at Mount Holyoke College where he also teaches in the Film Studies Program. He is the author of *Unlikely Couples: Movie Romance as Social Criticism* (1999), editor of *The Nature of Art* (2001), co-editor (with Cynthia Freeland) of *Philosophy and Film* (1995), and co-editor (with Angela Curran) of *The Philosophy of Film: Introductory Text and Readings* (2005). He is the film editor of *Philosophy Now*.

DALLAS WILLARD is Professor at the School of Philosophy of the University of Southern California in Los Angeles. His publications include translations of Edmund Husserl, and the following books in the philosophy of religion: *Renovation of the Heart* (2002), *The Divine Conspiracy* (1998), *The Spirit of the Disciplines* (1988), and *Hearing God* (1984, 1993, 1999). His *Logic and the Objectivity of Knowledge* (1984) is being revised for a second edition.

MARK A. WRATHALL is Associate Professor of Philosophy at Brigham Young University. He has edited *Religion After Metaphysics* (2003) and co-edited *The Blackwell Companion to Heidegger* (2004), *Heidegger Re-examined* (2002), *Heidegger, Authenticity, and Modernity* (2000), *Heidegger, Coping, and Cognitive Science* (2000), and *Appropriating Heidegger* (2000).

Index

Abelard, Peter. *See* Peter Abelard
Abraham, patriarch, 99, 207, 211
Achilles, 54
Adam, 28, 29, 30, 152, 221–25
Agreda, María de, 144
Albom, Mitch, 202, 203
Al-Gazali, 114
Allen, Woody, 112
Angelico, Fra. *See* Fra Angelico
Annas, 92
Anselm of Aosta, saint, 32, 201–03, 233
Anti-Semitism, x, xi, 2, 25, 42, 79–81, 83–85, 87–91, 93, 94, 101–03, 106, 108, 109
Aquinas. *See* Thomas Aquinas
Aristotle, 51, 54–57, 60, 177, 229, 233, 235, 236, 243, 245
Asclepius, Greek god (Plato's character), 180
Atonement. *See* Passion, meaning of the Criticism of 62–64, 67–75
Augustine of Hippo, saint, 31, 141, 195, 196, 233, 247
Aulén, Gustav, 49, 203
Avila, Teresa de, saint, 161

Bainton, Roland, H., 248, 258
Barabbas, Jesus, 33, 93, 104, 132, 147
Barney the Dinosaur, 53

Bassham, Gregory, xiii, 238
Baudrillard, Jean, 128, 135
Bazin, André, 86, 88
Begnini, Roberto, 53
Belief. *See* Reason/belief; Religious experience
Belluci, Monica, 15, 151, 153, 158
Benedict XV, pope, 200,
Bertocci, P., 42
Boethius, Severinus, 238, 245
Botticelli, Allessandro, 158
Bowne, B.P., 42
Brentano, Clemens, 3
Brickhouse, Thomas, 188
Brightman, Edgar Sheffield, 42, 49, 50
Bronson, Eric, 57
Brown, Dan 158, 159, 162, 172
Brutus, Roman politician, 235
Buber, Martin, 42
Buddha. *See* Siddhartha Gautama
Buford, T.O., 49
Bultmann, Rudolf, 187, 188
Burke, Edmund, 55, 56, 60
Bynum, Caroline Walker, 162

Caiaphas, High Priest, 21, 92, 102, 103, 108, 119, 129, 176, 225, 227, 228, 235, 254
Caligula, Roman emperor, 235
Camus, Albert, 15, 23

Carew, Rod, 112
Carr, Wesley, 216
Cassius, Roman politician, 235
Catharsis (*see also* Emotional
    response), 54, 55, 85
Caviezel, Jim, 151, 153, 161
Celentano, Rosalinda, 152
Chilton Bruce, 123
Christianity (*see* also Theology;
    Interpretation); devotion/piety.
    See Religious experience;
    institution, 64, 68, 79, 97, 158;
    spirituality, ix, 17, 18, 21, 23,
    33, 34, 37, 79, 83, 88, 112, 117,
    118, 121, 122, 202, 248
    revelation, xi, 66, 134, 135, 138,
    139, 142, 143, 145, 147, 149, 175,
    176; tradition 30, 68, 84, 95–98,
    117–120, 122, 144–48, 152, 156,
    171, 173, 174, 184, 185, 199, 201,
    249, 251–53
Claudia (Pliate's wife), 91, 122, 128,
    134, 135, 141, 152, 198
Confucius, 207
Consequentialism. *See* Utilitarianism
Constantine I, Roman Emperor, 97
Coppola, Francis Ford, 138
Corinth, Lovis, 9, 14, 16
Corlett, J. Angelo, 110
Cormack, Margaret, 203
Costanza, George (*Seinfield*'s
    character), 131
Coward, Noel, 1
Cripps, Thomas, 88
Crito (Plato's character), 180
Crossan, John Dominic, 99
Cullmann, Oscar, 185, 188
Cunningham, Phillip A., 144–45,
    150

D'Onofrio, Sandro, xiii
Da Vinci, Leonardo, 159
Dalai Lama, 207
Daniel, Jewish hero, 117, 118, 121
Dante Alighieri, 235
Danto, Arthur C., 55, 60
David, king, 206, 242
Dead Sea Scrolls, 117

Death. *See* Human nature
Descartes, René, 68
Detmer, David, 135
Diocletian, Roman emperor, 2
Dobson, James, 90
Donn, Allegra, 15, 23
Dostoevsky, Fyodor, 23, 24
Dracula (Stoker's character), 138
Dreyfus, Hubert, 23
Droge,Arthur, 193
Dylan, Bob, 112

Eckhart, Meister (Johannes), 68,
    69
Edwards, Jonathan, 239, 245
Eldred, Jody, 37
Eliezer, rabbi, 120
Elijah, prophet, 117, 118, 119,
    207
Emmerich, Anne Catherine, 3, 5, 92,
    93, 99, 100, 122, 144, 145
Emotional response/effect 10, 12,
    14, 17, 19, 25, 27, 37, 42–44, 48,
    51–59, 62, 67, 80–83, 85, 87, 88,
    90, 93, 101–03, 109, 112, 167,
    169, 209, 210
Epistemological theories 129–132
Ethics/morals (human) 41, 42, 44,
    45, 49, 52, 56, 58, 101–109,
    152–57, 162, 174–77, 182, 183,
    186–88, 193, 194, 196, 197,
    200–02, 206, 211–16, 224, 225,
    235–37, 239–244, 247–258;
    God's moral. *See* Evil
Eusebius, fourth-century church his-
    torian, 95
Eve, 28, 29, 152, 160, 221–25
Evil (*see* also Satan; Sin) 22, 23, 26,
    28, 36, 40, 41, 44, 47, 48, 57,
    106–08, 152, 168–170, 174, 176,
    194–96, 202, 210, 223, 227–29,
    235–38, 244, 254, 255; God and
    evil 28, 29, 32, 33, 62, 107, 171,
    174, 204, 207, 211, 215, 221–26,
    230, 235–241
Experience. *See* Religious
    experience
Ezekiel, prophet, 118, 119

Faith. *See* Reason/belief; Christian revelation)
Faulconer, James, 23
Freeland, Cynthia, 56, 58–60, 61, 135
Feinberg, Joel, 109, 110
Feminism, 152, 154–56, 158, 160, 161
Ferapont, Father (Dostoevsky's character), 23
Film language/technique, 19–22, 25, 31, 43, 53, 54, 56, 58, 62, 63, 67, 79, 80, 84–87, 107, 139–142, 167, 190, 193, 194, 197, 212
Firkes, rabbi, 121
Forgiveness. *See* Salvation
Fra Angelico, 9, 10, 12, 14, 16
Francis of Assisi, 47
Francis of Sales, 3
Frankfurt, Henry, 239, 245
Free will. *See* Predestination; Human nature/condition
Frodo (Tolkien's character), 48

Gadamer, Hans-Georg, 134, 135
Gandalf (Tolkien's character), 48
Gandhi, M.K. (Mahatma Gandhi), 43, 186
Gender role, 151–162
Gibson, Hutton (Mel Gibson's father), 94
Gilligan, Carol C., 154, 155, 162
Gingrich, Newt, 90
Glover, Jonathan, 41, 42, 49, 178
God and evil. *See* Evil
Gorman, Michael J., 216
Gospels, 2, 4, 17, 95–97, 102, 103, 135, 137, 139, 146, 149, 129–131, 159; Apocrypha, 159
Gracia, Jorge J.E., 135, 150
Greene, Graham, 1
Gregory Nazianzenus, 196
Gregory of Nyssa, 31, 195, 196
Griffith, D.W., 86
Gunton, Colin, 27, 38

Hanson, N.R., 178

Haskins, Susan, 162
Hegel, G.W.F., 63–76
Heidegger, Martin, 16, 24, 134, 135, 191, 192, 199, 203
Helms, Randel, 99
Herod Antipas, king, 83, 227, 228
Hilton, Paris, 122
Hitler, Adolf, 101, 107, 109, 235, 245
Hobbes, Thomas, 70, 177
Hoffmann, R. Joseph, 100
Hölderlin, Johann Christian Friedrich, 64
Holy Spirit (*see* also Trinity), 73, 74, 116, 145, 212
Honi the Circle-Drawer, 118
Huff, Benjamin, 23
Human nature/condition, 167–69, 174, 175, 177, 183–87, 191–93, 197, 202, 203, 211–13, 215, 222, 224, 225, 230–32, 237, 241–44
Human virtue. *See* Ethics
Human/divine nature, 1, 2, 26, 27, 40, 43, 170, 171, 183, 184, 195, 197, 199, 201, 202, 204–08, 225–232, 256

Incarnation. *See* human/divine nature
Inspirational experience. *See* Religious experience
Interpretation/criticism (*see* also Passion, meaning of the) absurd/unreal, 29, 30, 35, 94, 131, 151; aesthetic, 4, 51, 52, 54–57, 60, 67, 91, 134, 158–161, 167, 190, 193, 194, 200; anti-spiritual, 79, 82, 83, 137; Biblical/apocryphal, xi, 79, 85, 91–99, 102, 111–121, 127, 130, 131, 134, 137–145, 149, 152, 153, 157–59, 172–74, 194–99, 205–212, 214, 223, 244, 246, 251, 252, 253; commercialistic, 84; Catholic, 146, 149, 156, 158, 199–201, 247, 248; deceitful and manipulative, 85–88, 90–94, 99, 102, 111, 137, 138, 141, 142; dialectic (Hegelian),

67, 74, 75; Gnostic, 159, 160; historical/unhistorical, xi, 54, 55, 79, 80, 91–99, 102–06, 112, 131, 142, 145–47, 158, 159, 187, 251; Lutheran, 64, 65, 145, 249, 250; Orthodox, 158; pessimist, 23, 30, 43, 55, 63; polemical, ix, 25–27, 35, 40, 51, 53, 59, 65, 66, 79–81, 83, 85, 137, 149, 150; political 90, 91, 97–99, 112, 113, 120, 137, 138, 242; Protestant, 156, 248; racist, 86, 87, 101–03, 109

Interpretative approaches (to revelation), 142–47
Irigaray, Lucy, 161, 162
Irwin, William, xiii, 135
Isaac, prophet, 211
Isaiah, prophet, 200, 201, 206

Jackson, Andrew, 109
Jacob, patriarch, 211
James, saint and apostle, 93
James, William, 114, 115, 123, 131, 132, 135
Jesus as Messiah, 2, 101, 148, 156, 206, 227, 242
Jesus's identity (*see* also Theology; Christian: Trinity; Human/divine), 25, 26, 42, 43, 65, 68, 70, 71, 74, 95, 118, 119, 129, 133, 134, 204–08, 211, 216, 225
Jesus's trial and death (*see* also Passion, meaning of the; Salvation; Suffering; Resurrection), 104–08, 179, 181, 184, 185
Jewish tradition, 95, 96, 98, 99, 101, 112, 115–122, 137, 138, 159, 160, 193, 207, 249–252
Joel, Billy, 128
Johannes Climacus, 1
John Paul II, pope, 94
John the Baptist, prophet, 118, 120
John, saint and evangelist, 95, 96, 153 159, 198, 241, 244
Johnson, Luke T., 216
Joseph, saint (Jesus's father), 156

Joshua, rabbi, 120, 121
Judas Iscariot, 22, 46, 57, 83, 144, 168–170, 196, 213, 225, 227, 234–245
Julian the apostate, Roman emperor, 97
Julius Caesar, Roman ruler 235

Kant. Immanuel, 30, 36, 38, 51, 56, 58–60, 154, 241, 245, 257
Kazantzakis, Nikos, 172
Keats, John, 52
Kierkegaard, Søren, 1, 3, 4, 5
King, Karen, 153, 162
King, Martin Luther, Jr., 42, 186
Klassen, William, 235, 245
Knowledge/cognition (*see* also Reason/belief), 57, 58, 114, 115, 121, 122, 127–135, 139, 142–47, 173, 191, 204
Knudson, A.C., 49
Kohlberg, Lawrence, 154
Kolbe, saint Maximilian, 202
Krishna, 207
Küng, Hans, 248, 258
Kurtz, Paul, ix, xiii, 100

Lawler, James, 68, 75
Lazzeri, Antonella, 10, 24
Lewis, C.S., 47, 175, 178
Life, meaning of. *See* Human nature; Ethics
Longinus, Dionysius Cassius, 56, 60
Luke, saint and evangelist, 95, 96
Luther, Martin, 64, 145, 249, 258
Lyotard, Jean-François, 136

Macmurray, J., 49
Madonna, Louis Ciccione, 121
Maimonides, Moses, 114
Mainey, Linda, 216
Malchus, guardian of the Temple, 226
Malèna (*Malèna*'s character), 153–54
Mark, saint and evangelist, 95, 96

Markel (Dostoevsky's character), 23
Martin, Aryn, 122
Mary Magdalene, 2, 32, 34, 67, 73, 91, 135, 141, 151, 153, 154, 156–59, 163, 198, 225, 252
Mary, Virgin, 9, 17, 18, 23, 32, 52, 67, 73, 91, 93, 103, 115, 135, 141, 144, 148, 149, 151, 152, 154, 155, 156, 158, 160, 194, 198, 199, 200, 221–23
Matthew, saint and evangelist, 95, 96, 207, 241, 244
McCarthy, Vincent, 75
Maccoby, Hyam, 245
Meditation (on Passion). *See* Religious experience
Merleau–Ponty, Maurice, 16, 19, 24
Michelangelo Buonarroti, 51, 160
Miesel, Sandra, 162
Mill, John Stuart, 239, 245
Moore, Demi, 122
Morals. *See* Ethics/morals
Morgenstern, Maia, 151, 153, 158
Morris, Leon, 216
Moser, Paul, 216
Moses, prophet, 32, 98, 105, 116–121, 133, 207
Mother Teresa of Calcutta. *See* Teresa of Calcutta
Mounier, Emmanuel, 49
Muhammad (Mahomet), prophet of Islam, 99, 105, 134, 207
Mulder, Fox (*X-Files* character), 130
Myers, Abigail, xiii
Mysticism (*see* also Religious experience), 114–122

Narveson, Jan, 257, 258
Natural theology. *See* Reason /belief; Philosophy of Religion
Nebuchadnezzar, king, 117
Neo (*The Matrix* character), 56
Nero, Roman emperor, 235
Nietzsche, Friedrich, 2, 69, 128, 136, 230
Noddings, Nel, 155, 162

O'Reilly, Bill, 90
Olson, Carol E., 162
Origen, 31, 195, 196

Pagels, Elaine, 91, 153, 159, 160, 162
Pandya, Mitu, xiii
Paneloux, Father (Camus's character), 15
Pascal, Blaise, 16, 18, 24, 67, 75
Pasolini, Pier Paolo, 162
Passion, meaning of, 6, 12, 14–18, 22, 23, 27–38, 44–49, 52, 62–68, 70–75, 79, 85, 168, 170, 171, 174, 177, 178, 183–190, 192–203, 207–216, 223–29, 231, 240, 255, 256
Paul, Randy, 23
Paul, saint and apostle, 119, 120, 121, 129, 134, 195, 208–210, 214, 251
Persephone (*Matrix* character), 153
Personalism (theory of individuals' moral value), 41, 42, 49
Peter Abelard, 34, 37, 197
Peter, saint and apostle, 17, 93, 95, 111, 157, 206, 207, 226–28, 236, 237, 242–44, 247, 253
Phenomenology of religion (*see* also Religious experience), 17
Philosophy of religion, 17, 35, 40, 67–71, 114, 115, 137–39, 184, 201, 202, 204, 211, 214–16, 223, 225, 228–232, 237–39
Pico Della Mirandola, 174, 178
Pilate, Pontius, 19, 21, 70, 79, 83, 84, 91, 93, 95, 104, 105, 115, 122, 127–29, 131–33, 135, 145, 152, 176, 181, 195, 206, 227, 228, 235
Plato, 54, 60, 113, 129, 134, 177, 179–182, 186, 187, 188, 233
Postmodernism, 82, 128, 129, 239
Predestination and freedom (*see* also Evil; God and evil), xi, xii, 174, 175, 194, 205–07, 211, 221, 222, 224, 225, 227–232, 234–241, 246, 255, 256

Prophecy. *See* Predestination

Quinn, Philip, 36, 37, 38

Raba (Talmud), 193
Reason/belief (*see* also Christianity;
    Passion, meaning of the), 16, 17,
    21, 29, 30, 36, 37, 52, 59, 64–72,
    75, 82, 85, 95, 102, 103, 113–17,
    121, 122, 127–135, 137–39, 141,
    143–150, 159, 175, 191, 192, 204,
    205, 211, 213, 214, 216, 223–25,
    228–230, 232, 235, 236, 238–244,
    243–255, 257, 258
Reconciliation (human), 44;
    Reconciliation God-humanity *see*
    Passion, meaning of the; Salvation
Relativism (*see* also
    Postmodernism), 128, 129, 135
Religious conservatives/traditional-
    ists, 90, 91
Religious experience, 17, 18, 20–22,
    34, 37, 38, 44, 52, 55–58, 60, 66,
    67, 70, 72, 74, 80, 81, 83, 85,
    114–122, 133–135, 143, 144,
    175–78, 187, 196–98, 200, 202,
    212–15, 226, 253–55, 257, 258
Representation (of the Passion)
    linguistic or written, 19–21,
    139–142; mental (*see* also
    Religious experience), 19, 22,
    66–68, 139; visual (*see* also emo-
    tional response; film), 18–21,
    51–60, 63, 66, 67, 86, 107,
    139–142, 167
Resurrection, 29, 31, 40, 41, 43–46,
    48, 63, 69, 72, 73, 130, 176, 177,
    184, 187, 195, 205, 208, 209, 226
Rich, Frank, 90
Rooney, Andy, 90
Rosica, Thomas (Father), ix
Ruddick, Sara, 155, 156, 162
Russell, Bertrand, 105, 136

Sacrifice. *See* Passion, meaning of
Salvation (*see* also Passion, meaning

of) 29–37, 45, 47, 62–66, 69–74,
    160, 168, 170–73, 176–78, 183,
    184, 187, 192–97, 200–02,
    206–212, 214, 223–27, 231, 240,
    250, 256, 257
Sam (Tolkien's character), 48
Sandler, Adam, 112
Sartre, Jean-Paul, 174, 178
Satan, 22, 23, 25, 26, 30, 31, 32, 35,
    57, 63, 93, 102, 111, 141, 152,
    168–171, 176, 192–97, 199, 206,
    215, 221–23, 228, 234, 236, 237
Sayers, Dorothy, 1
Scheler, Max, 42, 47, 49, 50
Schelling, Friedrich, 64
Schindler, Oscar, 53
Schjedahl, Peter, 55
Scholem, Gershom, 123
Schopenhauer, Arthur, 230
Schweitzer, Albert 249
Scott, A.O. 12, 24, 111
Screwtape (Lewis's character), 175
Scully, Dana (*X-Files* character), 130
Sheena, Gail, 122
Siddhartha Gautama (the Buddha),
    207, 257
Simon of Cyrene, 34, 35, 53, 70, 73,
    103, 130, 171, 192, 196–99
Simon the zealot, saint and apostle,
    105
Sin (*see* also Evil; Satan; Passion,
    meaning of the), 21, 22, 27–29,
    32, 33, 36, 37, 62–66, 71, 73, 94,
    152, 160, 168–170, 176, 183, 185,
    186, 194, 195, 200–02, 205–216,
    223, 225–27, 231, 232, 234–37,
    244
Socrates, xi, 9, 113, 114, 115, 127,
    157, 179–183, 186, 187, 188, 191,
    253
Socrates's trial and death 180–83,
    186, 187, 191
Solomon, king, 116, 206
Spader, Peter, 49
Spears, Britney, 122
Spielberg, Steven, 53
Stalin, Josef, 235
Steele, David Ramsay, xiii
Steinsaltz, Adin, 123

Stoicism, 70, 71, 253
Stoker, Bram, 138
Stump, Eleanore, 38
Suárez, Francisco, 146
Sublimity, 55–60
Suffering (*see* also Passion, meaning
    of), x, 1, 9, 10, 12, 14–16, 18–22,
    30–35, 40–49, 51, 53–58, 62, 63,
    65–67, 71, 79, 80, 82–85, 87, 90,
    93, 101, 107, 108, 111–14, 121,
    141, 151, 159–161, 167–69, 171,
    172, 174, 176, 179, 184–87, 190,
    192, 194–202, 204, 205, 207–210,
    212, 221, 223, 225–28, 230, 231,
    234, 246, 256, 258
Swinburne, Richard, 36, 38, 130,
    136, 201, 203

Tabor, James, 193
Taliaferro, Charles, 35, 36, 39, 47, 49
Tarantino, Quentin, 52
Taylor, C.C.W., 188
Teresa of Calcutta, Mother, 186
Tertullian, 68
Theology, 1, 3, 16, 17, 26–28,
    30–32, 34–38, 41, 45–48, 62, 64,
    65, 67–75, 112, 113, 115, 138,
    147–150, 152, 173–78, 184,
    186–88, 192–97, 199–202,
    208–216, 222, 224, 225, 227, 229,
    231, 232, 237, 238, 248–253,
    255–58
Thielicke, Helmut, 216
Thomas Aquinas, saint, 2, 114, 146,
    233
Thomas, saint and apostle, 133
Tiberius Caesar, 21
Titian (Tiziano Vecellio), 158
Tolkien, J.R.R., 48, 49
Tolstoy, Leo, 250, 258

Trinity (*see* also Christian) 26, 27,
    62, 74, 231, 232
Truth. *See* Reason/belief;
    Knowledge and cognition; as
    Aletheia 134, 135

Utilitarianism, 254, 255, 257

Vanhoozer, Kevin, 150
Venus, Hellenic goddess, 158
Vermes, Geza, 123
Veronica, Christian traditional char-
    acter, 146, 152, 199
Violence, 10, 12, 14, 15, 19, 21, 25,
    26, 31, 33, 40–47, 49, 51–58, 62,
    63, 82–85, 87, 90–93, 101, 107,
    108, 111, 112, 141, 159–161,
    167–69, 176, 179, 185, 186, 202,
    207, 209, 221, 231, 246, 256;
    non–violence (doctrine) 186,
    246–257

Walls, Jerry L., 39, 46
Warhol, Andy, 138
Waternberg, Thomas E., 88
Wells, G.A., 100, 131, 136
West, Kenneth, 23
Wilde, Oscar, 1
Wolterstorff, Nicholas, 150
Wormwood (Lewis's character),
    175
Wrathall, Mark, 16, 24, 134

Yoder, John Howard, 250, 258

Zealots, 105

ALSO FROM OPEN COURT

Buffy the Vampire Slayer and Philosophy
Fear and Trembling in Sunnydale

VOLUME 4 IN THE OPEN COURT SERIES,
POPULAR CULTURE AND PHILOSOPHY

"In every generation there is a Chosen One. She alone will stand against the vampires, the demons, and the Forces of Darkness. She is the Slayer . . ."

So. If you're kind of killing time between apocalypses or just wondering about that meaning of life thing, here's some readage. . . . Look, these guys'll I-think-therefore-I-am you into the freakin' ground. And the happy is better than shoe shopping. What? If I don't consult the oracle I'll, like, turn to stone? Well, *yeah*, if not already.

"a thought-provoking philosophical intervention into the cleverest show on television."

— NORAH MARTIN
   Co-author of *Externalism and Self-Knowledge*

"Its erudite yet accessible chapters illuminate the work of philosophers from Plato to Kant to Feyerabend, all of whom benefit from emigrating to Sunnydale."

— DAVID LAVERY
   Editor of *Slayage: The Online International Journal of Buffy Studies*

"These doctors of philosophy x-ray the intellectual bones of Buffy. . . . reflects the deeply ethical nature of the Buffyverse."

— RHONDA V. WILCOX
   Co-editor of *Fighting the Forces: What's at Stake in Buffy the Vampire Slayer*

**AVAILABLE FROM LOCAL BOOKSTORES OR
BY CALLING 1-800-815-2280**

Distributed by Publishers Group West

For more information on Open Court books, go to
www.opencourtbooks.com